The Strange
Comrade Balabanoff

The Strange Comrade Balabanoff

The Life of a Communist Rebel

MARIA LAFONT

McFarland & Company, Inc., Publishers
Jefferson, North Carolina

Masha (now Maria) Lafont also wrote *Pillaging Cambodia: The Illicit Traffic in Khmer Art* (McFarland, 2004)

LIBRARY OF CONGRESS CATALOGUING-IN-PUBLICATION DATA

Names: Lafont, Maria.
Title: The strange Comrade Balabanoff : the life of a communist rebel / Maria Lafont.
Description: Jefferson, North Carolina : McFarland & Company, Inc., Publishers, 2016. | Includes bibliographical references and index.
Identifiers: LCCN 2016003942 | ISBN 9780786498789 (softcover : alkaline paper) ∞
Subjects: LCSH: Balabanoff, Angelica, 1878–1965. | Women socialists—Soviet Union—Biography. | Socialists—Soviet Union—Biography. | Lenin, Vladimir Il'ich, 1870–1924—Friends and associates. | Women socialists—Ukraine—Biography. | Women socialists—Europe—Biography. | Socialism—Europe—History—20th century. | Europe—Politics and government—20th century. | Soviet Union—Politics and government—1917–1936. | Soviet Union—Politics and government—1936–1953.
Classification: LCC HX313.8.B35 L34 2016 | DDC 335.43092—dc23
LC record available at http://lccn.loc.gov/2016003942

BRITISH LIBRARY CATALOGUING DATA ARE AVAILABLE

ISBN (print) 978-0-7864-9878-9
ISBN (ebook) 978-1-4766-2363-4

© 2016 Maria Lafont. All rights reserved

No part of this book may be reproduced or transmitted in any form or by any means, electronic or mechanical, including photocopying or recording, or by any information storage and retrieval system, without permission in writing from the publisher.

On the cover *clockwise* Angelica reading *Avanti!* 1939 (Collection of Giorgio Giannelli); Trevi fountain, Rome (© 2016 iStock/Thinkstock); View from Empire State Building, New York City, to Chrysler Building and Queensboro Bridge, low viewpoint (Library of Congress)

Back cover image: The Kremlin towards the Place rouge, Moscow, Russia, ca. 1890–1900 (Library of Congress)

Printed in the United States of America

McFarland & Company, Inc., Publishers
  Box 611, Jefferson, North Carolina 28640
    www.mcfarlandpub.com

For my mother

"I have so much, so very much of what makes life worth to be lived."
 —Angelica Balabanoff, letter to Ella Wolfe, December 4, 1960, HIA/BWC, Box 2, Folder 60

"I find something is wrong somewhere; we are either too far advanced or are lagging too far behind. Which is it?"
 —Rose Pesotta, letter to Emma Goldman, March 3, 1934. R.P. Coll. Correspondence, Emma Goldman 1934–1937. In Naomi Shepherd, *Price Below Rubies: Jewish Women as Rebels and Radicals* (London: Weidenfeld & Nicolson, 1993), p. 297

Table of Contents

Acknowledgments	ix
Preface	1
Introduction	9
List of Personalities	11
Abbreviations and Definitions	15
I A Natural-Born Rebel	17
II Professional Nomination	26
III Alone with Lenin	33
IV A Female Lecturer	38
V Forming *Il Duce*	50
VI Female Journalist	55
VII Expulsion	65
VIII International Spy	71
IX Lenin's Favorite; Mussolini's Most Trusted	74
X Mussolini's Elegy	82
XI A Well-Hidden Family	91
XII Back to Russia	97
XIII *De Facto* Ambassador to the Scandinavian Countries	104
XIV Dining with the Lenins	112
XV Post-Mortem Research	118
XVI Organizing the First and Only General Strike in Switzerland	121

XVII	Vice President of Foreign Affairs to the Ukraine	129
XVIII	Governor of Odessa	141
XIX	Lenin's Most Trusted Agent	149
XX	Freemason Without an Apron	156
XXI	An Adolescent Armenian Boy	164
XXII	Persona Non Grata	172
XXIII	The Spy Whom I Loved	178
XXIV	The Foundation of Angelica Balabanoff	185
XXV	Under FBI Surveillance	197
XXVI	The Red *Popessa*	201

Afterword: Ten Birth Dates	213
Chapter Notes	217
Bibliography	225
Index	229

Acknowledgments

My gratitude goes out to everyone who devoted time to this book.

First and foremost I would like to thank my husband, Jean-Loup Lafont, who constantly and tenderly supported me throughout the project.

Laura Blancq and Melissa Sodowick helped proofread the text. Federica Prina, Diana Maggiore, Patrick Mantell, and Fabrice Setta translated dozens of documents from Italian and German about Angelica's life, found in the Swiss and Italian archives. Patrice Mitrano helped to prepare the photos.

This book could not have been written without the following interviews. Marina Cattaneo spent two days with me in Milan at the Foundation of Anna Kuliscioff, taking me through the photos and correspondence that she had in her collection, which were in five different languages. Giorgio Giannelli, the executor of Angelica's will, who lives in Rome, gave long interviews about Angelica and shared the unique photo album with her photos. Roberto Olla, the author of *Il Duce and His Women*, spoke at length about the relationship between Angelica and Mussolini. Carlo Correr, a left-wing Italian journalist, shared his knowledge of the history of *Avanti!* Pierre Boichu, researcher at Bobigny archives, provided information about Angelica's stay in Odessa. Albert Tosoni-Pittoni, the son of Bianca Pittoni, a good friend of Angelica's, had much to say about the prewar years of the Italian socialists who lived in Paris. Jean-Jacques Marie of the Centre for Study and Research on the International Trotskyist and Revolutionary Movements, CERMTRI, personally knew some of Angelica's friends from her Parisian years. Judy Kelly lived for one month with Angelica in 1961 in Rome. All of them shared their memories and knowledge of Angelica with me and provided materials and photos from their personal collections.

My gratitude goes to more than 30 archives and universities in 11 countries that had documents about Angelica. Special thanks to Columbia University, which digitalized five-hour tapes of Angelica's interviews that she gave in 1965 to the Radio Liberty in Munich, making it possible for me to hear her voice and better understand her views and opinions on various events in her life. The staff of the International Institute of Social History in Amsterdam hosted me for one week. The Swiss Federal Archives in Berne prepared hundreds of documents in advance, enabling me to read them during my short three-day visit. The New York Public Library, State Archives of Rome, and the Archives section of the *Préfecture de Police* in Paris put together all information related to Angelica, making research and long stays in the libraries easy and enjoyable.

Last but not least I apologize to those whose names I have neglected to mention but without whom my work on this book would never be complete.

Preface

I first heard about Angelica Balabanoff by coincidence, on the Internet, while following a discussion on a forum about well-known Russian women who lived abroad. Someone mentioned Angelica Balabanoff, the socialist Russian mistress of Benito Mussolini. "Socialist," "Russian," and "Mussolini" in one sentence sounded intriguing, and so I decided to take a closer look at her. After some research, I found three short essays written about Angelica between 1975 and 1983.[1] Such a dearth of information was not surprising. In fact, this is rather common with women in history whose lives are lesser known than those of their male counterparts. Most of the information I found in the essays came from Angelica's memoirs, *My Life as a Rebel*. The book was out of print. I hurriedly ordered it from the secondhand-book website abebooks.com and read it immediately when it arrived. Dogmatic and monotonous, the book was a disappointment.

Ready to brush Angelica aside, I took a quick look at the bibliographies and noticed that all three essays provided completely different sources of information. After entering her name into the databases of the biggest archives in Europe and America, to my surprise I discovered a wealth of information about the life and secrets of this incredible person.

Born in 1878 to a dazzlingly rich family in Chernigov, present-day Ukraine, Angelica broke ties with her parents and left for Europe to become one of the leading female socialists of the European labor movement at the beginning of the 20th century. She was famous in Italy for "discovering" Mussolini, when he was an unknown socialist, and being the first person who "polished and educated" the future *Il Duce*. Only 5 fee tall, plump and unattractive, she was rumored to be the lover of Mussolini, Lenin, Trotsky, and Stalin. For a long time, it was thought that Mussolini's eldest daughter Edda was Angelica's daughter. Angelica returned to Russia at the beginning of the October Revolution in 1917. Highly respected within the European socialist movement, her mere presence in Russia during the Revolution served as real publicity for what was happening in the country.

After becoming one of the few women to occupy high-ranking positions within the all-male Bolshevik government, Angelica fled Russia because she disagreed with Lenin's policies during the Red Terror. She was accused by the European and American secret services of promoting communist propaganda, and by the Soviets of becoming a traitor. A brillian translator, she spoke 13 languages. An excellent speaker, she gathered crowds of men and women, addressing the most daring subjects at a time when many women stayed at home. A constant traveler, she lived all her life in small dorm-like rooms, moving, on average, every two years, going to places where her presence and work for the cause could help the poor and the oppressed, carrying two suitcases with documents she considered important. Angelica died in Rome at the age of 96, concluding her 65-year career by helping Giuseppe Saragat to become president of Italy.

The research I conducted into Angelica's life proved to be as incredible as my heroine. Because of her nomadic life, the documents are spread all over the world. It turns out that just about every police force and state archive of each country that Angelica visited during her life had documents on her. Luckily for me, most of them were in languages that I understand (some better than others)—English, Russian, French, German, and Italian.

During the course of my research, more than 30 different archives and libraries agreed to provide information in electronic format after a few e-mail exchanges, which greatly facilitated my work. Some locations held such vast documentation that they could not scan it all and send it to me, so I had to go there in person. Since I undertook this research on my own, it was a significant financial investment, which I made over the course of a few years. I live in Paris which made the French documents the easiest to consult, but I also traveled to New York, Rome, Berne, London, Brussels, and Amsterdam.

To understand the difficulty of the research, one has to imagine a stack 2.5 meters tall with Angelica's personal documents, letters, notebooks, drafts of articles, photos, business cards, and some personal items held in Amsterdam. A bit smaller but still impressive is the collection of documents in the Swiss Federal Archives in Berne. The documents that included references to Angelica's name totaled 400 pages. The Swiss police followed the Russian revolutionary for more than 60 years, meticulously putting together all articles and reports, considering her a dangerous agitator and her presence unwelcome on Swiss soil.

Speaking Russian was of vital importance. Most of the universities and state archives in the Western Hemisphere reply to inquiries within a few days of making a request. In Russia, the hierarchical government structure makes work extremely bureaucratic. In addition to sending e-mails to all Russian archives, I had to telephone all of them and explain again and again the reason for my call. Nevertheless, the people I had on the phone in Moscow, St. Petersburg, Chernigov, Kiev, and Odessa were helpful, and the documents were impeccably organized. I had the most interesting telephone conversations with FSB (the Federal Security Service), or the former KGB, in Moscow. I decided to contact them (the Archives) hoping to find some information about Angelica's work for Lenin as his secret agent. So I looked on the web, found the FSB contact information, and sent an e-mail detailing my request. Three weeks went by and I still had no response. I decided to call.

"Good morning. I sent you a request by e-mail about three weeks ago about Angelica Balabanoff, and I have not received any information so far," I explained to the person who answered the phone in the FSB information center.

"Good morning," answered a chilling, metallic-sounding voice that made my spine freeze. "You cannot say such things. You have to say: 'I have not *yet* received any information.'" The voice emphasized the word "yet." "Otherwise it means we did not send you any information on purpose and you could take me to Court."

I apologized and rephrased my question, giving my name and explaining my request. The metal voice responded: "We take 30 days to get back to you."

"Thank you," I said trying to sound as natural as possible. "When I receive your reply, if I have more questions, do you provide any contact details, or will I have to fill out another request form on the Internet?"

"Madame, we don't provide any contact information. You will receive an exhaustive reply," said the voice and added, in a way that made my spine freeze again, "With us there is no return."

Impatient to get news from the FSB, as the 30-day response time promised by the officer on the phone had long passed, I decided to call the FSB again. I dialed the number, remembering to start the conversation with "I have not *yet* received any information."

"Madame," said another equally chilling voice, "your response was sent out by letter, exactly 30 days after your request. However, we are not able to send the letter directly to you," continued the voice, prompting a sudden revelation.

"Your letter," went on the voice on the phone, "will be dispatched through the Ministry of Foreign Affairs to the Russian Embassy in Paris, who will then send it to you. We do not send letters directly to foreign countries."

I could only blame myself for this delay. When I filled out the request on the Internet, I gave my address in Paris. Now I regretted not giving my mother's address in Moscow. All I could do was be patient and continue with my research. A few months later, when I had given up any hope of receiving a response from the FSB, a letter arrived from the Russian Embassy in Paris. A very cordial response informed me that all documents concerning Angelica had been sent to the RGASPI (Russian State Archive of Social and Political History in Moscow), which I was invited to contact, and that FSB itself had nothing. Nonetheless, it was a good experience, which led me to discover yet another source of information.

My research brought me to the most unusual places, such as the Trotsky Center in Paris. It is maintained by ten people who believe in Trotskyism. On 25 April 2012, I entered a small office that opened directly onto the street in the 10th *arrondissement*, in the middle of an otherwise Indian- and African-populated neighborhood with ethnic restaurants and hair salons exhibiting all sorts of dreadlocks and style patterns. The Trotsky Center has an interesting collection of books, journals, and microfilms, kept in a back room, some of which were most useful for my research.

As the documents about Angelica came from a variety of different places, to advance in my research I needed a reliable reference document about her life that I could use as a base. As such, I chose her autobiography, *My Life as a Rebel*. This book is the only published document that follows the main trajectory of her life. I kept going back to it, reading it over and over again as if it were the Bible, following her steps and trying to read between the lines whenever I felt that some events had been embellished or obscured by Angelica herself.

Angelica's amazing and voluminous correspondence proved to be an invaluable source of information. Among dozens of different letters, the most interesting had been written by Angelica to her friend and the known anarchist Emma Goldman; her secretary in New York, Kitty Crowe; and last but not least Emma Wolfe, the wife of the well-known American socialist, Bertram Wolfe.

More noteworthy information came from the interviews. I was fortunate to get to know Giorgio Giannelli, the executor of Angelica's will, who considered the revolutionary his "surrogate mother." We met for an interview in his apartment in Rome on the piazza *Campo dei Fiori*. I arrived ten minutes early. It was a market day, and the small, picturesque piazza looked even more beautiful with vendors selling huge chunks of parmesan cheese, olive oil, and zucchini with golden flowers. To my surprise, in the center of the piazza, I saw the hooded statue of Giordano Bruno, one of Angelica's favorite historical figures and the first of the prosecuted free thinkers, who claimed that the Sun was one of the stars in the universe and that the universe had other populated planets. I thought it was quite amusing that two people so dear to her were united in one place after all this time.

The surprises of the day continued when I found myself in Giorgio's sitting room. I immediately understood that he considered Angelica, if not as his mother, then as a close member of his family. One of the walls in the room was entirely devoted to her, displaying her photos at all ages—Angelica in her sixties, half-reclined in an armchair with an issue of *Avanti!* on her knees, or another taken much later, in Rome, with her standing on the impressive marble steps of one of the historical monuments, wearing a turban, a simple grey trenchcoat, and sandal-like flat shoes. The central piece of this photographic exhibit was her will and testament, a carefully framed, yellowish handwritten paper. Giorgio was the only person to tell me how she had dressed, whether she used perfume, and what her favorite meal was. And most importantly: "What was the nature of her relationship with Mussolini?"

Just as interesting was my interview with Marina Cattaneo, whose grandparents were Angelica's friends. We made an appointment for February 14, 2011, at the Foundation of Anna Kuliscioff in Milan, where my husband and I had decided to spend Valentine's Day. The Foundation of Anna Kuliscioff is certainly an unusual place. It was created in 1987 by Giulio Polotti.

"Giulio collected all the documents about the workers' movement," explained Marina, while her grey boxer, Pea, was happily sitting between us. "He bought them from private collectors and at auctions, picked them up on the streets, tore them off the walls and signposts...."

Hailing from a well-off family, Giulio Polotti was in love with socialism. He decided to create his own collection of socialist-related documents. With his family money he bought a spacious ten-room apartment (plus four cellars in the basement) on *via Valazze*, in the center of Milan, and left sufficient funding for the maintenance of the property and archives after his death. The foundation was named Anna Kuliscioff, after one of the founders of the Italian Socialist Party. It contains thousands of books, posters, correspondence, and a full collection of *Avanti!*, the biggest Italian socialist newspaper, where Angelica and Mussolini had worked together in 1913. What had to be the dining room of the apartment became the main research and study room. Furnished with glass-protected oak bookcases along the walls, it also had a long table in the center, which Marina used to spread out all documents about Angelica. As usual, when it came to the Russian militant, the documents came up in five languages. Marina spent two days with me in Milan, answering my questions about the revolutionary and going through her photos and correspondence.

Because this research was sponsored entirely by my own funds, I could not afford to go to all the places I needed to see. I had to abandon the idea of a trip to Angelica's hometown, Chernigov. The journey promised to be interesting, but long and expensive. Going there without knowing in advance what the trip might entail was rather complicated. I decided to continue looking for more documents about her childhood while remaining in Paris, contacting the archives in the Ukraine by Internet, collecting any information I could from Google and reading Angelica's memoirs. Unfortunately, the archives in Chernigov had very little information for that time in her life. It is possible that going there directly could have yielded more results about her family or the place where she had lived. When I was about to give up finding any information about her early years, I received a parcel from the Princeton University Library. It contained Angelica's unpublished memoirs, a 30-page typed manuscript kept with the Saxe Commins Papers, in which she described her childhood and which came to be the major source of information for that time in her life. Saxe Commins was a chief editor at Random House between 1933 and 1958, where Angelica had tried to publish her memoirs.

Quite another experience was researching Angelica's university years in Brussels. The records of the New University, which she attended, are stored in the much more renowned Free University of Brussels. The folders with the complete records of Angelica's alma mater took up about one meter of space. The New University had existed for a total of thirty years. The entire archives were inventoried in a small A6 booklet.

Sometimes in my quest for information, I was purely lucky. When the time came for me to write about Angelica's role as possibly one of the main organizers of the one and only general strike in Switzerland in 1918, I was hesitant. Not much information was available about it. Besides, there are many books that tell the story of the one and only general strike in the history of Switzerland. Since I am not a specialist in the political history of the country, I had decided not to write about it, until one day, during my three-day visit to the Swiss Federal Archives in Berne, while taking a short break from browsing through 400 pages of Angelica's files and taking individual photos of each document, I literally stumbled upon an edition entitled

Switzerland-Russia: Contacts and Breaks.[2] The book contained correspondence between the Russian and Swiss governments dating from 1813 to 1955. Some letters cited the events of the 1918 strike, as well as Angelica and her stay in the country. These letters, completed by a few articles published in the Swiss newspapers of the time, revealed an astounding and little-known picture of the whirlwind Russian revolutionary's two-week trip.

Information about Angelica's Parisian period, between 1925 and 1935, turned out to be well documented in the Remembrance and Cultural Affairs Section of the *Préfecture de Police*, who keep archives of notorious refugees and lawbreakers. When I contacted the archives, the first response of the information desk officer was, "I cannot promise you anything. We have very few documents about this period of time." The second e-mail stated, "Yes, we do have some files, which you may consult in our offices."

It turned out that the documents about the revolutionary were more than abundant. They included a dozen A4 boxes, making me wonder what was so dangerous about her that she had to be so closely followed by the French police. More details related to this period came from the reports of the Italian secret police in Rome. The Russian muse of Mussolini was just as closely followed by Italian spies, who wanted to know her every move.

Angelica's stay in the United States between 1935 and 1947 was well documented by information from at least 15 different universities and archives, including correspondence with Leon Trotsky, by then in exile in Mexico; Norman Thomas, the charismatic six-time presidential candidate from the Socialist Party of America; German psychologist Erich Fromm, with whom she corresponded, and many others.

Finally, I think I should apologize to Angelica. I have always underestimated her. When I got to the moment in my research when she was about to leave the United States for Italy, in 1947, I thought to myself: "Oh, what else will happen to her? She is nearly 80 years old. She will probably spend her remaining years in Rome, reading books and making occasional speeches." Or so I thought until the moment I received reports from the FBI showing that upon her arrival in Rome, she was put under FBI surveillance. Her anti-communist speeches annoyed quite a few people, putting her life in danger.

I would like to say a few words about different currencies and monetary values used in this book. Whenever possible, I tried to convert the currency of the time into the present-day equivalent U.S. Dollar. Because of multiple currencies and a vast period of time, between 1897 and 1965, it turned out to be a difficult task. Inflation, different essentials of life, and purchasing power made prices vary widely and conversion gives only a rough estimate of the value.

Angelica's life was full of mysteries and unexplainable events, which I tried to elucidate in this book. I discovered the strangest of these when I least expected it. It was on a chilly December day when I visited her tomb in the non–Catholic cemetery in Rome, a beautiful place with cypress trees, wildflowers, and three-colored cats that followed me around. Reserved for foreigners or non–Catholics, the cemetery is a part of the tourist to-do list. It boasts the tombs of the English 19th-century poets Shelley and Keats, as well as many known personalities who died in the Eternal City at a time when bodies were not transported back to their native land.

To my astonishment, the modest white burial stone with Angelica's name and date of birth on it in dark grey letters was visible from afar. It was the only tomb that had fresh flowers: a pot of red azaleas. The most visited tombs, those of Shelley and Keats, did not have flowers. Standing in front of her tomb, I could only wonder who would have brought flowers 45 years after her death if she had no family or children, her name has been largely forgotten by history, and her friends have long since passed away?

Today, after finishing my book about Angelica and revealing most of the events in her life, this question still remains unanswered.

Introduction

Had she ever been married? Or had children? Was she really a mistress of Lenin, Mussolini, Trotsky, and Stalin? Was Edda Mussolini, the eldest daughter of the infamous dictator, her daughter? Angelica Balabanoff's life was full of mysteries and unexplainable events.

Born in Chernigov, a small town in the northeastern part of the Ukraine that at the time was part of the Russian Empire, she rebelled against her well-off merchant family and their traditional values, disagreeing from the age of five with the rules of upbringing imposed on the girls of her social milieu. She broke with her family when she became a young woman, refused the family inheritance, and, after being cursed by her mother, left for Western Europe to live with the poor and ease their lives. She never saw her mother or most of her siblings again.

After completing her graduate education, Angelica quickly became one of the primary female lecturers in Europe. The first person to discover, educate, and form the future *Il Duce*, she was also a close acquaintance of Lenin and Trotsky during their exile in Switzerland, stood next to them as their equal in the "all macho" Soviet government after the Russian Revolution, and became Lenin's most trusted agent, whom he sent on secret missions vitally important for the young Soviet State.

Disillusioned with the Revolution, Angelica was possibly the only high-ranking official in Russian history who left the country legitimately without being prosecuted. Rejected by many friends and colleagues, she became an anti-communist, but no one believed her because of her reputation as Lenin's associate. The Russians suspected that she worked for the BOI, the Bureau of Investigation, the predecessor of the FBI; the FBI that she worked for the NKVD, the KGB predecessor; and the Swiss, Germans, and French accused her of being a triple agent.

An unattractive woman, Angelica was five feet tall, plump, and slightly cross-eyed, with a practically asymmetrical face. And yet, it was said that she was also purportedly a mistress of Mussolini, Lenin, Trotsky, and possibly Stalin. She also had a string of other lesser-known lovers she met throughout her long career.

Angelica spoke many languages and moved to a new lodging on average every two years, each time renting tiny maid's rooms, often on the top floor with no heat, elevator, or cooking facilities, carrying with her two suitcases full of books and documents. She lived in Russia, Belgium, and Switzerland, and spent ten years in France, another ten years in the United States, and more than 20 years in Italy.

After settling in Rome at the end of World War II, she concluded her 65-year career by helping Giuseppe Saragat to become president of Italy. She died at the age of 96, leaving behind—as the only tangible proof of her existence—326 books, three mugs—one for herself and two for guests—three dresses, and two pairs of shoes.

Her life might have seemed odd, eccentric, and somber. Yet a few years before her death, she wrote to her friend, Ella Wolfe, the wife of the American socialist, historian, and writer Bertram Wolfe, the words that depicted her personality better than any other: "Believe me, even if I had much money at my disposal I would not like to live better than I do now. It was the dream of my life—since my childhood—to share the sufferings and deprivations of the poorest among the poor. As a matter of fact it so happened that I never did—I lived also [sic] better than the great majority of human beings, and so I do assure you, my dear, I have not met—neither in life nor in literature—a single person happier than I am!"[1]

The day she died, newspapers all over the world, from *The New York Times, Herald Tribune, L'Humanité,* and *Socialismo Democratico* to *The Weimar Republic,* came out with obituaries titled, "The Last Greatest Revolutionary Dies" and "The One Who Had Known Lenin and Mussolini." A few months later, no one remembered her, apart from a few friends.

This biography chronicles the life of an amazing woman forgotten by history.

List of Personalities

Alexander Berkman (1870–1936). A leading member of the anarchist movement in the early 20th century, known for his political activism and writing. Angelica met Berkman in 1920 in Moscow. She helped him to obtain a Russian passport (Berkman lost his U.S. citizenship after accusations of being a dangerous anarchist) and to meet Lenin. They remained friends until his death in 1936.

Louise Bryant (1885–1936). An American journalist and writer, wife of socialist and writer John Reed. She was best known for her Marxist and anarchist beliefs and her essays on radical political and feminist themes. Angelica met Louise in Stockholm in 1917 and was one of the few people to support Louise during the illness and death of John Reed in Moscow and during her last years in Paris.

Kathleen (Kitty) Crowe. An actress who became Angelica's "secretary" in New York. After Angelica left the United States, the two women continued a lively correspondence. Angelica's letters to Kathleen Crowe are kept at the University of Toronto, in the Claude Stewart Collection, and provide the most interesting information about Angelica's life after her departure from the United States in 1947.

Célestin Demblon (1859–1924). A poet, writer, translator of Shakespeare, politician, and Wallonian Deputy. Angelica's favorite professor at the New University of Brussels who supervised her thesis when she graduated.

Maria Giudice (1880–1953). An Italian socialist. During Maria's exile in Switzerland, together with Angelica, they published the first-ever newspaper for Italian working women, *Su Compagne!*

Emma Goldman (1869–1940). An anarchist known for her political activism, writing, and speeches. She played a pivotal role in the development of anarchist political philosophy in North America and Europe in the first half of the 20th century. Angelica met Emma in 1920 in Moscow, helped her and Alexander Berkman obtain Russian passports, and presented them to Lenin. The women remained close friends until Emma's death in 1940. Angelica's amazing correspondence with Emma proved to be an invaluable source of information for this book.

Maxim Gorky, **Alexei Maximovich Peshkov** (1868–1936), primarily known as **Maxim Gorky**. A Russian and Soviet writer, a founder of the Socialist Realism literary method, political activist, and friend of Angelica, whom she visited in Capri and worked with on a number of occasions in Europe and in Russia.

Robert Grimm (1881–1958). The leading Swiss Socialist politician during the first half of the 20th century. As a member of the Social Democratic Party of Switzerland, he opposed the First World War and was the main organizer of the Zimmerwald anti-war movement, closely working with Angelica.

Alexandra Mikhailovna Kollontai (1872–1952). A Russian Communist revolutionary and a close friend of Angelica, these women were considered the two most influential female revolutionists during the first years of the October Revolution. In 1923 Alexandra Kollontai was appointed Soviet Ambassador to Norway, becoming the world's first female ambassador.

Nadezhda Konstantinovna Krupskaya (1869–1939). A Bolshevik revolutionary, politician, and the wife of Vladimir Lenin. She was Deputy Minister (Commissar) of Education in Russia in 1929–1939. Angelica met Nadezhda in early 1900 in Switzerland. Despite years of close relationship, the two women never became good friends.

Anna Kulisciof, **Anna Moiseyevna Rosenstein** (1857–1925). A Jewish Russian revolutionary and prominent feminist, she was mainly active in Italy, where she was one of the first women to graduate in medicine. Good friends with Angelica from 1906, they separated in 1913 over Angelica's support of Mussolini and his management of *Avanti!* that Anna considered dangerous for the Italian Socialist Party.

Antonio Labriola (1843–1904). An Italian Marxist theoretician, the father of Marxism in Italy, and the main man in Angelica's life who initiated her into socialism.

Vladimir Il'ich Lenin (1870–1924). A Russian communist revolutionary, politician, and political theorist who served as the leader of the Russian SFSR from 1917 and as premier of the Soviet Union from 1922 until 1924. Angelica probably met Lenin in 1900 in Berlin. He highly valued and appreciated Angelica, assigning her important tasks and positions within the party, allowing her to leave Russia in 1921 when she became disenchanted with the Revolution and remaining her "protector" until his death in 1924.

Rosa Luxemburg (1871–1919). A Marxist theorist, philosopher, economist, and revolutionary socialist of Polish Jewish descent who became a naturalized German citizen. One of the best known female socialists of the 20th century. For Angelica, Rosa was an example of everything a woman could achieve in life.

Julius Martov (1873–1923). A Russian politician, leader of the Mensheviks in the early twentieth-century Russia and a friend of Angelica.

Benito Mussolini (1883–1945). An Italian politician, journalist, leader of the National Fascist Party, prime minister of Italy from 1922 until 1943.

Edda Mussolini (1910–1995). The eldest child of Benito Mussolini, Italy's fascist dictator from 1922 to 1943. For a long time it was thought that Edda was the daughter of Angelica.

Donna Rachele Mussolini (1890–1979). The mistress, wife, and widow of Italian dictator Benito Mussolini.

Christian Rakovsky (1873–1941). A Bulgarian socialist revolutionary, Bolshevik politician, and Soviet diplomat; he was also a noted journalist, physician, and essayist. A good friend of Angelica, he was her chief in the Ukraine when she was nominated the Vice-Minister of the Foreign Affairs of the Ukraine.

John Silas Reed (1887–1920). An American journalist, poet, and socialist activist best remembered for his firsthand account of the Bolshevik Revolution, *Ten Days that Shook the World*. He was married to writer and feminist Louise Bryant. Friends with Angelica since 1917, he took her to watch one of her first movies and insisted on her writing her memoirs.

Marghertia Sarfatti (1880–1961). A Jewish Italian journalist, art critic, patron, collector, socialite, a prominent propaganda adviser of the National Fascist Party, and one of Benito Mussolini's mistresses. Because of Mussolini, Angelica and Margherita became rivals and eventually sworn enemies.

Norman Mattoon Thomas (1884–1968). An American Presbyterian minister who achieved fame as a socialist, pacifist, and six-time presidential candidate for the Socialist Party of America. Norman Thomas nominated Angelica the "U.S. Socialist Party Ambassador to Italy" and created the Foundation of Angelica Balabanoff to collect money to allow her to work in Italy for the socialist cause.

Leon Trotsky, born **Lev Davidovich Bronshtein** (1879–1940). A Russian Marxist revolutionary and theorist, Soviet politician, and the founder and first leader of the Red Army. Angelica met Trotsky in 1904 in Switzerland. Friends and colleagues, they continued to work together until Angelica's departure from Russia in 1921.

Filippo Turati (1857–1932). An Italian sociologist, poet, and Socialist politician. Turati and Anna Kuliscioff were the most instrumental intellectuals in the founding of the Italian Socialist Party (PSI) in 1892.

Vatslav Vorovsky (1871–1923). A Marxist revolutionary, literary critic, and one of the first Soviet diplomats. In 1917 Angelica was allegedly nominated a Deputy of Vorovsky during his function as an ambassador of the Soviet Union to the Scandinavian countries becoming a *de facto* ambassador to Scandinavian countries. He was also the first person to initiate her into writing poetry.

Ella (1898–2000) and **Bertram** (1896–1977) **Wolfe.** Angelica met Ella and her husband, the well-known American socialist Bertram Wolfe, during her stay in the United States, where the Russian revolutionary had escaped from World War II and mounting fascism in Europe. After the end of the war, Angelica returned to Rome, but her friendship with Ella continued. Both women were good correspondents. In her letters to Ella, housed at the Hoover Institution Archives, Stanford University, in the Bertram Wolfe Collection, Angelica shared many poignant details of her long and interesting life, making them an invaluable source of information.

Grigory Zinoviev (1883–1936). A Bolshevik revolutionary and a Soviet Communist politician. Zinoviev is best remembered as the longtime head of the Communist International. Though she disliked him, Angelica was nonetheless obliged to work with him in 1919 as a secretary of the Comintern.

Clara Zetkin (1857–1933). A German Marxist theorist, activist, and advocate for women's rights. In 1911, she organized the first International Women's Day. Friends with Angelica since 1900, Clara considered Angelica one of her best friends and the only person she felt close with in life.

Abbreviations and Definitions

Archives

AB—Angelica Balabanoff
ACLU—American Civil Liberties Union
HIA/BWC—Bertram David Wolfe Collection, Hoover Institution Archives
IISH—International Institute of Social History, Amsterdam
IISH/AB—Anželika Balabanova Papers, IISH
IISH/EG—Emma Goldman Papers, IISH
NYPL/LML—Lola Maverick Lloyd Papers, Box 18, Manuscripts and Archives Division. The New York Public Library. Astor, Lenox, and Tilden Foundations, New York
NYPL/NT—Norman Thomas. Norman Thomas Papers, Manuscripts and Archives Division. The New York Public Library. Astor, Lenox, and Tilden Foundations, New York
PP/AB—Balabanoff Angelica N 1986, Remembrance and Cultural Affairs Division, *Préfecture de Police*, Paris
PSI—An initialism for the Italian Socialist Party, of which Angelica was a member since 1902
RGASPI—Russian State Archive of Social and Political History, Moscow
SAR/AB—Angelica Balabanoff. Folder 62, Secret Police Department, Directorate of Public Safety, Archive of the Ministry of Internal Affairs, State Archives of Rome, Rome
SFA—The Swiss Federal Archives in Berne
ULB—*Université Libre de Bruxelles* (Free University of Brussels)
UT/KC—Ms. Claude Stewart Collection of Kathleen Crowe/Angelica Balabanoff papers, University of Toronto, Thomas Fisher Rare Book Library

Definitions

Apparatchik—Russian term for a full-time functionary in the Communist Party.

Bolshevik—The Bolsheviks, name derived from *bol'shinstvo*, "majority," a faction of the Marxist Russian Social Democratic Labour Party (RSDLP), which split apart from the Menshevik faction at the Second Party Congress in 1903. The Bolsheviks were the majority faction in a crucial vote; hence their name. They ultimately became the Communist Party of the Soviet Union.

Cheka—Extraordinary Committee Combatting Counter-Revolutionaries, created in 1917 and led by Felix Dzerzhinsky.

Comintern—Communist International—also known as the Third International (1919–1943), an international communist organization initiated in Moscow in March 1919. The International intended to fight "by all available means, including armed force, for the overthrow of the international bourgeoisie and for the creation of an international Soviet republic as a transition stage to the complete abolition of the State." Angelica was nominated as the first secretary of the Comintern upon its creation in 1919.

International Workingmen's Association—an international organization that aimed at uniting a variety of different left-wing socialist, communist, and anarchist political groups and trade union organizations that were based on the working-class and class struggle. It was founded in London by Karl Marx in 1864 and was known as the First International; transformed in 1899 into the Second International; and in 1919 into the Third International or Comintern.

Menshevik—The Mensheviks were a faction of the Russian socialist movement that emerged in 1904 after a dispute in the Russian Social-Democratic Labour Party between Vladimir Lenin and Julius Martov, leading to the party splitting into two factions, one being the Mensheviks and the other being the Bolsheviks. The word is derived from the Russian word "minority," whereas Lenin's adherents were known as "Bolsheviks," from "majority." Angelica was commonly considered as a Menshevik, though she never accepted belonging to any party.

I

A Natural-Born Rebel

Angelica's story starts in Chernigov, hundreds of miles away from Paris, Rome, and New York, where she would spend most of her life. The 19th-century Chernigov was a quiet and provincial town with "two hospitals, several bank branches, a pawn shop and a society of mutual credit."[1] It was of little regional importance. The nearest railway station, Kruty, was nearly 50 miles away from town (at that time a four-hour trip). Most of the business activity was generated by the markets at which merchants from the nearby areas sold food, clothes, and domestic animals. Market days took place four times per year and went on for one or two weeks. However, they remained local, attracting only citizens of Chernigov, compared to the markets of the nearby town Nezhin, which attracted the whole region.[2]

Angelica came into this world on May 8, 1869, when the first lilac and chestnuts trees blossomed after months of cold winter and heavy snowfalls, at the sumptuous 22-room Balabanoff family estate in the suburbs of Chernigov.[3] The house, on the bank of the river Desna, surrounded by orchards and gardens, was lavishly furnished with fine-looking furniture.

Angelica lived the life of a *tsarevna* in Chernigov. Her father, Isaac Balabanoff, owned multiple properties in town: a factory that must have produced one of the main regional products—brick, vodka, or tobacco; and hectares of orchards and lands, which were harvested by hundreds of peasants who, after the abolition of serfdom in 1861, had been "liberated" but continued to depend on their landowner for work and remained a part of the household. As a christening present, she received her own garden, an aviary with birds, jewelry, and gold.

The Balabanoffs were a Jewish family. In Russia, Jews generally had to live within the pale of a settlement. Angelica's family was not confined by these rules. They could live where they wished and run their business freely, so her parents must have converted to the Russian Orthodox religion.

This would have allowed Isaac to become a member of the First Moscow Guild of merchants and a respectable citizen of Chernigov, and Anne Hoffmann, Angelica's mother to order clothes in the most fashionable boutiques in St. Petersburg. The shops kept custom-made mannequins with the Balabanoffs' measurements so that the family could place orders directly from Chernigov.

The family's regular tours in resorts like the Swiss Montreux, German Baden Baden, Austrian Bad Ischl, and French Nice culminated in visits to the extended family in Moscow and St. Petersburg—to the bourgeois mansions that Angelica would later remember as richly decorated with statues of cupids, crystal chandeliers, imposing staircases, and marbles entrances. Traveling became her favorite pastime and would remain so throughout her life.

As a child, Angelica was a short, chubby, and lively girl with masses of black curly hair. Her life was mapped out for her from the start. She was to receive a "worldly, conventional education" to achieve the only thing that was important in the life of a girl: "to marry well so as not to lose the social status befitting one of her class."[4]

To assure the marriage of her youngest daughter, Anna Hoffmann lovingly prepared her dowry. She filled up oak-wood flat-lidded dowry chests with silverware and furs. Angelica had "jewelry and gold instead of toys."

However, the relationship between Angelica and her mother was bad from the start. Angelica had an unusually independent and rebellious character. She never understood why marriage and living according to the rules and traditions established by society were obligatory and why they were supposed to make her happy.

Anna's expressions "Who will marry you if you don't drink milk?" and "What will people think of you?" had haunted Angelica since she was old enough to understand them.[5] Years later she exasperatedly resumed: "I can remember no issue or argument that my mother did not finally reduce to the ultimate in her eyes: marriage with a wealthy and respectable man."[6]

She tried to find explanations from people who surrounded her, but there was no one to help. She was terribly lonely on the vast isolated estate. By the time she was cognizant, her four older sisters were married and had left home. She saw them so little that, apart from her elder sister Anna, whom she would see regularly during her adolescence, she never mentioned their names in her autobiography and her correspondence.

Likewise, Angelica rarely saw her four brothers, Victor, Leon, Samuil, and Sergei. As was usual in well-off families, girls were raised separately from boys. They lived in different quarters of the house and had their own tutors, and much to the girl's jealousy and admiration, the boys were allowed to have friends and attend schools and universities to become lawyers and merchants.

The only children on the Balabanoff estate were those of the servants, but mingling with other social classes was out of the question. Instead Angelica was surrounded by French, German, and English governesses, French being the language of which she "first learned and appreciated the music, rhythm and rhymes," she would later recall.[7] The governesses were terrified of her mother, making Angelica's life stiff and rigid. They followed the girl's every move. She spent every day apart from Sunday in her study room to learn drawing, dance, embroidery, rules of behavior, and basic history and literature. During her play time she was allowed to go to her flower garden and observe the birds in her aviary. On Sundays she dined with her parents, and this was the only time she was allowed to see her father.

Angelica later remembered that the worst moments in her daily routine were the compulsory piano lessons, "one of the most vital and important accomplishments of a rich girl." Her mother hired "the best music teacher" from the Chernigov conservatory, who was brought to her villa every week in a sledge pulled by horses. "The very fact that the sole purpose of those lessons was to allow me to marry well," wrote Angelica, "prompted me to despise the lessons, as well as the cold, conventional teacher with the well-trimmed beard of which he was so proud."[8]

In the absence of supporters who could understand her revolutionary nature, Angelica turned to God. In her prayers she often asked Him to cancel the hated lessons. Once her governess announced to her that the teacher would not be coming because the horse that had been sent to pick him up died on the way. The death of the animal was the last thing that the girl had wanted. To her, it was caused by the same person who caused all her misfortunes: her mother, who had made the horse work too hard on the estate transporting water from the well to the house and to irrigate the orchards.

Lacking an understanding mother, Angelica fantasized about having a loving father. But Isaac was a busy man. Often away on business trips, much to his daughter's jealousy, he left home every day when she was still in bed, in a small two-wheeled horse-drawn carriage, to run the business. Anna used the hours reserved for meetings between her youngest daughter and Isaac to list everything that Angelica had recently done wrong, making the father-daughter relationship difficult. Angelica was persuaded that without such an authoritative mother, she could have had a tolerant and supportive father who would have comprehended his daughter's lively nature.

By the time Angelica turned five, everyone in the family knew that something was "wrong" with her. She had been born with an inexplicable guilt over belonging to the rich and privileged class.

She found it unfair that her family owned an estate consisting of the 22-room house, stables, and adjacent buildings, surrounded by gardens and orchards, while so many people lived in poor homes; that her mother could sleep late while the servants had to be up at dawn to start their work; and that peasants kneeled in front of her father to kiss his hem. She did not understand what was so charitable about giving away clothes her family did not need anyway. She quickly realized that the world was divided between those who ordered and those who obeyed.

The young rebel chose to side with "those who obeyed." At the age of five, she rejected her parents' authority, creating an open and ongoing conflict with her mother. Life at home was constant battle. When her mother scolded the servants for not doing their work well, the little rebel ran to them to hug and console them, begging them to leave the dreadful house and her tyrannical parents, assuring them that life could be much happier outside her family estate.

"Already at this very early age, the dominating feeling in me was sympathy with the humiliated people—and so it remained for the rest of my life," she admitted in her unpublished memoirs.[9]

Resourceful and inventive, she started her combat against the dictatorship of bourgeois conventions. She remembered the story of a beggar woman who had habitually come to their estate in Chernigov. Once her mother asked Angelica to give this woman a scarf, which she did. Then Angelica knelt down and kissed the woman's hand, thus establishing equality between her and the woman.

The young rebel soon realized that the beggar woman seemed happy to come back and get more secondhand clothes and that the servants, for the reasons she failed to understand, continued their work for her parents even when badly treated. Her attention turned to the family horses, who worked hard on the family estate and from her point of view were insufficiently fed and taken care of and thus needed her protection. The working conditions of the horses, the cleanliness of the stables, and portions of extra oats became Angelica's first social combat.

Whenever she could, she asked her mother for the keys to the stables and ran to look after the horses, caress them, and take care of them. This new passion also allowed her to spend more time away from the governesses and their stiff daily routine. At first amused, Anna Hoffmann quickly became fed up with the fantasies of her daughter. Angelica recalled how one day when she was ill and stayed in bed, she overheard Anna complaining to her son-in-law, who was also their family doctor and had come to treat Angelica:

"I do not want her to get so fond of horses and so close to the servants. Why should a well-bred girl be so concerned about horses? If it were a boy—but it is a girl—most shocking! As soon as my husband comes home, I will induce him to get rid of the horses."[10]

Anna did not need to repeat her words twice; once Isaac was back from the business trip, the horses were sold. Devastated over the loss of her favorite animals, Angelica never forgave her mother.

All things considered, from Angelica's description, Anna Hoffmann comes across as modern and progressive woman. She helped her husband to run the business, skillfully negotiating the rent of orchards and lands with peasants, and busied herself with charitable activities, which was as much as a woman could do in strict-mannered and patriarchal Russian society. She also kept her maiden name, Hoffmann, adding her husband's name with a hyphen after the marriage. Though not entirely unknown in aristocratic families, such a practice was still an exception. Angelica admired her mother's talents but blamed Anna for forcing her to live according to the rules of her social class.

She considered that her unhappy and lonely childhood was the fault of Anna Hoffmann, who failed to understand and accept her daughter's revolutionary nature. "In fact, I could (*sic*) scarcely remember any childhood," claimed Angelica.[11]

One of her refuges was books. Her favorite was *David Copperfield* by Charles Dickens. During long winter evenings, she recited to herself again and again her preferred passages from the novel, sobbing and rejoicing together with her hero, who succeeded in his life despite becoming an orphan, being forced to work hard and living in poverty: "I know I do not exaggerate, unconsciously or unintentionally the scantiness of my resources or the difficulties of my life.... I know that I lounged about the streets insufficiently and unsatisfactory fed...," Angelica wept while reading, triumphing at the happy ending, "I might easily have been, for any care that was taken of me, a little robber or a little vagabond."[12]

When Angelica was ten, Isaac Balabanoff died. After many tears and much drama, the young rebel achieved her first victory. She was the first girl in her family allowed to go to school; however, she quickly decided that this triumph was insufficient. She did not want to go to any school but a public one. Her dreams of socializing with girls from middle-class families were crushed by her mother from the start. Anna's verdict was the best private school for girls in the region, or nothing. The fight was unequal. Eager to leave home at all costs, Angelica agreed to attend The Princess Obolenskaya Institute in Kharkov, 330 miles away from Chernigov.

Angelica later understood why Anna Hoffmann had agreed to send her to school. She expected that her daughter would fail the entrance exams in Russian. The language was not spoken in the family. Anna did not know that her daughter had been learning Russian secretly from the servants and books. Both ladies traveled to Kharkov, where Angelica brilliantly passed the entrance exams. Anna returned to Chernigov alone, leaving her youngest offspring in the care of the teachers.

Anna's last hope was that in the absence of her husband, the school would do well for her daughter's temper, which was unusually disobedient for girls at the time. A prestigious boarding school should certainly affirm Angelica's understanding of traditional values, and she would come back home a more tolerant and quiet person, with all her feminine virtues in place. Besides, Angelica's elder sister Anna lived in Kharkov with her husband and could look after her.

The newly admitted student was the happiest person in school. While other girls complained about wearing the same sky-blue uniform dresses every day, their short sleeves trimmed with white lace and white aprons; sleeping in large dormitories together with thirty other students, in rooms that were so badly heated in winter that water froze in the wash basins in the morning; eating stale, dull food; strict teachers; austere daily life, and obligatory mass early on Sunday mornings, Angelica was delighted to finally have friends and to have escaped from her mother and those stiff governesses.

During her seven years in school, Angelica spent much time with her sister's family. Anna's son was Angelica's age. The children and the sisters became close. Angelica finally had someone she could call her brother, while sister Anna's love filled the empty space in Angelica's heart created by the lack of understanding with her mother. Angelica even called Anna "Mama."

The school provided only a temporary respite. Seven years later, when Angelica's school days were over, the young woman was back in the much-despised household, where, with her siblings gone, she now lived alone with her mother. There seemed to be no way out. Angelica must have heard about the radical leftist movement, which was spreading its wings in Russia; about the creation of the first revolutionary organization, *Narodnaya Volya*, which demanded the abolition of the monarchy, the distribution of lands to peasants, and freedom of speech, it certainly had its sub-group in Chernigov; and about strikes by workers and the assassination attempt on the highly conservative and widely disliked Tsar Alexander III, whose organizers included Lenin's brother Alexander—subsequently captured and hanged. It is difficult to say whether she wanted to join them and be a part of the movement. Despite her rebellious nature, she had spent all her life in a cloistered family environment and was not familiar with the world outside her home. Suddenly an opportunity presented itself.

A few months following Angelica's return from school, she went with her mother for their regular autumn sojourn in Montreux. They settled in an upscale hotel with a picturesque view of the azure Lake Geneva, cruising boats, and the Swiss Alps. On the itinerary: walks along the scenic Riviera-style streets, with cypresses, palms, and flower beds full of lilies and dahlias. Angelica was unable to stroll idly for days at a time. To occupy herself, she enrolled in the language school for girls. One of the teachers said she had the necessary capacity to become a teacher. She was beyond happy. For the first time in her life, someone had suggested that she could have a vocation.

Back home, she immediately started to give language lessons to girls from the middle-class families in Chernigov who planned to study abroad, as higher education for women was not available in Russia. Anna Hoffmann accepted her daughter's teaching activity, deeming it charity and helping the poor. When Anna commented that her daughter gave too many lessons, Angelica waited for her mother to leave the estate to visit poor homes or go shopping in Chernigov and gave appointments to her students in one of her hideouts in the garden.

She would have liked to study abroad herself. Shy and self-conscious, she was afraid of sophisticated universities like Heidelberg that accepted female students. That is, until sometime after her return from Montreux, when one of her pupils told her about the New University of Brussels—a newly-created, low-cost, democratic institution. Angelica's mind was set on going.

She called a family meeting and calmly explained to her mother and brothers that she planned go to the university in Brussels, taking with her a small suitcase with only few belongings, and that she intended to do so even if she had to break ties with her family. To say that Angelica's announcement of her plans caused shock in the family would be an understatement. The response of her mother and her brothers was easy to predict. In addition, her brothers had heard about the school. It had a reputation as more a leftist political center than as a reputable institution. Their refusal was followed by months of tears. Angelica was hysterical. She stayed for days in her room, refused to eat or go out, and eventually became ill. The summer of 1897 was at its peak when her mother saw that nothing could be done. With a heavy heart, Anna Hoffmann decided to accept her daughter's wish to study at the university.

At the time when Angelica decided to leave her home, she was 28. For her time she would have been a mature and most certainly married woman. Information about her marriage is contradictory. It appeared on the Internet a few years ago from unknown Russian sources indicating a certain Mikhail Balabanov as her possible husband, a social democrat and a distant cousin, which explained the same family name. Never in her life did Angelica refer to this marriage, making the whole issue questionable. A few years after leaving her home, she would change her date of birth from 1869 to 1878 (and switch her day and month of birth from May 8 to August 5) implying that she had left Chernigov at 19. Considering her real age, no matter how much she was against marriage, the pressure of family and society were difficult to resist in a small provincial town, making her marriage with her cousin highly possible, though most probably short-lived and unsuccessful.

When Anna Hoffmann finally agreed that Angelica might leave Chernigov, another family meeting was called, during which Angelica's brothers told her something she had not thought of before. She would need money for everyday life. After some discussion, her brothers suggested that she would receive a monthly allowance as an anticipated inheritance. Angelica gave it some thought and asked for 50 rubles per month, an average worker's salary (an amount that women of Angelica's socio-economic milieu could easily have spent on a few bottles of French perfume). Astounded by their youngest sibling's proposal, persuaded that she would not last more than a few days on this amount, her family agreed. Her first monthly allowance was supplemented by a one-way train ticket to Brussels, in third class, as she had insisted.

Anna Hoffmann started to pack her daughter's suitcases. She unlocked Angelica's trunks and drawers with her daughter's "trousseau" and dresses made to order in the best shops in Europe. But Angelica refused to hear of it. She would not need any of these things in her new life. Anna finally understood that despite her efforts during all these years to keep Angelica within the acceptable boundaries of her social class, her grown-up "Nihilist" daughter was committing an unimaginable "sin." She was leaving her home forever to live with the "poor" as she had wanted to do since the age of five. Worst of all, she would probably remain a pathetic spinster, as no respectable man would want to marry her. For Anna, her daughter's life did not follow any customary ground rules and was no longer worth living. She cursed Angelica.

The execration was not unheard of in Chernigov. Everyone knew the legend of a young woman, Motrya Kochubeevna, who was cursed twice by her mother for escaping from her parents' house to get married to her godfather. The beautiful young woman died quickly after that and started to appear to strangers at night, wearing a long white nightdress with her hair down. She begged them to cross her twice to liberate her soul from the curse. As no one dared to bless her, out of fear of stumbling into a ghost, she disappeared at sunrise with moans. Each person in Chernigov knew that the youngest child in the Balabanoff family was doomed to suffer for the rest of her life. But Angelica's life was just beginning.

Her last meeting with her mother before starting an independent life and leaving Chernigov took place in the three-story stone-built mansion in the city, a rarity in a place where most of the constructions were of wood. It was centrally located "on the corner of Boguslavskaya street and the Red Square" and served as a family business base and as a necessary stopover for trips outside Chernigov. Angelica would always remember the last words of Anna Hoffmann.

"I'm throwing you out of my house," her mother said.

"No," replied Angelica, "I'm leaving because it is my decision to do so."

They never said goodbye.[13]

II

Professorial Nomination

Angelica's family's disapproval of her decision to leave Chernigov was not surprising, considering the peculiarity of the New University of Brussels, chosen by the rebellious young woman for her studies. Opened in 1894, three years prior to her arrival, it would continue its existence for a total of 30 years. The place was a cauldron of anarchists. A staggering number of 139 anarchist and socialist professors taught for free in the afternoons and evenings. The Belgian authorities, horrified by the dissident faculty and equally disruptive students, threatened to close the establishment. The government regularly accused the institution of promoting political propaganda.

By the time Angelica arrived, the issue of the university's accreditation and, more importantly, the acceptance of its diplomas, had been debated by the Belgian government. According to Belgian law, universities were obliged to have at least four colleges to be considered a university. The New University claimed to have a college of Philosophy and Letters, where Angelica studied, as well as Law, Science and Medicine, and consisted of five buildings. In reality, the colleges of Science and Medicine most likely did not exist.

The diplomas awarded at the college of Philosophy and Letters were accepted only after exams in front of a mixed jury consisting of New University teachers and government representatives. Students from the colleges of Medicine and Science had to pass additional exams to validate their diplomas. Student fees of 150 Belgian francs per year (approximately $810 today) and occasional private donations composed the main income of the university.

The conflict between the university and the government was regularly and publicly discussed in the press and in Parliament. During each conflict, the university's professors admirably defended the school's importance. Among those professors were some prominent political figures. They included the founder of the university, the well-known anarchist, geographer, and traveler Élisée Reclus; his equally anarchistic brother, Élie Reclus; and the handsome and wealthy Belgian socialist Emile Vandervelde, who was also the president of the International Socialist Bureau[1] for many years, of which Angelica would soon be a member.

The school continued to exist largely because of foreign students who enrolled at the university each year. Out of 231 students that registered in 1897 together with Angelica, more than half came from Eastern Europe, including 56 Romanians, 54 Bulgarians, and 31 Russians. When the university finally closed at the end of World War I, it was due to the fact that because of the war, the students from Eastern Europe could not travel as freely as they had done previously.

On a rainy grey October day in 1897, Angelica pushed open the door of her "dream place" located in a middle-class neighborhood on the *Rue des Minimes*, "housed in two old residential buildings" made out of brick, to register, pay the tuition fees, and receive a class schedule. There was neither elegantly forged gate, landscaped gardens, nor a doorman to greet her at the entrance, but just a shabby-looking door in the middle of the street, which was hardly ever closed.

Angelica upon arrival in Brussels, c. 1897 (collection of Giorgio Giannelli).

Angelica asked to defer payment of the already modest enrollment fee because she could not afford to pay the entire amount. She was allowed to pay 50 Belgian francs out of 150 on registration day and the remaining amount at the end of the following month.

She arrived in Brussels as a shy, introverted, and babyish-looking young woman. The surviving photo of the time shows her with childish round cheeks and a stubborn look on her face, wearing a dark dress and a straw hat. Dazzling the faculty members with her knowledge of Russian, English, French, German and Italian, she easily passed the entrance exams for the college of Philosophy and Letters.

Nothing could show more starkly

the difference between her new existence and her family home than her lodgings. A tiny, unheated room situated at 11 *rue Rollebeck*, her new apartment was only a few minutes away from the New University and about ten minutes on foot from the Central Square.

> It was a miserable little room without heat and furnished with only a bed, a table and two rickety chairs. It was one of the most poverty-stricken districts in Brussels. But even on the coldest days and at a time during the winter when I was sick and half-dead from a combination of cold and undernourishment, I would not have surrendered one dark corner of my room for all the big, well-heated houses in Chernigov.[2]

One year later, Angelica moved to a similar room on 353 *Chaussée de Waterloo*. Such student-like, "microscopic," as she described them in her letters, rooms became her trademark.[3]

She was rarely overly excited with her pursuits or happy with the results of her work. The New University was one exception. It was exactly the place she needed to be in order to establish herself. The subjects available for study at the college of Philosophy and Letters provided plenty of opportunities for political discussions and included ancient, medieval, and modern political history.

Overwhelmed with her life, Angelica did not worry about the issue of diploma accreditation; the small auditoriums that "could not boast of million-dollar endowments"[4]; the classrooms furnished with long narrow benches that were closely arranged to seat more students; or the insufficient classroom lights that came from the small bell-shaped lamps, attached to the edges of inverse-T-shaped sticks that hung from the ceiling. None of that mattered to Angelica. She could learn and soak up the foundation for the political spirit that would be the heart of her existence for the next 67 years.

The professors who had the delicate mission of nurturing and developing the boisterous spirit of this young Russian woman were, in her own words, "Olympians not to be approached by ordinary mortals."[5]

Out of all the outstanding professors, the one who impressed her most was Célestin Demblon, a poet, a socialist, and the poorest of them all. The first love of Angelica's intellectually liberated life was ten years her senior. Oddly enough, she remembered him as unattractive, yet his photo depicted a handsome man. Demblon had a high forehead, gleaming eyes, a long straight nose, slicked-back chestnut hair, and a neatly cut fringed beard and moustache. Only much later in her life did Angelica realize that Demblon's simple conventional clothes hid a carefully constructed romantic image. Demblon taught French literature at the New University. As a Wallonian Socialist Deputy and a freemason, his political credo was to defend all oppressed people. Angelica fell for him immediately. She wrote him an eight-page letter. Addressing him as *"vrai 'homme"* ("a real man"), she expressed her admiration and asked to meet him outside classes.[6] He agreed to supervise Angelica's studies and her thesis when she graduated.

They met in her small room to drink her favorite black Assam tea, with *varenye* (fruit jelly). She introduced her teacher to the Russian custom of eating *varenye* with the tea. They discussed Demblon's recent translations of Shakespeare. He cited Victor Hugo, Chateaubriand, and his own poems, which she had learned by heart.

> *Volons! oh! Mais, plus vite! à l'immense idéal,*
> *Loin des ces jours goujats, loin du passé féal,*
> *Eperdument! volons vers l'avenir splendide,*
> *Mystique, aimant, grenat, orangé, gai, lucide!*[7]

Open-mouthed, Angelica listened to the words of her much-beloved professor. Losing track of time, as though it did not exist, she was forgetting that she was sitting on a sagging chair in her poorly heated room.

Some afternoons, Angelica followed Célestin Demblon to Parliament. The romantic walk to the House of Representatives passed through the Park of Brussels with its double-row lime-tree alleys, Greek marble statues, and lily pond. Together they entered the Iron Forged Gates of Parliament and parted only at the last minute. Demblon would then take his place on the floor of the chamber. Angelica hurriedly climbed the wooden stairs to the visitor's gallery to listen to his speeches on protecting the working class against tyranny.

Nearly 30 years later, on the occasion of a socialist propaganda lecture, Angelica would visit Brussels. At the end of the conference, to her disbelief, she would be approached by an elegant brunette in her forties. The stranger presented herself as the daughter of Célestin Demblon.

The two women would spend the entire evening in Angelica's hotel room. Miss Demblon would tell Angelica how two tombstones had been erected for her father after his death in the Robermont cemetery in Liege, the first one by socialists and the second by communists. The two parties argued about his political views, and each decided to erect its own tombstone. Miss Demblon would then confide to the stupefied Angelica that her father had always talked about her and followed her career.

"Please come to the house tomorrow," Miss Demblon said before getting up to leave. "I still have some of my father's items. I would like you to have something that belonged to him."

Unable to take any hefty object, Angelica would choose her professor's black fountain pen with which he had written his poems.

During the university years after spending her Brussels afternoons with Demblon, Angelica restrained from prologing her evenings in the company of friends or lovers. She had other, more pressing, things to do. She quickly swallowed a bowl of vegetable broth, accompanied by bread, and then went alone to the People's House, where she slipped into the crowd of listeners to attend political lectures and discussions, organized, among others, by Russian students.

Convinced that every inch of her body screamed out her bourgeois background and unpreparedness for life, she timidly "worshipped them from afar," avoiding the heated debates. Nonetheless, it was at these lectures that she made her first leftists contacts. Her attitude would radically change over the next few years, when Angelica would become one of the greatest female speakers in Europe.

With all these activities, Angelica did not notice how quickly her two-year course in Brussels came to an end. In April 1899, advised by Demblon, she completed her education with a two-month pilgrimage to London, obligatory for all young leftists. The city had become the new Mecca for Marxist followers since Karl Marx had been buried in the East Side of Highgate cemetery. During the week, Angelica went to the British Library. She spent her Sundays in Hyde Park's Speaker's Corner. She remembered with fondness the speeches by the popular, modern and serious-looking Trade Union speaker, Tom Mann, with his thick moustache and beer belly, and speeches about overthrowing capitalism and the authoritarian lectures on universal suffrage by the social-democratic writer Henry Hyndman, who, with his long beard that reminded Angelica of Orthodox priests and a dreamy philosophical look in his eyes, seemed to belong to another century.

The short stay in London proved to be more complicated than Angelica had planned. The city was expensive. Her stipend was insufficient, and she had to work as a babysitter for what she described as a "stuffy, bourgeois family," which painfully evoked her home and everything she had so despised—from the unbending rules of behavior to the poor treatment of the servants.[8] She made her way back to Brussels in time to defend her thesis: "The Feminine Characters in French Literature in the First Half of the 19th Century." On 6 June 1899, she received her title of Doctor in Letters in the presence of seven university professors, headed by Célestin Demblon and Elisée Reclus.[9]

During her studies, Angelica must have made quite an impression on the entire faculty. As soon as she defended her thesis, the university proposed that she become a professor at the New University. They were the first to remark upon her oratorical skills and her agreeable deep voice, which, combined with clear and simple speech, made her audience understand and remember her words. Despite the flattering proposal, Angelica decided to leave Brussels.

She knew for certain that professorship was not the kind of "new life" she had in mind when she "escaped" from home. She wanted to explain to her favorite professor during one of their last meetings that it would be a pitfall into a liberated but bourgeois lifestyle, but she did not want to hurt him. So instead she told him that she did not feel ready to settle down. She still needed to learn.

Angelica missed her chance of becoming one of the first female professors, who at that time numbered about 10 in Europe and the U.S.

The young woman left Brussels more reassured, but she was still unable to imagine what her life might entail. Lost between her dreams of helping the poor and not knowing how to apply her dreams to her real life, she then spent one academic year at the University of Leipzig, followed by a few summer months at the University of Berne and by one and a half trimesters in Humboldt University in Berlin. None of the universities have any records of her. She probably chose an unofficial education. At that time, some students, mostly women, attended some lectures after receiving authorization from professors and without registering.[10]

She wrote in her memoirs that she did not like any of the above places. The so-called liberal university of Leipzig did not accept women when Angelica arrived there. "If there were any radicals among the Leipsic [sic] students, I did not discover them—and this was one of the most revolutionary Socialist centers in all Germany," Angelica later recalled.[11]

Describing this period as "full of disillusionment," she waited until the end of the academic year and in May of 1900 arrived at the University of Berne. Whether it was because of an amorous escapade or a thirst for a better political education, for some reason no one ever knew that she had been to Berne. Angelica kept this secret to herself until 1945, when she mentioned having attended the University of Berne in her curriculum vitae, required for submitting a bill providing for the legitimization of her stay in the U.S.

By the end of the summer, Angelica was in Berlin. She decided to study political economics at Humboldt University, the alma mater of Karl Marx, taught by the famous left-wing professor Adolf Wagner. The female students were admitted only into the Arts and Letters department. Angelica's desire to study political economics created a small uproar. Her request was doubly unusual: not only was she a woman, but she already had a diploma from the New University in Brussels and wanted to study more. She had to explain her interest in studying political economics in front of the stupefied faculty members.

The course was another disappointment. Political economics was not her field. An even greater disenchantment was Professor Wagner. She was appalled when she saw that his lectures were attended by members of the Hohenzollern family.[12] Suspecting that the "supporter" of the left wing was in reality devoted to the Bismarck regime, she quickly lost interest in the celebrated professor and his teaching. Her education was at a halt. However, her intuition in choosing Berlin had not failed her. She made her first revolutionary acquaintances. Among them was a small, thin, neurotic, bald man with piercing brown eyes and a short, red beard who presented himself as Vladimir Oulianov-Lenin.

III

Alone with Lenin

At the age of 31, Angelica was small and plump, with grayish skin and messy hair. One could not call her beautiful, but she had a lot of charm and personal charisma that attracted different people to her and that were more important than her physical looks. As such, her numerous romantic liaisons remained for years a subject of discussion in many households of her friends and enemies. Marina Cattaneo, the granddaughter of Maria and Ivan Matteo Lombardo, secretary of the PSI (the Italian Socialist Party) who were Angelica's close friends in Milan during the last 30 years of Angelica's life, confirmed that according to her grandparents, Angelica's lengthy list of lovers included Lenin, Trotsky, Stalin, and Francesco Misiano—the Italian socialist filmmaker who came to live in Russia to avoid fascism in Italy—and many others.

Out of all her encounters, the most peculiar was with Lenin. Angelica never told anyone under what circumstances or where they had met. She always insisted that the first time she met Lenin, she had found him so "plain and uninteresting" that she could not recall when or how this meeting took place.

Yet there is something odd about her explanations. Angelica usually remembered how she had met most of the people she knew. She eagerly described her first encounters with Benito Mussolini, Leon Trotsky, Josef Stalin, Rabindranath Tagore, and John Reed and gave interviews about her friendship with Ben Gurion and Golda Meir. Somehow she could not remember one single detail about her meeting with the main Russian political figure of the 20th century. How many women *just happen* to stroll into the life of Lenin?

All things considered, Angelica and Lenin might very likely have met in Berlin in the autumn of 1900. Angelica arrived there to attend the coursers of Professor Wagner at Humboldt University. It is the first time that both were in the same place at the same time. Lenin came to Berlin at the end of 1900, after a three-year exile in Siberia, to visit his elder sister Anna. He traveled alone. His wife, Nadezhda Krupskaya, was still serving her sentence in Ufa for her red underground activity. Lenin was one year Angelica's junior. By the time he arrived in Berlin he was considered one of the leading revolutionaries in Russia, a well-known figure for anyone interested in this movement and a person not to be missed for Angelica. Of course no one could ever have imagined that one day he would lead one of the biggest countries in the world.

Angelica was still more of a socialist sympathizer than a real supporter of any left-wing party in Europe. But she was eager to enlarge her revolutionary contacts and had already made a few impressive friends. She had met Rosa Luxemburg and Clara Zetkin—the most prominent female leaders of the socialist movement in Europe—and Lenin's elder sister Anna.

There is a striking difference between Angelica's description of meeting Rosa and that of meeting Lenin. She always remembered how nervous and excited she was about meeting Rosa. She recalled in much detail how Rosa had come to Berlin to deliver a lecture and how she rushed to the meeting room where Rosa was to speak. The young Russian woman was so afraid that it would be too obvious that she was not a member of any socialist party that she did not dare to enter without getting Rosa's permission first. She was waiting for Rosa at the entrance to the meeting room when she saw an unattractive, short-legged, lame Jewish woman with a disproportionally large head. Angelica approached this female star of the socialist movement.

"Comrade, would you allow me to attend your meeting?" muttered Angelica, bravely explaining that she was not yet a member of any socialist party.

"Of course, I'll be happy to have you," replied Rosa.[1]

All the chairs were taken in the high-ceilinged meeting room. Angelica managed to squeeze into a far corner. Large windows let the light stream in as Rosa was about to speak. While observing Rosa, Angelica came to the conclusion that for her, Rosa was the best example of everything a woman could achieve. Rosa had incredible intelligence and passion, which she gave to the socialist movement. Her rare style of work, speech, and personality singled her out in any crowd. Angelica would successfully adapt Rosa's oratorical skills to her own, acquiring Rosa's simplicity, enthusiasm, and ability to address both men and women.

Approximately around the time that Angelica met Rosa, Angelica created her famous altar. She collected photos of people she admired and who inspired her, framed them, and placed them on a windowsill or on the only table in her small room. The iconic-like collection startled more than one of her visitors. Some found it touching, whereas others considered it naïve and outmoded. But she kept "praying" to her gods. With time, most of the photos would disappear. Friends and teachers would disappoint her or betray or change their political views and beliefs. But Rosa always remained.

The respect was mutual: "I have enjoyed a lot your Balabanova," Rosa wrote to Clara Zetkin in 1906. "She has a good nature, only a bit too whining for my taste." Rosa was referring to Angelica's prevailing tendency to talk about the "bitterness of disappointment and dissolution of reality."[2,3]

Clara Zetkin, or "Wild Clara," as she was called by her colleagues for her incessant fight for women's rights and for marrying a man 18 years her junior, was another source of inspiration for Angelica at the beginning of her career. Clara immediately understood how unique Angelica's language and organizational skills were in the preparation and handling of international socialist meetings, making Angelica an indispensable part of the movement.

Twenty years after meeting Angelica, Clara—aged, lonely, and expelled from Germany—would find her last refuge in Moscow amid the October Revolution and the beginning of the Red Terror. In a large, unheated communal flat, with heaps of snow falling outside, the hunched, thin Clara, her face marked with deep, long wrinkles, would whisper to her *Liebe gute* (dear, good) Angelica:

"You are the only person I have ever felt close with in life."

When Angelica met Clara and Rosa, she was worlds away from imagining such a turn of events. She was beyond happy that life had given her a chance to meet and observe two women who did that which Angelica could not yet imagine doing in her wildest dreams.

Being well indoctrinated into female revolutionary circles, it is possible that Angelica knew Lenin's sister Anna. The women might have met in Brussels where they studied and attended political gatherings in the People's House. Having similar views, they might have continued seeing each other in Berlin. Angelica's encounter with Lenin probably took place in Anna's apartment or in one of the *Berliner* coffee shops. However, she first mentioned it only in 1961, four years before her death, in her book *Impressions of Lenin*, devoting a few lines to her meeting with the greatest of all revolutionaries. Her narrative was much less exhilarating than that of meeting Rosa. She had forgotten how or where her meeting with Lenin took place. All she remembered was that it was "brief and unsuccessful."

He "did not seduce" her. She found him "unappealing and at times rude." She failed to see what was so exceptional about him and his disagreeable voice which sounded full of "metal shavings." "Neither the content of his speech nor his handling of the topic [the European workers' movement] made a deep impression on me," she wrote later, remembering her conversation with one of the most prominent speakers of the century.[4]

Strangely, despite an apparently bumpy start, their relationship continued for years, making her one of the oldest friends of the revolutionary leader. Lenin's stay in Berlin was short. Before the end of 1900, he went to Munich to continue his underground work and launch the publication of the political newspaper *Iskra*—prohibited by the Tsarist government—for which he found a publisher in Munich.[5] Not only would Angelica travel to Munich during the next two years, but she would continue seeing Lenin and his wife Nadezhda in Switzerland, where all three would soon move. They were far from knowing at that time that during the 1917 Russian revolution they would be at the heart of the major changes in their homeland.

So there is a disparity between her description of meeting the "uninteresting" Lenin and the friendship that followed. It was as though Angelica was trying to obscure the details of the first months of her acquaintance with Lenin. There are two possible explanations for this. She described it during the Cold War, when the fear of Russia was eminent, and she probably tried to down play her early involvement with the revolutionary leader. Another explanation for such vague recollections of the early years of friendship could be an affair that she later wished to conceal.

The private lives of both figures are still shrouded in mystery today. Subject to a secret in Russia, Lenin's "official" biography did not include the non-revolutionary part of his life. His name is usually connected with two women: his wife and his mistress, Inessa Armand. His marriage with Nadezhda Krupskaya always seemed to be more of a political union than a marital one. Suffering from Graves' disease, which resulted in bulging eyes and a tightened neck, nicknamed "The Herring" by her comrades, Nadezhda was an intelligent, knowledgeable, and deeply devoted woman who lived in Lenin's shadow.

Rather different was Lenin's French-born mistress, Inessa Armand—a pretty, petite, green-eyed, long-haired woman with a sharp birdlike nose. After meeting the multilingual and music-loving Inessa in 1909, he would be close with her for years while still remaining married to Krupskaya.

The best word to describe Angelica's private life would be "unconventional"—the word she liked to use when she talked about herself. As a young woman, she came to see marriage as a lonesome routine that had deprived her of the childhood she wanted and that would cut her off from real life. She decided to devote herself to the socialist cause. Afraid that family or children would take up too much of her time, she was against marriage and, indeed, any long-term relationship. For Angelica, being a revolutionary was a life lived not only in ideas but in everyday life. Upon leaving Chernigov, the Russian revolutionary became an adept of "free love."

Quite a few people close to Angelica, such as her long-term friends in Chicago, Doctors Renee and Emil Jonas, confirmed that her relationship with Lenin was more than friendship.[6]

Angelica's amorous liaison with Lenin could also explain her otherwise surprisingly distant relationship with Nadezhda Krupskaya. Being Russian with similar political views and spending much of their lives outside Russia, the women might have been friends. Yet Kruspkaya was the only person to openly accuse Angelica of hypocrisy.

"What strikes me is her insincerity," she wrote, remembering the years they spent together in Switzerland. "To you she always says that she agrees completely, but behind your back she agitates against you; she does not fulfill her formal promises, and so on. It is difficult to work with such a person."[7]

Angelica's other good friend, the famous French communist Marceau Pivert, described Angelica's private life as "rich and adventurous."[8]

Angelica had always been discrete about her private life. She did not like to discuss it except in conversations with a few of her close friends, years later, when most of the people she knew had long passed away. The gap between her silence and the vague recollections of her friends was so vast that it started many rumors. The number of her supposed partners became over-exaggerated. One thing was sure: the main revolutionary figure of the 20th century was not the most important man in Angelica's life.

IV

A Female Lecturer

In her memoirs, entitled *My Life as a Rebel,* Angelica devoted five entire pages to her professor in Sapienza University in Rome, Antonio Labriola, admitting that he was the most important man in her life. In comparison, she dedicated only a few paragraphs to her parents and her female revolutionary heroine, Rosa Luxemburg, a few mere lines to Leon Trotsky and Joseph Stalin, and not a single sentence to six of her eight siblings.

Angelica had met Labriola in a rather desperate moment of her life. It was the spring of 1901. She was 32 years old, a middle-aged woman according to the life expectancy of the time. And she was still not sure what she wanted to do. So far in her quest for justice, in her discussions with Lenin and gatherings in People's Houses she attended, she kept hearing a rather standard explanation of the Marxist theory of communism as possible historical evolution, but she did not know how to apply it to her life. In Berlin she had heard about the Italian professor Antonio Labriola, apparently known for taking a more human and emotional approach to Marxism. With his voice weakened from years of sniffing tobacco, he gave his lectures in the university courtyard, standing on a chair, as no classroom was large enough to fit all the students who came to listen to him. Nothing worked better to seduce the Russian rebel than an unconventional approach to teaching. She decided to attend his course.

She packed her two suitcases and took an express Berlin-Rome train, interrupting her studies at Humbert University in Berlin. Upon her arrival, she did not know a single person in Rome. Her friend the Italian anarchist Alfredo Talamini, whom she had met in Brussels, gave her the address of his lover Elena Pensuti. He had suggested Angelica could contact his friend if she needed assistance. Elena helped Angelica to get a room in the same boarding house in which she lived. The district, which Angelica described in her memoirs as "new," near the Church Santa Maria

Maggiore, had picturesque, mountainous narrow streets and closely built three- and four-storey pink, terra-cotta, and yellow houses.

Angelica quickly enrolled in the Faculty of Humanities at Sapienza University to meet the famous professor. She joined the course in the middle of the academic year, and all absence of information about her studies in the university archives could be explained yet again by her attending courses after receiving permission from the faculty but without registering, as some women did at the time. By the end of the first lecture, she had fallen under the spell of Labriola and his slogan "to put knowledge at the service of the masses." It corresponded well with her ideas about the state of the world and allowed her to understand what she could do to combat poverty and inequality, which she considered the greatest evils in the universe. Under Labriola's guidance, she finally accepted Marxism as the starting point of her understanding of a balanced international order.

It is possible that the young woman was looking for a father figure. Her father, Isaac Balabanoff, had had died when she was ten. All she remembered was a busy and inaccessible man, who had been present only when she had done something wrong and when her mother had asked him to intervene. For years, Angelica had fantasized about a kind, gentle man, capable of understanding and loving his rebellious and unusual daughter. Something in Labriola's appearance may have reminded Angelica of her father—the professor's long face, thick, Mediterranean wavy hair, dense round eyebrows, curved-up moustache, and a sad, tender look in big black eyes with lizard-like hooded eyelids. Whether Angelica was in search of such a Marxist father figure or Labriola first recognized something in her because of her tormented and revolutionary thirst for justice, the two became close friends.

Together they went for long walks in the Gardens of the Villa Borghese, wandering along its hills, beautiful villas, and fountains. She was often invited to dine at his house. Then the rumors began, claiming that there had had to be more to their relationship than that of student-professor, despite their 25-year age difference.

As spring came and the academic year of 1902 neared its end, Labriola told Angelica to come and stand next to him in front of the class:

"Look here, Signorina," he said, sadly, "I'm the only Marxist in Italy. When I die, you will be the only one. You must be the executor of my Marxist will."[1]

That same spring Angelica joined the PSI (the Italian Socialist Party). She did not particularly support it over any other socialist party; she had thought it was something she owed to Labriola. He gave her the support she needed to affirm herself and become a prominent female socialist and speaker of the 20th century.

Italy became her "beautiful adoptive country." She saw Italians as easygoing, open, and warm. The country's ruins were romantic, landscapes breathtaking, and colors gay—not to mention the splendid selection of her favorite "candy, chocolate and stationery."[2]

Most importantly, Angelica finally knew what she would like to do with her life. Italy underwent waves of emigration while Europe looked for extra labor. She would help Italian immigrant workers, for whom she had felt an unexplainable bond since her childhood trips with her family in luxurious French and Swiss resorts:

"One of the striking and startling examples of inequality and injustice which added to my misery [of traveling with the family] was the aspect of the Italian labourers," Angelica later recalled. "The necessity for leaving their homes in search of work and the inferiority of their standard of living made them accept any kind of work at very bad conditions. Then a passionate feeling of solidarity would well up in me. I was happy and honored at any opportunity to speak a few words to them in their own language."[3]

Her childhood dream of helping "the underprivileged" was finally coming true. On February 25, 1903, one day before her passport was to expire, she crossed the border to Switzerland and arrived in St. Gall, heading directly to the Trade Union Headquarters and armed with reference letters from the PSI.

Angelica chose St. Gall over other places because she spoke German and Italian. St. Gall is a German-speaking town located apart from the larger towns of Zurich and Basel. At the time when Angelica arrived there, it was one of the largest centers of the textile industry in Europe, hosting thousands of Italian immigrants who did not speak German. Her knowledge of both languages could be useful. Besides, the overall situation of immigrant workers in St. Gall was worse than in other parts of the country. Cheap Italian labor was over-exploited. Young girls and women worked in dreadful conditions and were more poorly treated than the men.

As soon as the train arrived at St. Gall, she rushed to the Trade Union reception, a shabby room in one of the buildings on a cobblestone street in the old part of town.

With a slight Russian accent, Angelica announced to the two Trade Union officials that she was looking for a job, handing them her reference letter from the PSI in Rome. Startled, they looked at the tiny person. It was the first time that anyone in this small, provincial German-speaking town had seen a foreign and visibly educated woman asking for work.

After a short pause, one of them finally said that there was no work and no money to pay her.

"I'll work for free," answered the peculiar woman. "Could I have a table and two chairs?" With her monthly family allowance of 50 rubles, she could devote all her time to this work.

"At the time women were seldom seen in the offices," Angelica later recalled, "and in addition to this circumstance, my whole case was so unusual. To find a young girl, [a] university graduate who was eager to give her time without remuneration of any kind was strange indeed."[4]

The Trade Union officials agreed to provide her with the necessary equipment. She could start the next day. Angelica hurried to tell the good news to Elena Pensuti, who had traveled with her to St. Gall. The women planned to share an apartment. Aside from their quarters, they shared several beliefs—notably in free love and membership in the PSI. The reasons for their trip to St. Gall were, nonetheless, different. The "the avant-garde and open-minded Elena" was interested "in reuniting with her lover, Alfredo Talamini," while Angelica was interested in "working for the socialist movement."[5]

Prior to their arrival, Talamini had found for them a small two-room apartment in the Italian workers' neighborhood. Each room was furnished with a bed in one corner and a table with two rattan chairs in another. The decoration was completed with a plain china pitcher and ewer washing set on a chest of drawers and a rectangular wooden-framed mirror hanging above it. The kitchen, shared with Elena Pensuti, was equipped with a few shelves, and a curved-leg black coal stove was of little interest for both "libertarian" occupants of the apartment.

Angelica began to work at the Trade Union the day after her impromptu interview. She started by helping out those who were illiterate or did not speak German to fill out administrative forms necessary for their work and visas and organizing German lessons and meetings among workers to help them to get to know each other and settle in. She looked for financial aid and warm winter clothes or simply talked to people and heard them out. For her there were no big or small tasks.

She became one of the most in-demand people in the Trade Union. Her apartment was literally open day and night to her Italian neighbors. The first to rise, she greeted them from her window early in the morning when they went to work and welcomed them back home at night. If it started to rain, she would lend her only umbrella or a raincoat, throwing it through the window to the first person passing by.

The Trade Union officials quickly noticed that she also spoke Russian, French, and English (In fact she spoke 13 languages, including Japanese). She never commented on her extraordinary linguistic talent, explaining once during an interview at the end of her life that she had learned Yiddish "from a woman who came to the family estate in Chernigov to sell eggs."[6]

Her secretary in Moscow, Suzanne Girault, recalled asking her in 1920 when she had learned all these languages. Angelica thought for a second and then answered: "I do not remember. I might have known them forever."[7]

One day in St. Gall, she was approached by the director of the People's House, who asked her to make a speech in German about Russian revolutionary activity.

She flatly refused. For probably the first time, she used what would become her favorite expression: "I feel too small, too insignificant." She explained that she was entirely comfortable with her simple administrative duties, which helped people. It was all she had ever wanted to do since she was a little girl enraged by the way her mother had treated the servants and her governesses. The life of an active, outspoken revolutionary was not for her.

The director of the People's House did not give up. She was the best person in St. Gall to do the job. Eventually a dutiful Angelica reluctantly agreed and immediately became nervous. In vain, Elena tried to encourage her friend, telling her that speaking in front of a modest gathering was no more difficult than being one of the first women to publicly ride a bicycle in Rome. Angelica was inconsolable. Not only had she never spoken in public before, but her bourgeois background was surely too obvious and out of place. Six years after leaving her parents' remote estate in the suburbs of Chernigov, she was still haunted by her upbringing in a wealthy family who owned a factory, lands, and entire streets with buildings.

The frightful meeting date finally arrived. Angelica remembered this first speech very well. After days of anxious rehearsing and fears that no one would come to listen to her and that people would get up to leave after the first few words, she decided to take Elena's small dog with her as an escape plan. In the event that she failed to interest the audience, she would excuse herself and take the dog out for a walk, making her escape seem natural. The meeting room in the People's House, with its poorly plastered walls and old wooden armless chairs, quickly filled up. In spite of the late hour and chilly night, the German workers of St. Gall, mostly men, were eager to know how their comrades from Russia were fighting against the imposed long working hours and unfair pay.

Angelica stood in front of her audience. Despite Elena's insistent requests for Angelica to buy a new dress, she decided to wear one of her formless skirts. Her splendid heavy black hair, which she had last brushed early that morning, was braided with two strands overlapping at the back of her head. She suddenly realized that she had so much to say, so much compassion for the people in front of her, that the words began to flow of their own volition. Years later she still seemed to be surprised that not one person moved during her one-hour speech and that the participants stood up to applaud at the end.

Fame came to Angelica literally overnight. After her first successful speech, she was invited to give lectures in other towns.

In her speeches she explained to the workers that "they should be aware of who they are, that they are human beings who have the rights to everything produced by art, science, etc."[8]

However, her preferred audience was women. She did not hesitate to address all sorts of pertinent but taboo issues with them that were hardly ever raised in the working-class milieu—their right to vote; the right to initiate a divorce; or to not get married at all and to be paid as well as men. The first women granted voting rights would be in Finland in 1907, followed by Russia nearly seven years later.

Travel and public appearances ended up becoming a habitual part of the life of the Russian revolutionary. She

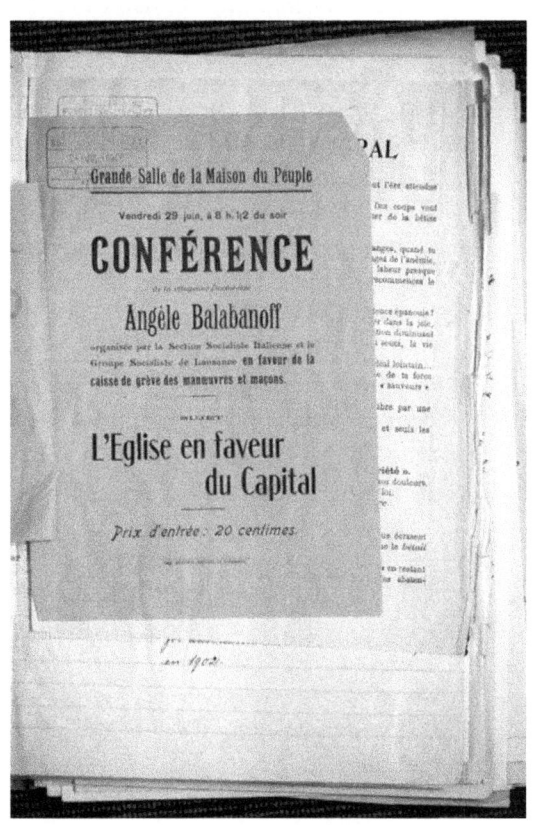

Leaflet announcing Angelica's speech in Lausanne, 1906 (SFA, CH-BAR#E21#1000/131, Nr. 8599. 2012. Photograph by Jean-Loup Lafont).

felt at home in the coffee shops and restaurants, rented for such occasions, lit with pagoda-like ceiling lamp shades. The attendees listened to her while sipping beer, house wine, or absinthe, seated at the round wooden tables or leaning against the bars. She ended up knowing most of the small local theatres, where she spoke before a performance or a play, and all piazzas "overcrowded, so that traffic had to stop during my speech," she confided to Ella Wolfe.[9]

Angelica later remembered that during the weekdays, the speeches started "between eight and nine in the evening and lasted for up to two hours." On Saturdays and Sundays, she delivered between three and five speeches per day, with discussions often ending well after midnight.

Her public appearances were advertised on blue, pink, and pistachio-colored leaflets, marking her name in bold Arial letters. Distributed among the workers, the leaflets announced a small entrance fee from which Angelica received either a percentage or a flat fee, which could be as little as 10 Swiss Francs (about $2 today). The organizers of the meetings covered her travel fees and an overnight stay in a hotel, unless someone in the audience offered her a place to stay.

Travel was time-consuming. A trip by train from Lugano to Lausanne took 22 hours, with transfers in Lucerne and Berne. Some villages were too far from the train station, with no train to catch until the next day. For Angelica, wasting time was out of the question. Rising early in the morning, she would see if she could organize an improvised literacy class for girls before dashing off to her next destination.

Her back must have ached from sleeping on old mattresses and from carrying the heavy brown leather and brass travel bag that she kept with her everywhere, filled with books, newspapers, and documents. She went for days without changing clothes. But she did not think about the hours she spent on the trains and in the meeting rooms and believed that it was normal to be exhausted all the time.

"I live in a perpetual high degree of exertion," she said, describing her lectures years later in another letter to Ella Wolfe. "Speaking to a proletarian audience has always requested the tension of my whole being: the endeavor to present complicated problems in the most easily comprehensible form, take advantage of the interest you may arouse to convey a thought, a desire for knowledge, an aspiration to act accordingly with the ideas or principles you want to inculcate ... not to be influenced by applause, observe the most rigid 'supervision' of yourself, of the absolute correspondence between thought and word, feelings, and their expression, between suggestion and possibility to realize them.... And then the permanent scruple: am I worthy, morally and intellectually prepared...."[10]

In her most daring childhood dreams, Angelica could not have imagined that life would offer her so much more than she had ever wished for. Petitioners queued in front of her desk at the Trade Union, which exploded with papers, demands, and appeals. She lost track of time and food and had to work impossible hours to meet all demands.

"I'm happy to be here where I can not only listen to others, but also do something," repeated Angelica to those who were surprised by her vigor.[11]

Provocation was second nature to the boisterous revolutionary. When she saw that her audience and her enemies were becoming used to her unorthodoxy, she came up with new ways to challenge them. From female workers she found out that some priests, in their sermons, condemned women who lived with men out of wedlock. This was the situation of many Italian women who resided in Switzerland alone and were secretly involved with men to whom they were not wed. Angelica saw no reason why affirming sex out of wedlock could not be a valid subject for her speeches. She openly called for the right to free love.

Priests fumed in rage. During a Sunday mass in St. Gall, one of them reportedly called her a "she-devil" whose lifestyle showed that "she rejected the two most sacred missions of a woman—being a spouse and mother," promising that Angelica would go directly to hell, avoiding the Last Judgment.

Not in the least affected by such threats, a year after her first speech, thriving more than ever, Angelica went on her first propaganda tour. She was seen in Lausanne, Zurich, Lugano, Siena, Geneva, Neufchatel, "and many other cities and towns of which you may even ignore the existence," she would describe her lecture tours later to Kitty Crowe.[12]

The impression that she left on her audiences was truly unforgettable. She reported to Ella Wolfe in 1947 that after her recent lecture in Rome, "a young man got up from his seat to give me a letter and a bar of chocolate—both came from Switzerland from a woman who had been a maid—43 years ago in a house where I was boarding...."[13]

She simplified her daily routine to a minimum of tasks. The main meal of the day consisted of a cup of tea, a cheese sandwich bought at the train station cafeteria, and a few apples. It was also one of the ways for her to battle traditions, which she would maintain all her life. At the age of 84, describing her daily routine in Rome to Ella Wolfe, she added: "I got boiling water twice a day for my tea. I feel very well physically and my 'regime'—mostly sandwiches and fruits—agree[s] with me perfectly. Also as far as food is concerned—I enjoy absolute liberty and enjoy it. I eat very regularly and sufficiently just what I need and what I like even if it means going against the stream, against tradition."[14]

Angelica's public appearances attracted a lot of attention, gathering crowds of people. Her unprecedented success could be explained with a few reasons. One of them was her ability to speak in two or three languages at a time. She gathered, in one room, Russian students who numbered nearly 2000 in various Swiss universities, Italian and German workers, socialists and anarchists—increasing her audience from a few dozen to a few hundred. As a rule, she made about two-thirds of the speech in the language understood by the majority of the attendees and then summarized or answered questions in the native language of other participants.

Angelica's undeniably effective strategy was to aim her discourse at the most uneducated people. It made her lectures simple and understandable: "It was clear to me," she recalled, "that the most sincere, well-meant statements may be utterly ineffective if the form in which they are presented is not the adequate one…. All the listeners might at once have the impression that the speaker is not a stranger to them, that he is dealing with their destiny, with their cares and sorrows, with their interests, with their future."[15]

Another, more trivial reason for her fame was that many residents of Italian and Swiss villages where Angelica was invited to speak found it novel to see for the first time a female, not to mention a Russian, lecturer.

Unexpectedly, it was her future sworn enemy and the mistress of Mussolini, Margherita Sarfatti, who would later remark on a vital factor that contributed to her eminence as a speaker—a sudden transformation that happened to her when she spoke. According to Margherita, Angelica's whole body would suddenly undergo a transformation, making her irresistible, convincing, unforgettable, and altogether rather exotic. Her fervent voice with trilled "R"s and exaggerated "S"s and "Z"s pierced the audience. Her magnetism made her black eyes radiate and enveloped the public. Her passion made her listeners believe in achieving their dreams for a better life.

By the summer of 1904, Angelica's speeches had become unwanted in residential areas. She gathered large audiences. The attendees carried by her inflamed words stayed in the meetings late into the night and shouted out anti-capitalist and anti-clerical slogans. The police of the Swiss cantons decided it was time to put an end to her public activities. The pretext was easy to find. She had not renewed her leave-to-remain in Switzerland.

IV. A Female Lecturer

Police file of the "political agitator" Angelica Balabanoff, Switzerland, 1903–1930 (SFA, CH-BAR#E21#1000/131, Nr. 8599. 2012. Photograph by Jean-Loup Lafont).

Angelica received a letter asking her to present herself at the police station in St. Gall. The police wanted to see her passport and her leave to remain in Switzerland. Angelica had no other choice than to hand them her navy-blue booklet-like Russian passport, worn out around the edges after years of traveling. She knew what they were looking for.

Her leave to remain had expired a year prior. She violated the law by not renewing it on time. To the genuine surprise of the policemen, her passport was only valid until February 25 of the year before, which meant a double violation.

Angelica had entered Switzerland in 1903 ONE day before her passport had expired. The newly made lecturer had been too busy to get to the Russian Embassy in Berne to exchange it.

At the end of the interview, she was issued a fine of 800 Swiss francs. It was an enormous amount, representing most of her annual income. She did not have this money. In the end she was bailed out by the PSI. For them, she was irreplaceable.[16]

Carried by her success, a perpetual mocker, she decided to exact more revenge against her bourgeois childhood. No subject was better than fashion. With her portly figure, Angelica had been allergic to fashion from the time she had been forced to accompany her mother on the endless shopping tours in Chernigov. In her new life, Angelica's choice of simple clothing was clearly made to underline her new social status as a "working girl." Following a general "socialist-democratic fashion," she wore long, loose-fitting skirts, even if they made her look more voluminous than she was, simple turban-draped covers for her head, to avoid constantly brushing her hair, and an occasional long necklace.

Angelica photographed by Swiss police, 1903 (SFA, CH-BAR#E21#1000/131, Nr. 8599. 2012. Photograph by Jean-Loup Lafont).

In her public speeches, she

launched a *de facto* war against corsets. The only reason for wearing corsets, she maintained, were marriage and pleasing men—more than enough for her to intensely dislike this fashionable accessory. When she was interested in attracting men or expressing her sexuality, she did not do so with what she was wearing. Captivated by her work, she attracted men with her convictions, her charm, and the burning fire of her words. One day during her lecture, she met a man who looked like a beggar and who immediately understood how much he could profit from Angelica. His name was Benito Mussolini.

V

Forming Il Duce

On a chilly evening in March 1904, Angelica arrived in Lausanne to give a lecture marking the anniversary of the Paris Commune, the two weeks in 1871 during which the workers took over Paris from the elected governance. To commemorate the event, the organizers rented what Angelica remembered as a "murky room on the second floor of a restaurant hidden in the back streets of town."

By that time, Angelica had been living in Switzerland for a year. As often happened during her presentations, the room was full. After her one-hour lecture, the participants, Italian immigrant workers, mainly men, employed in low-paying jobs in mines and wineries, launched into an animated discussion about their fight against the capitalist exploiters. Suddenly Angelica saw a man about 10 years her junior, of medium height with masculine figure, heavyset lower jaw, and restless bulging eyes. She had never seen him at these meetings before.

Angelica was immediately attracted to him. She was not sure what she found so appealing in the beastly appearance of this stranger. Was it the insolent adolescent look in his eyes? Or was it the contrast between the well-trimmed moustache above his sensual lips and the thick black tousled hair that badly needed to be cut? He was poorly dressed. His ill-fitting lounge-suit jacket, contrasting soiled trousers, and worn-out double-soled shoes stood out even in this modestly-dressed gathering. His speech revealed a sharp mind and the abilities of an excellent speaker. Both, however, needed to be refined. Angelica did not fail to notice his lack of original ideas, obviously stemming from insufficient education. But she was impressed with how aggressively he defended his views. This man was a real socialist.

Angelica asked her colleagues about him. They shrugged. His name was Benito Mussolini. A primary school teacher from Romagna, he came to Switzerland to avoid his military service in Italy, claiming illness. He slept under the bridge. Some tried to help him to find a job but in vain. She was alarmed. In front of her was a man urgently in need of help.

"There is nothing that can be done for anyone like me," Mussolini reportedly said. His notorious womanizing was becoming well known, and he was unsure of what to do with this petite, not overly appealing female creature who had dazzled the crowd with her speech, only to approach him and personally offer her help.

"I am the son of a drunkard, am diseased with syphilis and am condemned to suffer for the rest of my life.... Don't waste time and words with me [sic]. There is nothing for me but hunger and death in a mad house," he said.[1]

Angelica persisted. She offered to help Mussolini with the translation of a brochure by a Marxist thinker, Karl Kautsky, that Mussolini had mentioned in a previous conversation. Mussolini's publisher in Italy, *Avanguardia Socialista*, was willing to pay 50 Swiss Francs for the translation of "On the Day after the Social Revolution" from German into Italian, but Mussolini hardly spoke German.

The work on the translation did not take long; Angelica's and Mussolini's relationship continued for more than ten years. Angelica was the first person to spot, form, and educate the future *Il Duce*.

Such was the story of Angelica's meeting with Mussolini, depicted by her in her memoirs *My Life as a Rebel* in 1938, 35 years after their first encounter. Quickly picked up by the journalists, it was retold dozens of times by all Mussolini's biographers and by a few people who had written about Angelica, deemed, as a rule, the main event of her life.

But even this well-known part of Angelica's life is contradictory. Giorgio Giannelli, a distinguished Italian leftist journalist whom Angelica had considered as her son and with whom she shared many of her life-stories, insisted, "When the revolutionary and Mussolini had met, he was chewing his hat." So according to Giorgio's version of events, during Angelica's stay in St. Gall, she gave German lessons to Italian immigrants and helped them to write letters to their families. In one of her classes in Lausanne, she noticed a shabbily dressed man with a long beard. He was sitting at the end of the table, biting his hat. Angelica thought that he was mad. After the lesson, everyone left, but he continued to sit at the table. "What is happening? Are you nervous?" she asked. "Leave me alone," he answered, "I have to commit suicide, I'm sick." At which point Angelica offered him help with translation of the Kautsky brochure.[2]

So which of the two versions of their first encounter is accurate? Their early relationship is difficult to discern. Little is known about it. In the beginning, the camaraderie of an unknown Russian woman who was educating an Italian vagabond passed unnoticed by colleagues and friends. By the time their names had become hot items in the news, few witnesses would remain to give testimony about them. Angelica and Mussolini made an effort to refer as little as possible to their Swiss romance. She did not want to publicize her relationship with the Italian dictator, nor he his with a socialist Jewish woman.

Angelica was the only person to leave a detailed description of their meeting in Lausanne. A bit of simple math showed that her story was not that straightforward. She insisted that they had met during the 33rd anniversary of the Paris Commune, placing their meeting to March 1904. However, this celebration had been held in Geneva, and not in Lausanne, in the presence of Lenin. Historians say that in all likelihood Lenin and Mussolini never met. Mussolini himself provided contrasting testimony of knowing and not knowing Lenin, finally admitting that in March 1904 he attended an altogether different meeting in Zurich. Angelica and Mussolini must have met before that, possibly as early as 1903, making Giorgio's version of events possible.

The union of these two people must have looked surprising, even during their early years in Switzerland. Angelica was already a known personality in the Swiss and Italian socialist communities. She had a solid reputation. Mussolini's real beliefs in life and in politics were unclear. He wrote articles, gave Italian lessons, and officially represented workers. Many did not like him for his violence and extremism. He was known for spending his evenings in the company of mostly Russian bohemian students, drank heavily, made love with the first woman he met on a given day, and entered into the most subversive and confrontational political discussions with anyone who was willing to talk to him.

Mussolini enjoyed telling the story of one of his arrests in Geneva for attacking two English ladies while trying to steal their sandwiches. Starving, he had seen them in the park eating their breakfast.

"I could not restrain myself. I threw myself upon one of the old witches and grabbed the food from her hands. If they had made the slightest resistance, I would have strangled them," Mussolini confessed at the end of the tale.[3]

Nonetheless, Angelica and Benito were not as improbable a couple as some would think. They had common interests. The son of a blacksmith, Mussolini came from a simple family with communist traditions. He was violently against inequality and full of hatred for the rich. Angelica came from a rich family. Her father was a merchant of the First Moscow

Guild. She was just as violently opposed to inequality, considering that the rich did not help the poor as much as she believed they should. Both of them would end up occupying high-ranking positions within their parties.

Angelica's efforts flattered Mussolini. For the first time, he was seeing a woman from a well-off family willing to invest so much of her personal time in him. Angelica's background was a secret to no one. Her manners and education were so vastly different from the working-class women he had met before, the wives of soldiers and innkeepers. It did not matter to him that her black clothes were obsolete and that, at times, her hair was unruly. Instinctively, he understood how much he could profit from Angelica. He needed her. In his early years, Mussolini was unsure of himself; his ideas came from the last book he had read.

Under the guidance of his Russian muse, he blazed through a substantial part of Marxist literature. He would use his new knowledge to his advantage, becoming a renowned speaker. She helped him improve his French and German. He even managed to enroll at the university in Geneva, and all that despite his problematic stay in the country—he was in and out of prison for falsifying his passport and for violent behavior.

The nature of the relationship between Angelica and Mussolini is much debated. Mussolini mentioned his encounter with Angelica in Switzerland only on one occasion, in his letter to his sister Edvige, where he talked about Angelica in a way that implied much more than friendship:

"She knows and understands a lot of things; she's read all the Marxist texts. But while her body is full of juice, her mind is full of dried ideas."[4]

Angelica and her close friends always denied any personal involvement between the Russian revolutionary and the future *Il Duce*, explaining that she simply "felt sorry for him."[5]

And yet how can it be possible that a Don Juan of Mussolini's magnitude spent so much time with a liberal and charismatic young female comrade for over ten years without anything passing between them? By the time Mussolini was the Prime Minister of Italy, his sexual image had become a legend.

"It was commonly thought—and confirmed by his private valet—that the Duce slept with a woman a day—an impossible number; even if we halve it, it's still highly improbable. If we say that on average he slept with a different woman once a week, the total would be in the order of several hundred, which begins to look more plausible as a realistic estimate..."[6] wrote Roberto Olla in his book *Il Duce and His Women*.

There must have been more to their relationship than simple friendship. In Switzerland, they lived separate lives in different towns. But then they often participated together in the PSI meetings in Geneva and Zurich.

Angelica once wrote that she "was the only human being he has ever had absolute confidence in and to whom he spoke openly and frequently of himself."[7]

They might have met in her place or in a hotel room, Angelica drinking her favorite thoroughly steeped black tea and Mussolini the cheap house wine, making love and talking for hours about his upcoming speeches and his future as a politician.

It was always about him. Never about her. She did not mind. It was because her love was unreserved. She was willing to give him everything without asking for anything in return.

In the Swiss Federal Archives in Berne, there is a rare document—a police report about their meeting in 1904 in Geneva in the Handwerk Brasserie. This regular socialist gathering place on 4 *Rue du Mail* was a traditional brewery with large dim windows and black marble-tiled exterior walls that advertised a sizable selection of beer and simple food. On the first floor, it housed a restaurant and two meeting rooms, one of them large enough to fit a few hundred people. Sitting across the bulky wooden bistro table from Mussolini, in the presence of about a dozen comrades, Angelica openly admired her pupil. In front of her was a forceful, reassured politician. Mussolini was imposing order, prioritizing the agenda items he considered important, and criticizing the Swiss socialist party for insufficiently helping their Italian colleagues in exile.[8]

Angelica was worlds away from envisaging all the misfortunes that helping Mussolini would bring to her life. Sensitive and energetic, she dreamt of how much both of them could do for the cause. In the spring of 1904, Angelica firmly believed in it. *Kak v kamennuiu stenu,* as they say in Russia.[9]

VI

Female Journalist

There are not many photos of Angelica. Most of them are kept in private collections and date to her later years. Among the few photos available that relate to her early career, one of the most interesting is a photo of the front page of the magazine *Su, Compagne!* (Arise, Comrades!) the famous newspaper for Italian women that Angelica launched when she lived in St. Gall. The paper being impossible to find now, this photo allows us to see what it looked like. It shows the paper layout, the type fonts, titles of the articles, name of the publisher and editorial team, its sale price, and all details an image can tell more clearly than any words.

After Angelica became a successful speaker, she wanted to do more for the cause. Journalism was the most any daring woman could do at that time. She did not know how much success launching this journal would bring to her career. She started the paper with Maria Giudice, whom she had met by coincidence in St. Gall.

Maria arrived in town in the spring of 1904 after escaping from Italy to avoid being arrested for publishing a provocative pro-socialist article. She needed a place to stay. The Trade Union officials thought of Angelica. Her room was always available for those who needed shelter. Angelica agreed to lodge the stranger until Maria found a permanent place to stay.

The woman who arrived at Angelica's doorstep the same day looked like the twin sister she had never had. Maria was a small, chubby, thin-lipped, stubborn-looking brunette, only about 10 years Angelica's junior. After a quick talk with her guest, Angelica learned that, apart from resembling each other physically, they had many things in common. Both were unconditionally devoted to socialism, and like Angelica, Maria did not accept compromises. She was ready to sacrifice herself and her children for her beliefs.

"My duty as a socialist is greater than my duty as a mother," were Maria's words addressed to the judge in Turin during one of her court hearings about her leftist activity.[1]

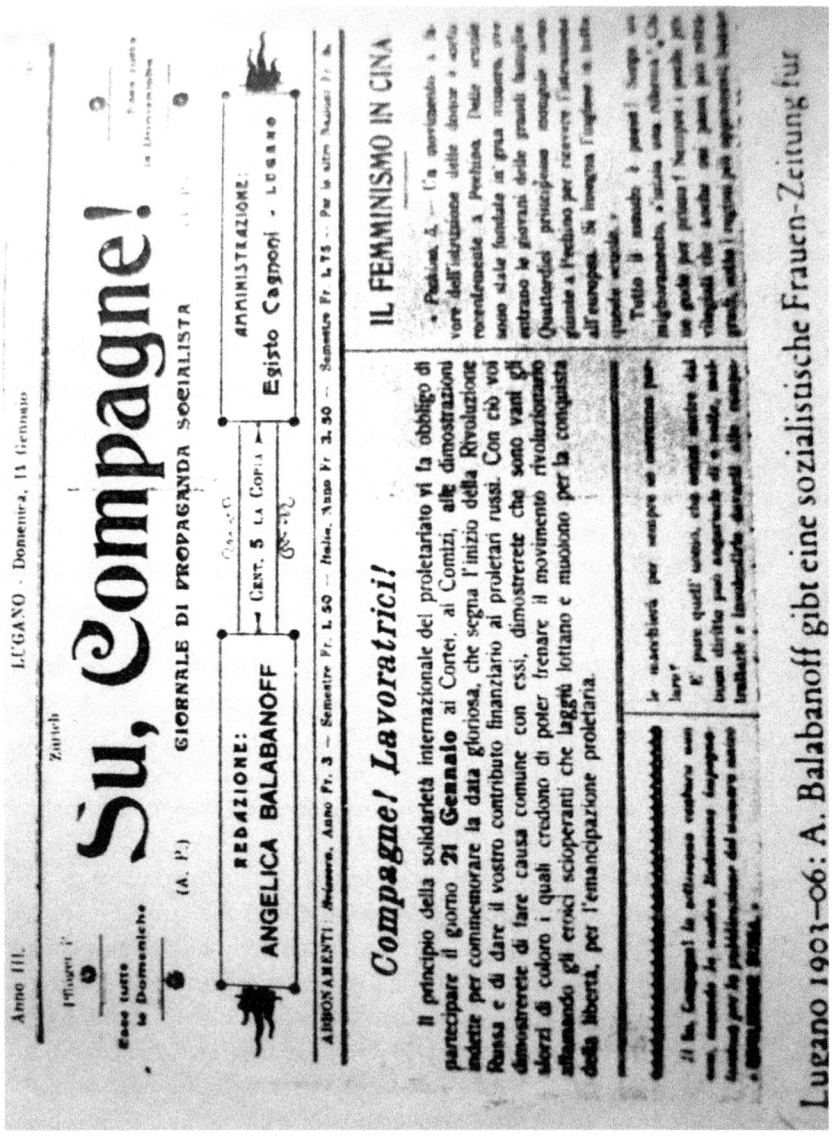

One of the issues of *Su, Compagne!*, the first-ever weekly newspaper devoted to Italian women workers, launched by Angelica in the summer of 1904, 1906 (collection of Giorgio Giannelli).

Maria was welcome to stay with Angelica as long as she needed. Onlookers considered them an unusual twosome. Whether they slept top-to-tail or found an extra mattress to put on the floor, no details were ever revealed by either of them in their memoirs. But it was hardly a Sapphic relationship.

Burning with a desire to do something for the cause, within a few weeks, the two roommates came up with an idea, secured financing for the project, and started publication of the first-ever weekly newspaper devoted to Italian women workers—*Su, Compagne!* The new weekly came out on Thursdays. The articles for the first few issues were written mainly by Angelica. In her editorials she encouraged women to fight for better wages, academic and physical education, birth control, and time for leisure activities. One of her articles—and how can we not applaud Angelica for the ideas that remain pertinent even today—proclaimed:

> You are told that you are weaker, yet must work as hard as man for less pay.... You are given the responsibility for the new generation, yet you have neither time nor the necessary preparation for nurturing, raising, or educating your children.... We instead urge you to wage war against your enemies: war against the exploiters, war against those who wish to cloud your consciousness, war against war.[2]

Instead of being praised by their comrades, Angelica and Maria became the laughingstock of the Swiss and Italian communities. Their publication was viewed as a marginal, plain, and unsophisticated newssheet. The photo of *Su, Compagne!* explained the reasons for this harsh judgment. The weekly did not look like a real paper. It was printed recto-verso on a single page, had an oversized, though elegant, Calibri font title and characters larger than usual, making it look like a girly newssheet. No one thought that two women would be able to regularly edit a newspaper in Angelica's room, seated at her unique table, on the only two chairs she had.

But they enjoyed immediate success. It sold out. It was the simple style of the articles that pleased. For once all women could read it, even the semi-literate. Not to mention its price, only 5 centimes, twice as cheap as other daily papers.

After the first few issues, the editors started to receive letters from women who told their stories, described their lives and working conditions. These letters became the main source of information for the paper.

The accomplices quickly faced the problem of finding a publisher willing to do this job for little money and ready to confront the police and censorial laws. They found a printer who worked for the Trade Unions in Lugano. His company name was Paradiso, a Paradise. Angelica and Maria moved to Lugano, where they continued to share an apartment. Located in a scruffy workers' neighborhood, far from the picturesque paved walkways along the azure shores of Lake Lugano and romantic misty views of the Pre-Alpine Mountains, it was still only a walk away from the shops selling the delicious chocolate of which the Russian revolutionary was so fond.

After settling in the modestly furnished small rooms, Angelica resumed her traveling from Friday to Sunday to the French and German cantons to deliver propaganda speeches and getting back on Monday morning, weary after nights of traveling, and putting herself to work on the next issue of *Su, Compagne!* due on Thursday.

One day, among the voluminous correspondence she and Maria received weekly from the readers of the newspaper, a letter arrived. It was from Italy. In large, awkward handwriting, the author of the letter poured out all her grief and sorrows onto a small faded piece of paper and caused real shock in the small editorial team.

The desperate woman who wrote it explained that "unable to feed her family," she, as many parents were at the time, was "obliged to send her 15-year-old daughter to work away from home to do 11-hour shifts in the textile factories in St. Gall." The girl lived "in the monastery with the nuns, not far from the factory." Living alone was considered inappropriate for unmarried women.

Up to this point in the letter, there was nothing alarming. The appalling living and working conditions of the girls in the monasteries had already been addressed a few times in the press. The Italian traveler Amy Bernardy had even described the day-to-day routine in such *madchenheime*: "To make time for the obligatory prayers, all the girls had to be up at five. By six they were at work in the factory, and upon their return home in the evening the girls were expected to perform domestic chores until nine. Sunday mornings, the girls were required to attend mass, while in the afternoons—their only free time—they had to listen to biblical readings ... some seemed malnourished...."[3]

But as Angelica and Maria continued to read the woman's letter, they understood that they were far from the end of the revelations that awaited them. The unpleasant surprise of this housing arrangement was that the girl's salary was received directly by the nuns. Out of the salary the nuns deducted money that they helped the girl to send to her family, a fee for lodging and other "peculiar" extra expenses they called sins and penalties. The final amount the girl received left nearly nothing of her wages. This story about withholding money from the salaries of the girls had been unheard of prior to this letter.

VI. Female Journalist

Distraught, Angelica decided to look for more information and write an editorial. She traveled to St. Gall for an arranged meeting with a few girls outside the factory after their work. The results of her research exceeded her most pessimistic expectations. She was greeted by a group of pale, undernourished, and exhausted adolescents. All they wanted to know was when they would be able to eat to their fill.

Each girl had her own notebook, which listed by month the expenses deducted by the nuns. They ranged from 5 Swiss francs for talking too much to 140 for the new statue of Madonna and included 10 Swiss francs for charity, 30 to 80 for rosaries and 50 for the visiting sisters from Lourdes.[4] This from less than 200 Swiss francs per month, or about a quarter of average female textile worker's salary.[5]

After meeting the girls, Angelica wrote to their families and took a train to Sienna to meet them. At the end of her research it became evident to her that the nuns had an arranged agreement with the managers of the factories to proceed with their deductions from salaries, or what Angelica called racketeering.

She wanted to stop the financial scheme in which too many interested parties gained money. It was at that moment that her serious problems with the police started. The authorities started looking for any pretext to stop her from further investigation. The minister plenipotentiary of the Italian Legation in Berne wrote to the Swiss federal attorney general a letter that said:

> Dear Mr. Attorney General,
> The named Angelique Balabanoff, originated from Russia, residing in Lugano, a member of the editorial team of the newspaper "Su Compagne," ... has been staying for the last few days in Sienna.
> Further to the orders received from my government, I have the honor to request you to provide me, by confidential courier, with information you have at your disposal regarding Balabanoff.[6]

Totally ignorant that she was under surveillance, Angelica continued her journalistic work. She came back to Lugano and immediately published the results of her investigation in *Su, Compagne!* Her article "Church in Favor of Capital" enjoyed unprecedented success. For the first time, Angelica's work was reproduced in other papers in Switzerland and as a separate brochure, a small booklet printed on Kraft paper, with Angelica's name on it in thick Arial bold letters.[7]

The article made her famous outside the socialist communities. The name of the Russian militant became known to the general public.

After the publication of Angelica's article, life became a living hell for her. The clerics had had enough of the "she-devil." They organized attacks on her during her public speeches. Often she had to escape by running to avoid getting hurt by heavy clods of dirt and stones that right-wing Church supporters threw at her during her appearances on the piazzas of small villages, and she was hissed at by the public. When safe in her room in Lugano, Angelica had only one thing in mind—to get back to her audience and address as many people as possible.

The most considerable event of the summer happened in Stabio, a small agricultural community very close to Lugano. Invited by the few socialists in the town, Angelica was asked to come and talk to local women about their rights. She immediately agreed and started to note down ideas for her speech.

On the day of the meeting, she arrived in Stabio at the hotel indicated to her by the organizers, not far from the train station. Much to her surprise, upon entering the reception area of the hotel, instead of the female audience that Angelica was expecting to see, the welcoming committee was composed of priests and police. Angelica overheard a few worrying phrases: "dangerous Russian agitator," "high risk of disturbing security and peace in Stabio," and "would put the hotel reputation in peril."

The hotel owner could not understand what was so dangerous about the chubby brunette who had just shown up at his door and who was the height of a ten-year-old. Nevertheless, after receiving such an official forewarning, he announced to the organizers that he could not allow such a risky event to take place in his establishment. The organizers, troubled by such a turn of events, and afraid that their lives would become even more difficult in the small Stabio community, decided that it was best to cancel the event.

Angelica had not come to Stabio on a field trip. Not easily embarrassed, she was made for emergency situations. "A revolutionist does not yield to threats," she said, proposing to find another location.[8]

Guided by the organizers, and keeping calm, Angelica found herself in the place which was probably the least suitable for such event—the piazza of the Saint Giacomo e Cristoforo parish church. Standing with her back to its white porch entrance with Ionic columns, she faced the small cobblestone piazza, the tall imposing houses of respectable Stabio citizens with linden-tree gardens, and a hesitant crowd of about 30 people who followed her from the hotel and now gathered around her. A bit farther away, she saw a few tensed priests and policemen who were waiting to see what would happen.

As she pronounced the first words of her speech, the bells started to ring. Her voice was barely audible. Her little black figure looked more and more solitary. She knew that in such situations, the unbreakable rule was to continue. Interrupting speeches could provoke chaos and riots. Suddenly someone in the crowd shouted: "Why don't they let this woman speak? I want to hear her. Let's go to my place."

Guided by the unexpected host, they went to a large half-empty wooden farm shed with a gable roof. By then, the news of a woman who wanted to give rights to other women had spread around the town. Her audience was growing by the minute. The shed was full, and more people were gathering outside. Angelica finished her speech by saying: "[The] time [has] come to wake up and fight against capitalism and religion. It is not when we are freethinkers that we eradicate religion, but when we abolish private property."

Pleased with her work, she was about to go back to the train station when one of the organizers pulled her aside.

"Quick," he said, "you must get out of here. Peasants are coming armed with sticks. They will kill you."

Immediate escape was the only option.

"The doctor's house is a safe place," shouted someone. "We can get there by going round through the fields."

Helped by her welcome committee, she ran through the narrow back streets, along the three-story red and yellow village houses and the pasture fields with tall, emerald-green, sharp grass, wet from the rain. She had never been a great runner, but she could not risk stopping. In her memoirs, Angelica wrote that the men who accompanied her suggested they take turns carrying her in their arms.

It was not the first time she described men willing to carry her in their arms. Similar stories came up on a few occasions. Most often it happened before or after her speeches, in a crowded place, with her having difficulty getting up to or off of the podium. Did she imagine them or not? Possibly these anecdotes show her anxiety over being a small woman in a public position.

Anyhow, during the Stabio chase, Angelica rejected their suggestion to carry her. The escape was successful, and they finally arrived in an empty stone-built house that belonged to a doctor, situated on the edge of the village. After barricading themselves in the house, closing the door and the window shutters, they could still hear the crowd outside the house. But at least Angelica was able to catch her breath.

Her eventful trip did not end there. As Angelica sat down, thinking that it would be nice to dry her shoes near the stove, one of the men who had accompanied her kneeled down in front of her and started taking off her shoes.

"Please, don't," said Angelica, startled.

The man calmly looked at her, finished removing her shoes and put them to dry. Then he took out a pen and a piece of paper and started to write a letter that Angelica reproduced in her memoirs:

> Dear Comrade Balabanoff:
> I would like to give my life to sa[v]e yours. I'm a stammerer [sic] and have always felt inferior to others. My parents died when I was very young.... During my childhood other children teased and laughed at me. I can't take part in the discussions of the workers. But when I heard you speak I understood that you feel and speak for people such as I—for all the unhappy, the unhappy, the downtrodden.[9]

It's difficult to say today whether the man portrayed in her memoirs could write such a note or whether she was able to reproduce it so many years later, word for word. Her admirer certainly wanted to thank her for her work.

After some time, the noise outside the house calmed down. The crowd had finally left. As the time to catch the train approached, Angelica's new admirer proposed to get a carriage. Thinking that the worst was over, Angelica found herself half an hour later at the station. The second she alit from the carriage, she was surrounded by "a frenzied horde" of people who, after leaving the doctor's house, had come to the station, thinking that the "she-devil" would also get to the station to catch her train.[10] They threw dust in her face and spat on her dress. Angelica looked around. There was nowhere to hide. A one-room station house with an arched doorway and red-tiled roof was the only refuge on the platform. On one side were the rails, on another a row of linden trees followed by the fields, with the nearest village houses about a quarter-mile away.

One of the socialists who accompanied her to the station reached into his pocket. Angelica knew what it meant.

"Don't touch that revolver!" she screamed as loud as she could.

We will never know whether it was the revolver that scared the crowd or not, but they did let Angelica get on the train.

As Angelica's fame spread beyond the Swiss and Italian socialist parties, she received an invitation to participate as a speaker in the much-publicized Congress of Freethinkers.

The Congress of the Freethinkers was a biannual congress and "a must" for all people who considered themselves progressive. It attracted to Rome members of the European parliaments, scholars, thinkers, philosophers, and economists from Europe, North and South America, and Russia. To receive a speaking engagement at the congress, as Angelica did, was an honor. The year she was invited to speak, in September 1904, *The Nelson Evening Mail* reported a staggering attendance:

"Four thousand had attended the Freethinkers international congress in Rome and 10.000 attended their procession to Portapia...."[11]

The culminating moment of the congress was to contradict the Pope and to commemorate the memory of Giordano Bruno—one of the first prosecuted freethinkers, who claimed that Sun was one of the stars in the universe and that universe had other populated planets, and Angelica's favorite historical figure.

A demonstration in memory of Giordano Bruno forced the Pope to close the Vatican during the time of the demonstration.

A bit unsure about such a sophisticated audience—certainly anti-clerical but anti-capitalist—Angelica arrived in her favorite city on September 20, just in time for her speech, equipped with her leather doctor's travel bag with books and unfinished editorials for *Su, Compagne!*

The revolutionary was in her best spirits. She loved Rome in September, with the summer heat gone and the perfume of jasmine still in the air. Her arrival was delayed a few hours by railway strikes and a demonstration outside the congress. She was so proud of what she considered a true union of people that she hardly paid any attention to missing the opening ceremony of the congress. Most importantly, the congress was taking place at her alma mater, her dear University of Sapienza.

The renowned courtyard of the university, with its elegant clay-hued two-story arched windows, welcomed Angelica with an influx of memories of her professor. She knew by then that Labriola would not come to listen to her speech at the congress. He had died only eight days before her arrival.

Thinking about the man to whom she owed so much in her life, she entered the main room of the congress just in time to speak. She calmly took her place on the podium. With her hands clasped in front of her stomach, she decided to speak as vividly and passionately as Labriola would want her to do.

As she spoke, the noise in the room ceased. A few minutes later, the meeting room was fully packed. She spoke ardently about poor, undernourished Italian girls forced to leave their homes, about the unbearable living conditions the nuns provided in the monasteries, and about deceitful clerics who robbed the girls of their salaries and their lives. Not only did her speech ended with a standing ovation, but a resolution was passed and unanimously approved condemning the working system of the nuns and factories and calling for the abolition of private ownership of the means of production.

For the first time, Angelica understood that it was her talent as a speaker which moved the audience, rather than the subject of her presentation. Suddenly she saw in the crowd a familiar face with a fringed beard and chestnut colored hair. It was Célestin Demblon. He had come to assist his former pupil's first public success.

"It so [sic] happened quite unexpectedly," she wrote to her friend Ella Wolfe, "that I became one of the chief speakers.... A worker published an open letter in the papers 'Depressed and offended have I entered the hall where freethinkers had gathered, and heard Angelica B. speaking: her words made me forget my misery and depression. I began to believe in the future. I did not feel anymore [sic] as a slave. I was newborn. A new life began.'"[12]

Angelica sarcastically remarked later that all of a sudden, everyone seemed to know her in Sapienza University. At the café Aragno, where she used to go with Antonio Labriola, she was recognized by professors and ex-students. They had known her when she had lived in Rome but had not been interested in her before this speech.

For Angelica the explanation of her success was always simple, if slightly dogmatically expressed:

> I was personally and particularly interested in reaching those who in my mind were the most unhappy and discouraged ones and in comparison with whom an average proletarian may be considered privileged.... If in the most huge audience of intellectuals or workers already more or less trained and conscious of their rights there should be a single man or woman more backward—I would chiefly try to reach these even at the expense of the other ones.[13]

By the time she came back to Lugano, Maria needed both her table and her bed to lay out the letters and articles about her speech. The Russian revolutionary was invited to speak at more congresses and conferences than she could handle. For Angelica, this began what might have been the best period of her life. As for the Swiss authorities, stirred up by the nuns and the factory owners, they decided that they had had enough of her.

VII

Expulsion

At the end of June 1906, the police team of the Department of Justice and Police of Lausanne, headed by Robert Cossy, was stressed. The political terrorists, or anarchists and socialists, as they liked to call themselves, had been causing too many troubles in the canton of Vaud. Most of all, they were annoyed by the Balabanoff case.

During their professional careers, none of them had a recollection of any Russian woman or, in fact, any woman at all, being such a nuisance. She was probably one of the least attractive and most hysterical female types they had ever seen. The worst part of it was that nothing could be done to calm her down. She had no family, was in no apparent need for money, did not take drugs, did not even drink, and was motivated purely by her obsessive goal of establishing equality between the rich and the poor.

In previous years, the "Russian harpy" had limited herself to criticizing the Russian monarchy, which was none of their business. Recently, she had started to attack Switzerland, maintaining that it was not a free country and that the poor had to rise against the authorities, which were, in her opinion, just as capable of mass killings as the working classes in Russia.

The latest reports that Robert Cossy had received about her activity in Lausanne included worrying

With Valentino Pittoni, a well-known Italian Socialist deputy in Trieste, 1906 (collection of Giorgio Giannelli).

statements: "The speeches of Angelica Balabanoff are anarchistic, of the utmost violence..." and "She is strongly against the Swiss Democratic Republic, which, according to her, shamefully exploits poor Italian workers and prostrates [them] in front of the [Italian] monarchy." He could not ignore these any longer.

The police department needed to do something urgently about this woman to avoid more trouble. It needed a pretext, even if slightly exaggerated, to expel Balabanoff at least from their canton and create as much publicity about it in the papers as possible.

As the authorities were contemplating their plans, Angelica only increased their anxieties by her audacious behavior and multiple exuberant activities. Her public appearances were more popular than ever. Crowds of people who attended her meetings, keyed up by her words, remained on the streets late at night, shouting out slogans: "We shall have revenge!" and "Long live Socialism!" These were heard on all nearby streets as the militants walked back home. An article in the *Gazette de Lausanne* of January 1906 commented on a few hundred people who attended one of her meetings: "All these in spite of the furiously blowing wind," reported an astonished journalist, "that lasted throughout January, able to chill off any crowd."[1]

As the year went on, Russian Tsar Nicolas II and Tsarina Alexandra arrived in Italy on vacation during the summer. Riots were organized to protest against the oppressors of the poor, Angelica being one of the most violent protestors. Margherita Sarfatti, Angelica's future rival over Mussolini, attended Angelica's speech:

> Then I saw this woman, this blunder of the celestial typography which prints Cyrillic characters, transfigured by her speech and spirit. She made her speech in a correct Italian, blazing and efficient, her wet, sparkling eyes got larger, to the point of devouring her pitiful grey face. Her strident and cracked voice, warmed with strange guttural intonations, skinned you [to] the bottom of your guts with its mystical and hysterical force of persuasion. She ended up by evoking Mother Russia and the "Saint Russia," which suffers and passionately hopes, and suddenly fell on her chair, all pale, in tears; and all of us around the table cried, just as saddened and pale.[2]

When Margherita wrote these words, the women were sworn enemies, and she did not hesitate to grant Angelica as many "compliments" as she could come up with. However, Angelica's approach to work was certainly well detected by Margherita. As a result of the protests, the Tsar found it safer not to leave his yacht. The official visits in Rome were cancelled and moved to other places. Margherita even hinted that this turn of events was mostly Angelica's work.

In the meantime, Maria Giudice went back to Italy. *Su, Compagne!* became Angelica's sole responsibility. She published and distributed it on Sundays. Eager to keep up the paper, she found a new administrative assistant, Egisto Cagnoni. The Italian socialist was hiding in Switzerland from the Italian police, as Maria had done a few years prior. He was happy to do this work while Angelica continued hopping from one meeting to another, while remaining the editor of the paper.

Angelica's rebellious activities did not end there. Dozens of files in the Swiss Federal Archives mention her name as an active participant of the leftist group the "Nucleo-Socialista" (The Socialist Core Group).[3] Reports on the work of *Nucleo-Socialista* provided by under-cover agents, meticulously listed on lined paper used for such recording, show meetings with time, dates, names of the attendees, and subjects discussed. The group showed an impressive pace. The meetings were held at least three times per month, mostly in Geneva and Berne, and could last for two days, making one wonder how Angelica found time for all this work. She was regularly cited as an active co-organizer of political conferences, lectures, musical evenings, and staged plays to collect funds, support strikes, and assist Italian and Russian workers.

By midsummer of 1906 Angelica knew that the police followed her everywhere she went, and she expected to be arrested. She changed her name to make it sound French: Angélique. But because of her accent, she was obliged to say that she was Russian, and her covers were easily detected. The agents, disguised as workers supportive of the labor movement, waited for her at PSI meetings, at conferences, and at the hotel entrance when she returned at night, reporting her every move throughout the day. They even noted down the names of those who came to talk to her after the meetings.

One such report, made two days prior to her arrest, stated:

[T]wo meetings in Lausanne on June 29 *The current strike of Masons* and on 30 June *Church in favor of Capital* gathered two hundred fifty participants, mostly Russians and Italians. The organizer of these events, the anarchist Ugo Gailland, presented Angelica to the audience, apologizing for the lack of audience and "not having time to make any publicity in the press." He just distributed a few leaflets with her name on them.

On the second day, in her speech, she pronounced herself against all religions, insisting that:

"The main aim of the clergy is to scare, oppress and keep people in ignorance as to their rights."

She ended her speech by saying that:
"In Switzerland people were not freer than in other countries."[4]

That all took place on Saturday. Robert Cossy might have interrupted his Saturday dinner and seized this occasion to sign papers for her arrest and extradition from the canton of Vaud on the same day. Sunday must have been a day off for everyone, including the police, for it was not until Monday morning that she was arrested at the Lausanne post office, where she came to pick up the letters left in her name.

Without any explanation, two officers brought Angelica to the police station, where she was measured and fingerprinted. Then came in a photographer. He took at least eight pictures—front, profile, portrait, and three-quarters. Measuring and fingerprinting were humiliating, but she did not want to show her feelings. The flash of the camera was blinding. She looked directly into the camera, without blinking. The photographer captured her determined, tense look and her weary face with deep shadows under the eyes, which showed a lack of sleep she had accumulated during the last months, and the first wrinkles around her eyes and chin.

Just as quickly as Angelica was brought into the police station, she was taken in front of a magistrate. He began by reading out the accusation. She was guilty of registering at the Hôtel de France under a false name on June 28. Her signature indicated that room N 32 was occupied by Angélique Poloponost.[5]

Angelica tried to protest, insisting that she was in a hurry and surely the magistrate could decipher "Balabanoff." Besides, how could she hide if her name was printed on dozens of pink leaflets, which announced the speeches in the Large Room of the People's House of Lausanne on June 29 and June 30? Hundreds of people saw her there, starting from 8:30 in the evening.

Her pleas did not help. "You are expelled from the canton [of] Vaud and must leave immediately," the magistrate informed her. "You will be accompanied to the border of the canton."[6]

Moreover she was refused the right to collect her luggage from the hotel on the grounds that she did not want to accept the charges. The luggage belonged to the client of the hotel, Angélique Poloponost. Angelica did not worry about clothes, but it would be a pity to leave behind her books and the editorials she was working on.

The same two policemen who brought her to the police station took her to the train station, boarded the 6 p.m. train to Berne, and stayed with her in the same train compartment until Romont, to make sure that she arrived in the Canton of Fribourg, where they descended, reassured that

VII. Expulsion

she had left. They did not even have to buy her a train ticket. She had her second-class train pass with her. The arrest took most of the day. With no prior engagements, Angelica suddenly had a free evening, which did not happen often in her busy schedule. She went to Berne and stayed overnight with her Russian friends, who had guests. Berne had a large Russian community, which included Grigory Zinoviev and Trotsky's sister Olga, whom Angelica knew well and whom she might have visited on that day.

It had been a long time since Angelica had joined in on such a *vecherinka,* an evening gathering with friends, and she had almost forgotten how relaxing it could be. She allowed herself to be rocked to sleep in a cozy family apartment with a spacious living room. Guests stayed late, sang Old Russian romances—"The Night is Bright" and "Beggar Woman":
"Winter, snow falling, strong wind.
At the church entrance there stands an old woman,
She is alone, dressed in rags,
waiting for alms," hummed Angelica.

The hostess served tea with marmalade. Angelica did not realize that she had fallen asleep in her chair.

The next day, all French-speaking papers carried articles about her extradition, completely falsifying the events. Even the liberal *Gazette de Lausanne* announced: "The Department of Justice and Police extradited from the canton Ms. Balabanoff—at least she insists it is her real name—originating from Russia, who conducted a conference of rare violence against the government, bourgeoisie and capital in French and in Italian in Lausanne. This charming person, declared the Head of Security of Lausanne, is 'four times more anarchist than all other anarchists.'"[7]

Angelica was not easily discouraged. No matter how hard it might get, no matter how threatened she felt, the truth and telling the truth right into the eyes of her enemy was what mattered the most. She quickly found a new place for her speeches: Stand des Armes Réunies (The United Arms Club), in La Chaux-de-Fonds in the canton of Neuchâtel. The photos of the time show an elongated building with picturesque Swiss-style attic and roof. The club had the shooting stand facilities on the left side, while the right side was occupied by a restaurant on the first floor and a concert hall on the second floor. The place was excellent for promoting Angelica's political activities.

Judging from the number of reports from *La Chaux-de-Fonds* in Angelica's file in Berne, her presence in the small town created quite an uproar with the local police. Panicked by the presence of the unwanted visitor, they immediately issued a report stating that the Swiss population was in general "indifferent to the socialist propaganda made by the immigrants and for the immigrants" and started to follow her into each meeting. They soon felt that these measures were insufficient. In August, the federal attorney general granted authorization to send a request to Russian colleagues in St. Petersburg to inquire about Angelica. The reply received on September 20 from the Russian Ministry of the Interior was brief and unexpected: "Balabanoff, born in Chernigov, left Russia about eight years ago to travel abroad and has never come back. During her stay Chernigov, nothing suspicious was noticed in her behavior and she was not a suspect of a political nature."[8]

Undisturbed, Angelica continued to show up freely for her conferences in The United Arms Club. All the Swiss kept guns at home. Lenin might have been right after all when he thought that Switzerland was "the country which was most prepared for a revolution." Commencing her refreshed attacks from the club, she managed to maintain international audience. Many immigrants were employed in the watch-making business.

"The government says that education in Switzerland is equal and obligatory for everyone," proclaimed Angelica, who regained more energy with each new audience. "Who believes their promises? It is no secret that the working-class children have to leave school at one p.m. to help in the fields and with cattle stock. Is this equality? If the workers want equality, they have to fight for it."[9]

Angelica's file with the police grew thicker. By now the authorities could have accused her of anything, even if she were miles away from the event. Remaining in Switzerland was dangerous. On December 19, 1906, she moved to Nervi, near Genoa. To the relief of the police of Lugano, *Su, Compagne!* was closed with her departure.

Angelica's frequent travels, fearlessness, and open attacks against the Tsar and Swiss government surprised her enemies as much as her colleagues. Both accused her of being an international spy.

VIII

International Spy

Throughout her life, Angelica faced frequent accusations of being a spy. The Italians thought she spied for the Germans, the Germans and French were persuaded that she was a double or even a triple agent, and as for the Swiss, they preferred when she was not around. When Angelica left Russia in 1921, the Soviets would accuse her of working for the BOI, the Federal Bureau of Investigation, and the BOI for the NKVD, the predecessor of the KGB. As the indictments continued, in 1933 the French secret services decided to open a counter-espionage file on her. The file being mysteriously empty, it is hard to know whether they found nothing or whether the documents were moved to another unindicated place.[1]

The FBI as well as the secret police in the UK, Austria, Switzerland, Italy, and Sweden had files on the revolutionary ... and no proof whatsoever of her being a spy.

The only published document that was even remotely based on some evidence was an article that appeared in 1918, in *La Gazette de Lausanne*, which exposed Angelica's life starting from the time when she had left Switzerland in 1906 and moved to Italy. It said:

> Upon her arrival to Terni ..., Ms. Angelica Balabanoff lived there with Walter Träger, German, who allegedly made his living by making photographic reproductions. After three months, the couple suddenly left Terni to go to Nervi-Bogliasco, where Ms. Balabanoff found lodging for her protégé at the house of a known Russian, from whence Träger disappeared on one sunny day without leaving a trace, ... Träger and Ms. Balabanoff were close friends with Seiling, who under the pretext of editing illustrated post cards, photographed all establishments and sites of the province of Ombrie and its surroundings, and who escaped at the beginning of war, leaving the impression on everyone who knew him that he was a German officer on a spy mission. Among others things, Ms. Balabanoff declared living in Terni on 120 Livres, while the life she had led

At the Socialist Congress in Terni, 1911 (collection of Giorgio Giannelli).

should have cost her much more. Notably, in 1911, she went on a long trip, travelling through Italy, Switzerland, Germany and Belgium, during which she incurred some significant expenses.

A few years ago at the train station of Aoste, Ms. Angelica Balabanoff was called an "international spy" in the presence of many socialist comrades and none of them protested.[2]

Though the charges against Angelica were numerous, they provided little evidence of wrongdoing. One of the things such a compilation of different testimonies emphasized was her eccentric lifestyle. At the age of 37, her notions of life remained unusual, making her friends smile and, at times, worry for her, and her enemies suspect her of all evils. She had neither home nor money. After leaving Lugano in December 1906 and arriving in Nervi, a small picturesque resort near Genoa, famous for its ocean-cliff walkways, the homeless revolutionary stayed with friends for three weeks and then traveled 270 miles to the south of Italy to settle in Terni, where her friends found her a job. She was suddenly nominated to be secretary of the Terni Chamber of Commerce, a job she kept for a few years. Not exactly the James Bond girl, but still a highly unconventional trajectory for a woman.

When Angelica had free time, she opted not to go out to dance events or raffles. She stayed at home to write letters, read, and prepare for her upcoming lecture tours. Her unique distraction was an occasional evening at the theatre to see a pro-socialist play, *Anne Frank* being her favorite in her later years.

Her daily habits were ascetic to the extreme. Angelica's wardrobe, which consisted of plain, often secondhand clothes, did not exceed three dresses, two skirts and blouses, a coat, and a pair of cheap stockings for the winter season. Her toiletries were reduced to a strict minimum of a soap bar, tooth powder, and an occasional moisturizer. In no time she could pack her belongings into her two suitcases and move to a new location. At any rate, she rarely spent more than a few nights in the same place—more than sufficient for the locals to assume her to be the source of all things evil. In the Middle Ages, she would have been considered a witch or a heretic and burnt at the stake on the basis of pure suspicion.

Despite such heavy accusations, Angelica's fame in the socialist community was more prominent than ever. Lenin and Mussolini could not get by without her.

IX

Lenin's Favorite; Mussolini's Most Trusted

Angelica always insisted that her work had to be anonymous. It was the results she produced, not her, that held importance. She succeeded quite well in this quest for anonymity. The only town in which her memory is well commemorated is Rome—a street and a music school are named after her in the suburbs of the city. Only a handful of encyclopedias such as *Women in World History, German Universal Encyclopedia*, and some Italian political history dictionaries carry short articles about her. Otherwise, her name was practically forgotten after her death. The record of anonymity is held by Russia. In her homeland, Angelica's name was mentioned in one encyclopedia published sometime in 1919, which listed all prominent socialists and which had a short lifespan, being quickly replaced by other publications. And yet all of this only proves how subjective history can be.

At the turn of the 20th century, Angelica was at the height of fashion with her revolutionary colleagues. Solicited by the leaders of European Socialist parties, she was at the organizational core of the movement. No notable international event could take place without her linguistic skills. Often the only woman in such meetings, she found herself at large, exclusively male gatherings, sparkling in her white dresses, which contrasted with the dark, masculine suits. She received standing applause for her impressive, swift translations of the speeches delivered at these congresses, into three or four languages at a time, and she was publicly embraced and congratulated by the leaders of the movement.

Lenin was one of her immediate "fans." In his constant efforts to look for new party members, Angelica was one not to miss. If many Russian émigrés tended to stick together, thinking that the Swiss were boring, the Germans stiff, and the English stuffy, Angelica at least did not divide people by countries and imaginary cultural and social boundaries. For her, all socialists and all unprivileged people were a part of the one nation to which she truly belonged.

Lenin and Balabanoff regularly met in Geneva, running into each other in the Public Library and Café Landolt, the place for Russian revolutionaries to meet and a necessary stopover for Angelica during every stay in that town. She loved to treat herself to a cup of tea and a chocolate, sitting at one of the round tables on the terrace under the famous white-and-grey-striped sun shades.

"Angelica Isaakovna, you know everyone," Lenin would say. Her network of contacts was so impressive that when he wanted to know more about one of the European socialists, he would ask Angelica. "What do you think about X? His wife, who does she vote for? Do you think she could influence her husband?"[1]

Lenin had no doubts that Angelica was also an excellent fundraiser. In January 1905, there was a revolution in Russia. There were strikes and civil and military mutinies directed against the government. The mutinies ended up bringing long-needed democratic changes to Russia, like establishment of the State Duma, a multi-party government system, and the first-ever constitution, but the revolution itself was brutally suppressed on the orders of the Tsar. This crackdown resulted in the murder of at least 1,000 people, killed during a peaceful demonstration in St. Petersburg on 9 January, later known as Bloody Sunday.

Many leftist activists launched campaigns to support the revolution, its organizers, and the families of the victims. After talking it over with Lenin, Angelica decided to lunch her own campaign. Her Spartan habits enhanced by her bachelor lifestyle allowed her to devote a stunning number of hours to organizing meetings, inviting speakers, assuring attendance and press coverage, sales of socialist literature, and collecting funds.

During her lecture tours, she raised three times more money than Maxim Gorky, who was by then a prominent writer and the most famous Russian revolutionary personality. Gorky went on a similar lecture tour in the United States, invited by Mark Twain. He was traveling with his mistress, a well-known Russian dramatic actress, Maria Andreeva, while still married to his wife. When the news got out, his campaign went downhill and his U.S. trip was largely boycotted. He escaped back to Europe.

For once, Angelica was extremely proud of the results of her work. Discounting her usual habits of maintaining anonymity, she even reported on it in her memoirs.[2]

Incidentally, it was Angelica, of all people, whom the journalists in

Italy wanted to question about Gorky and his calamitous fundraising trip. They showed up uninvited in her small room in Lugano.

"It was as if they had thought I was hiding him under my bed," she commented later regarding their unexpected visit.

The next day, the papers announced that she was hiding Gorky in a "secret villa."

To Lenin, Angelica had many irreplaceable skills, but she also had handicaps. No doubt Lenin immediately sensed the main one. She was incapable of any theoretical or strategic undertaking. She had never developed or published any theoretical work of her own. Most annoying for Lenin, she failed to understand the importance of political factions. Angelica was clearly unable to grasp the simple Bolshevik idea that Russia needed a small, powerful government that would be able to impose its views on the rest of the masses. Instead she tended to think that it was better to have a large socialist Democratic Party and openly supported the Russian Democratic Menshevik leader, Julius Martov, Lenin's opponent, whom Lenin dubbed an "insect."[3] She even had the nerve to tell Lenin that "all socialists" in Russia were "fighting for the same cause."

In spite of this, Angelica's major drawbacks did not dissuade Lenin. He desperately needed simple agitators like Angelica as well as more complex propagandists like Trotsky or Zinoviev. He had enough ideas of his own that she could disseminate for him. Overall she was a real treasure. As such, Lenin entrusted her to perform the most important tasks.

In May 1907, Angelica was nominated to be the treasurer and a finance committee member of Russia's 5th RSDLP (Russian Social Democratic Labor Party) congress that took place in London. It went on for three weeks and was the largest such Russian socialist gathering. The redbrick Brotherhood Church on Southgate Road, rented by the congress organizers, managed to fit all 338 participants.

Angelica's job was to collect 10,000 German marks donated by the German Social-Democratic party in Berlin and bring the sum to London. She was appointed to such a prestigious position for two reasons. First, everyone knew of her honesty and accuracy with money. Second, she was possibly the only Russian able to placate her good friend and the leader of German socialists, August Bebel, who kept complaining that "Russians wasted money and spent weeks on [sic] talking and fighting. A socialist congress does not last for more than five days."[4]

Unaccustomed to working with Russians, Angelica was totally out of her element, lost track of time, and kept insisting in her memoirs that the congress went on for six weeks. Eyes wide open, she observed the "delegates," mainly from Russia, who arrived in London with no money and no extra clothes. One of them explained to her that it was to divert the attention of the Russian police, who were looking for potential congress participants on the westbound Russian trains.

Angelica thought that at least one did not need police to trace them in London. The sheepskin *shapkas* of participants from the Caucasus stopped the London crowds.

She was abashed by the greeting of her countrymen—"To which faction do you belong?"—instead of the more habitual and elegant "What is your name, comrade?" and an utter lack of unity among them.

"To me, attending a Russian Congress for the first time and unaware of the factional intrigues, all this was incomprehensible and exasperating," she wrote later.[5]

Bemused, she watched the participants spend the first week on approving the agenda and deciding who would be the president of the meetings. The conflicts between the Bolsheviks and the Mensheviks were so violent that that the congress had to be interrupted to avoid a fist fight. Angelica, who represented the Russian Marxist University students, was more than content with her role as an observer and a finance committee member.

Ten days after the beginning of the congress, the participants, who had barely managed to elect their president, ran out of the money donated by the Germans. Angelica, together with the writer Maxim Gorky and charismatic politician Georgy Plekhanov, was sent to look for more money. They were invited for dinner to the glamorous London-based house of the Russian-born American soap magnate Joseph Fels, who promised to give a long-term loan to the revolutionaries. Before dinner, the guests were invited to admire the magnate's glamorous picture gallery with paintings exhibited in massive golden Rococo frames. Strolling through the sumptuous gallery, Maxim Gorky, who found it too richly and vulgarly decorated for his taste, remarked in Russian: "How terrible!"

Angelica's heart sank. She was wondering how to translate it to their host. The industrial magnate would surely feel insulted and would never loan them the money they needed for the RSDLP congress in London to continue. Plekhanov saved the entire event by reassuring Fels: "Comrade Gorky has merely exclaimed, 'How remarkable!'" The soap magnate, entirely happy with such understanding revolutionary friends, issued them a much-needed check for £1,700 ($273.500 today).[6]

During the congress, Angelica saw all the Russian "titans" of the movement in action—Lenin, Trotsky, Plekhanov, and Martov, with whom she was by then good friends. By the end of the London congress, the split between the Mensheviks, led by Martov, and the Bolsheviks, led by Lenin, was definitive. As for Angelica, she was still unable to understand why one needed to belong to a faction when they all had one aim—to fight against the oppressors.

When it was time to return home, the congress participants followed the same strict conspiracy rules as they had upon their arrival. Without any luggage, they took trains to get back home. This time it did not work as well. The Russian police officers Okhrana, who had traveled to London for the occasion of the congress, noted down all participants, including Angelica, and added another line to her file.

Besides making a strong impression on the leaders of the entire Russian red movement and being noted by the Russian police, Angelica must have had quite an effect on the generous soap magnate who had co-sponsored the event. She heard from him ten years later, just after the October Revolution.

"I ... received a letter from Fels, asking for the restitution of the money loaned us in London," remembered Angelica. "What I did with it? [sic] I forwarded the letter to the government in Moscow for the settling of the account," she dryly remarked.[7]

Angelica could hardly believe it herself when the issue of the loan restitution came up again, more than 30 years later, when the eighty-year-old Angelica lived in Rome, where Fels managed to track her down. This time she had been long out of favor with the Russian *apparatchiks*. She suggested that Fels write once more to Moscow. She knew that the loan receipt had been long exhibited in the Museum of Political History under plate glass.

After the London congress, Angelica started to receive regular invitations to join one of the Russian parties. "Comrade," Lenin kept saying, "why are you not with us Bolsheviks? You views coincide with ours."[8]

Angelica was not persuaded that it was such a good idea. There were many disturbing rumors of robberies, corruption, and the other malicious means that the Bolsheviks used to get financing for their party and that were slowly becoming public knowledge. The best known was the bank robbery in the Caucasian nation of Georgia, only a month after the congress in London. On June 26, 1907, at half past ten in the morning, the post office of Tiflis had to transfer to the Russian Bank an amount estimated at 250,000 rubles, about $1.7 million today. Suddenly a bomb explosion stopped the car transporting the money and blew up the escorting cars. All the bills were numbered and listed, and the money could not be used in Russia. A few months later, many Bolsheviks were arrested in Berlin and Geneva trying to exchange, unsuccessfully, notes of 500 rubles. A large part of the notes would be burnt in Paris in 1910 by the leftist comrades, who decided to get rid of the unusable notes. The act was committed by two Caucasians known as Koma, or Ter-Petrosian, a renowned Georgian revolutionary, and his friend Koba, much better known as Joseph Djugashvili—Stalin.

Angelica met Lenin again two months later, after the London congress, at the Seventh Congress of the 2nd International in Stuttgart. She attended the congress as an observer, but following the chaos created by the presence of 850 delegates, she took on a role as an interpreter. Angelica asked Lenin to explain some of the rumors to her. The answer left her in dismay: "Everything that is done in the interest of the proletarian cause is honest."[9]

"Did human feelings exist for Lenin at all?" she wondered.

After this discussion with Lenin, Angelica made her final decision. She had nothing in common with the Bolsheviks. Siding with Lenin was out of the question once and for all.

For Angelica, 1907 ended in a flattering and unexpected proposal.

"Comrade Balabanoff," Castelli, the Italian publisher of Maxim Gorky, addressed her during one of her trips to Milan, "would you agree to translate Gorky's novel *Mother* into Italian? It had been well received in the United States, England, and Russia. I would like to publish it as quickly as possible in *Secolo*. I have spoken with Gorky; we both think that you would be the best person suitable for the job."

Angelica's rejection was firm.

"There are too many illiterates in Russia and Italy! They do not read what we write; only oral propaganda can educate and emancipate them. Spend time and energy on a work that would deprive me of the possibility of making propaganda that is so desperately needed? Never."[10]

A "Comrade" to Lenin, Angelica was "*Carissima*" to her Italian protégé. Mussolini continued his rapid ascent to power at the beginning of the 20th century, and he often needed her help. No matter when or where she received his messages, starting with "*Carissima*, we need you here," she went right away to help. Proud of her pupil, she was confident that she was grooming the main revolutionary man of Italy. The future *Il Duce* became an editor of the small paper *Lotta di Casse* in the region of Romagna. A brilliant journalist, his simple, understandable language attracted new readers; the newspapers he was working on gained eminent success.

At the end of April 1910, Angelica received the usual *"Carissima"* "invitation" calling her to Forli to participate in the meeting to celebrate Labor Day on the first of May.

"Only you, *Carissima*, can create such enthusiasm," he wrote.

Eager to assist, *"Carissima,"* who at the time lived in Milan, rushed to Forli. Mussolini was waiting for her outside the arched entries of the train station. On that day, Forli was torn by internal struggle between the Republicans, who were against the meeting, and the socialists who organized it. Together Angelica and Mussolini made their way through the small, irregular streets of town all the way to the piazza Saffi, where the meeting was scheduled to take place. Angelica looked anxiously around her at the groups of people who spoke agitatedly and screamed out menaces.

After a twenty-minute walk, they arrived at the trapezoidal piazza Saffi, surrounded by an abbey and imposing palazzos. A disorderly crowd of those who were in favor of as well as against the Labor Day event fumed around the stage, which was set in one of the corners of the piazza with the police forces nearby, ready to intervene.

"Maybe we shall have to call off your speech," proposed Mussolini.

"I don't think we should break the promise we made to the people when we announced our meeting," replied Angelica, and she immediately went on stage.[11]

She later remembered feeling how the earth moved under her feet. Then she heard an explosion. She understood that a bomb must have exploded in one of the nearby streets. From the shouts, she concluded that there were victims. Knowing that in such a situation, the abrupt end of the speech might provoke riots, Angelica calmly ended her presentation. Only then did she join Mussolini near the stage. To her astonishment, he did not even try to speak.

Angelica was unpleasantly surprised by her pupil's sudden fear of death, but she did not have time to give it much thought. They were about to leave the piazza Saffi when they were approached by two policemen. "The police authorities, fearing for our lives," remembered Angelica, "provided a coach for Mussolini and me to drive in."[12]

Mussolini did not need to be asked twice. The three policemen got into the first car and Angelica with Mussolini into the second. Driven by a chauffeur, they started to advance through the disorderly streets of Forli. As both cars slowly approached the station, making their way through the crowds of people, Angelica heard shots fired and the noise of windows shattering. The first car had stopped abruptly. As they passed the car, she saw the lifeless head of a policeman against the window frame, with blood running down his temple. Mussolini seated next to Angelica "shrunk down in his seat, trembling and cursing," she remembered later.

Together with her disciple, she safely got to the station. Only after getting back to Milan did Angelica understand why he had asked her to join him at the meeting in Forli. He had wanted her next to him on stage not for the public speeches, nor because he missed her. She had been used for one of two things. If the event had gone well, her presence would have brought more fame to Mussolini. If the event had failed, she would have been the one blamed. He was too afraid to take responsibility alone.

Angelica's first doubts about the true nature of her protégé had entered her mind. But she brushed them aside. After years of tutoring Mussolini, her desire to see him becoming an important and gifted player within the socialist movement was coming true.

X

Mussolini's Elegy

So what role did Angelica play in Mussolini's life? Supporters on both sides, who had witnessed their story, tried to avoid any discussion about the Russian Jewish Socialist and minimalize her involvement in *Il Duce*'s affairs. A rare, possibly unique testimony of the time, was left by the Mexican painter Diego Rivera, who had met the Russian revolutionary during his trip to Europe. "Mussolini, then an Italian Socialist leader, became Angelica's lover," wrote Rivera in his autobiography. "Soon he was the puppet of the fiery Angelica, echoing her every word and thought; for a time in fact, Angelica was Mussolini's brain."[1]

Mussolini mentioned her only once, in a conversation with his personal biographer Yvonne de Bergnac, but in a rather impressive way: "I repeat, I owe Angelica more than she thinks that I owe her. Political wisdom, fidelity to the ideas.... Her generosity does not know the limits, just as her friendship and her intimacy. If socialism could have a liturgy, religious rites, Saint Angelica of Socialism should be placed at the front of a political empyrean with Marx as a creator of earth and heaven. If I had not met her in Switzerland, I would have remained a small party activist, a Sunday revolutionary."[2]

This makes Angelica possibly the most important woman who contributed to Mussolini's accession to power during his early years. It was Angelica who helped him to get his first serious appointment, that of chief editor of *Avanti!*, at that time the main Italian socialist newspaper in the world. This position was offered to Mussolini during the National Socialist Congress of July 7, 1912, in Reggio Emilia. As a representative of the small federation of the town of Forli, he did not have many chances to be noticed. But he knew how to seize the right opportunities that life presented to him. Prior to the congress, an anarchist had tried to kill the King of Italy, Vittorio Emmanuel II. Some of the socialists, Leonida Bissolati, Angelo Cabrini, and Ivano Bonomi, went to see the king to express their joy that the attempt on his life had not been successful.

Mussolini, supported by the intransigent and anti-reformist Angelica, pronounced an imposing speech at the congress advocating for the exclusion of all pro-royal right-wing socialists from the party. "The king is by definition a 'useless' citizen," he proclaimed.[3] His speech was supported by the majority of the participants.

The future Italian prime minister was noticed for his oratorical skills, youth, and potential as a future leader. He had not yet acquired his famous pose, "with his two hands on his hips, chin raised and chest pushed out," but he was noticed by the PSI leaders.[4]

Furthermore, the victory of the leftist socialists at the congress made news all over Europe. Lenin publicly praised Mussolini. British, Swiss, and German socialist journalists devoted articles to the historical event, attributing this victory largely to the tactics of the young Italian politician. *Il Duce* was elected to the Executive Committee of the PSI and was offered to take the important position of chief editor of *Avanti!*, the major propaganda tool of the PSI, read by all Italian workers.

Angelica had been grooming him for this triumph since the day they had met. She then convinced the hesitant Mussolini to accept the prestigious job of the editor-in-chief. He was afraid to accept it. It took her hours to persuade him. In her play, *Traitor*, written about Mussolini, an interesting historical document, she describes how they met in a small restaurant near the headquarters of *Avanti!* after Mussolini had been offered this job:

"Life gave you one chance, do not miss it," insisted Angelica. "It would be the starting point for your political career. I'll help."

"I cannot take the responsibility alone." Mussolini seemed to be afraid.

"I won't leave you alone," she replied.[5]

By the end of the shared meal, "delicious macaroni with cheese, *past'asciutta*," house wine for Mussolini and water for Angelica, he was ready to accept the job. So when the

Anna Kuliscioff, 1908 (collection of Albert Tosoni-Pittoni).

PSI leaders reunited to nominate him to this position, Mussolini stood up in front of them and suddenly said: "I'm accepting this appointment under one condition only. Comrade Balabanoff has to come to Milan as a member of the editorial staff."[6]

Opinions differ on why he insisted on her nomination to such a position. Angelica had always said that she did not want any of it, and Mussolini proposed that she join him because of his "pathological feeling of intellectual inadequacy." Quite another version of the facts was provided later by Margherita Sarfatti, who insisted that Angelica imposed herself on Mussolini, as she usually did.[7] A more plausible explanation was provided by Mussolini's biographer Renzo De Felice. He thought that Mussolini plotted to attract all those who supported Angelica to his side, making the management of *Avanti!* a shared responsibility, knowing from the start that Angelica was one of the most difficult and inflexible people to work with.

No matter how, Angelica was elected to the quite prestigious position of co-editor, and both moved to Milan.

With her daily presence required at *Avanti!* her life became completely different—settling in one place, working with Mussolini, coming to the bright, clean offices, guarded by the old doorman Colomo, listening to the sound of the printing machines, and staying in until late at night, when it was quiet. She probably imagined herself orchestrating the management and running of *Avanti!*, with Mussolini directing it, succeeding, and winning all his battles under her guidance.

However, for Angelica, the trouble had begun the day after their nomination to the *Avanti!* positions. Her responsibilities, mainly administrative, included doing all the unpleasant work for Mussolini, from going to the meetings that did not interest him because his opinion was not supported by the majority to protecting him against PSI members, firing staff, and explaining questionable editorials. To everyone's astonishment,

Filippo Turati, c. 1908 (collection of Albert Tosoni-Pittoni).

Mussolini started his new job by dismissing his predecessor, the brilliant and experienced journalist Claudio Treves. The future prime minister would not tolerate any other authority next to him. It was Angelica who had to announce this dismissal to her long-time friend Treves, explaining that even his articles would no longer be accepted.

Mussolini's radical management of the paper and decision about Treves created uproar in the PSI. He was immediately summoned to the salon of Anna Kuliscioff, the co-founder of the PSI and the partner of the party's leader, Filippo Turati. She wanted to know why a provincial youngster and novice like Mussolini would fire one of the most professional leftist journalists. Mussolini dutifully went to see Anna.

The exquisite Milanese salon of Anna Kuliscioff was situated on 23 piazza Duomo, near the Duomo Cathedral, in one of the palazzos above the arcades of Galleria Vittorio Emmanuel II (one of the arcades still bears a plaque with her name). For years it remained the place to meet in Milan if one was considered a socialist. Attending the weekly gatherings, participating in discussions and sitting on or next to Anna's by-then-legendary emerald velvet sofa were absolute musts.

A few years Angelica's senior, Anna Moiseyevna Rosenstein originated from a well-off Ukrainian family in the Crimea. Her adoptive name, Kulisceva, stood for "a woman from a far-off Eastern land."[8] She was a known beauty. Those who had met her when she was young reminisced about her natural elegance and good looks, her blue eyes, "blond, thick, wavy hair and very white skin."[9]

Contrary to Angelica, Anna did not give up her family inheritance. Her wardrobe included a wide selection of white cotton high-collar and lace-infill blouses, which her maid arranged in a spacious dressing room next to black tailored suits—fitted jackets with three-quarter-length insets, braided and embroidered cuffed sleeves, and ankle-length matching skirts.

Dubbed "the most intelligent *man* of Italian Socialism," Anna was a prominent feminist, a socialist leader, and a doctor. After attending the universities of Zurich in Switzerland and Naples and Pavia in Italy, specializing in obstetrics and gynecology, she opened one of the first medical practices for poor women in Milan. Anna was also a talented politician. Some said that her partner, Filippo Turati, a Milanese lawyer, poet, and socialist, with whom Anna had established the PSI, did nothing without consulting her first.

In our days, Anna could have made a career as a Member of Parliament. In her time she was limited to developing the most elaborate strategies and giving instructions while remaining in her salon, but she was not admitted into big politics. Nonetheless, Anna was an extremely self-assured and no-nonsense person. Mussolini knew that the socialists who were given appointments in her palazzo to discuss PSI policy had it in their interest to be well prepared if they intended to debate.

Anna had never liked Mussolini. She had never gotten carried away by his charm as a leader and had thought differently about him from anyone else. Considering him a "perfect anarchist," she had wondered about the dangers that could arise from entrusting a paper of the party to such a man.[10]

However, the first meeting between Anna and Mussolini on December 2, 1912, was quite positive. Mussolini won her over. His talent as a journalist worked miracles. With time, *Avanti!* sales practically doubled, once Mussolini took it over from Claudio Treves. The publication of each issue at times reached 64,000 copies instead of the 34,000 maximum prior to Mussolini's ascension, while the special issues sold at 100,000.

Just two weeks later, he was back in Anna's salon again. He was ready to get rid of Angelica. Anna reported their conversation with Mussolini about the newspaper management in a letter to Turati, saying that Mussolini "hinted" that he "found the way it was being done to be very bad" since the revolutionaries did "not know, not even they, what they want."[11] He persuaded Anna that it was Angelica's inexperienced co-ordination that was dangerous for the paper. He did his best for this decision to be made by Anna rather than by him, and he was close to succeeding.

Anna began to suspect that Angelica was not so "intelligent," the word she used to describe Angelica after meeting her in January 1906. In another letter, Anna wrote to Turati that she considered Angelica "intellectually shallow and an unreliable person to work with."[12] She complained that Angelica "does not understand anything in politics or in the socialist movement" and that she came to seek her advice for every little thing, "unable to make her mind on anything." Already by mid–December 1912, Angelica's cherished relationship with Anna was going down the drain.

Long past were the days when Angelica had entered the meeting room during Turati's speech and he had interrupted himself mid- speech by saying: "No more words of mine. We have with us … Angelica Balabanoff."[13] All this was forgotten. Turati agreed with Anna, admitting that Angelica was "not a woman of genius" and went further in his private correspondence, saying that she "had the brain of a chicken."[14]

It was quite possible that the position of co-editor exceeded Angelica's capacities. She was an excellent organizer, but power and political games were not her style, while this position required much more than being an able administrator. Suddenly everyone was against her.

X. Mussolini's Elegy

As for Mussolini, he no longer needed his Russian muse. There were a few reasons for this. One was his wife, Rachele. So far she had lived in Forli. But shortly after Mussolini became the editor-in-chief, she decided to join him in Milan. Out of all the women of *Il Duce*, she was jealous of Angelica.

Just as everyone else in the PSI did, Rachele suspected the Russian revolutionary of having a relationship with her husband. Angelica and Mussolini lived only a few houses apart. They often walked back home together, after the long office hours, in the shadows of the trees, along the broad, quiet Castel Marrone street in the working-class district of Milan. Angelica's house was at number 9, an imposing red-brick building with plastered balconies and windows adorned with reclined cupids, holding marble wreaths in their hands, grey from the dust and long-needed renovation. Mussolini lived farther away, at 18.

There was no proof that anything was going on between them. Angelica told everyone that not once did he help her to "open the heavy street door" bound with metal, and that he just kept walking farther, "hands in pockets," insinuating that he had never been to her room. Nonetheless, a persistent rumor soon began to circulate that Mussolini's daughter Edda, born in 1910, was in fact the daughter of Angelica, who did not want to take care of her, and that Rachele had agreed to raise her in a token of acceptance of revolutionary free love.

The rumor that Edda was Angelica's daughter remains one of the greatest mysteries in Angelica's life. However, the story is hardly true. It was probably based on the fact that Mussolini and Rachele did not get married until 1915, and according to the traditions of the time, when little Edda was born, her birth certificate, issued at the Forli Town Hall, stated "mother unknown."

Once in Milan, Rachele had had enough. She started to make scenes in *Avanti!* accusing Mussolini of a liaison with Angelica and insisting that she should be fired immediately. In the Duomo salon, the rumor quickly spread that Mussolini had screamed back loudly: "Even if I had found myself on a deserted island, I would have rather made love to a female monkey," and swore that he had never had a relationship with Angelica.[15]

However, Rachele was not the main reason why Mussolini wanted to get rid of Angelica. A new woman entered his life.

The dark-haired beauty, Margherita Sarfatti originating from a rich Jewish family in Venice, was the wife of a Milanese lawyer, Cesare Sarfatti, and was an ardent devotee of the socialist movement. She had been working for some time as an art critic for *Avanti!* Just as Anna did, Margherita had her own salon in Milan supporting writers and artists. Her house on 93 *di corso Venezia* had a remarkable painting collection, carefully selected by Margherita herself. It included the first of her many portraits by Emilio Gola and Romolo Romani, soon to be followed by Oscar Kokoschka and Achille Funi, who, with her support, became prominent painters.

Margherita served as vice president of the international jury at the International Exposition of Modern Decorative and Industrial Arts in Paris and actively supported the International Monza Biennale of Decorative Arts and exhibitions in Milan. On Wednesday evenings, her popular salon, richly furnished with chandeliers, consoles, and cabinets decorated with ebonized woods and inlaid with ivory and bone, gathered artists, musicians, poets, politicians and economists.

The photos of the time taken in her salon and at social outings she attended showed Margherita wearing silk and satin dresses and evening gowns, pearl necklaces, and small tiaras with precious stones. She breathed connections, elegance, and higher class.

Margherita's immense fortune and lifestyle had been critically viewed by many socialists. One evening, in Anna's salon, Anna's 12-year-old daughter, Andreina, passed around a plate of *petits fours* and stopped in front of Margherita, who was wearing a magnificent brooch—butterfly with diamonds, sapphires, emeralds, and rubies. The child attracted her mother's attention to the brooch. "Yes, my dear," said Anna, "yes, of course, the demands of the proletariat ... yes, very beautiful, yes ... these diamonds, the Engels scale of salaries...."[16]

Mussolini thought that there was nothing wrong with being immensely rich and a socialist. He was attracted right away by Margherita's money and style. She was worldly and wealthy. Angelica's deliberate choice to live a life of poverty bored and annoyed him. He started to find her too maternal, too watchful, and too critical of his behavior.

He must have felt uncomfortable in the company of the educated and sophisticated socialists from Milan. A provincial teacher from Forli, he probably looked odd in this crowd of lawyers and Parliament deputies. The photos of the time show that he replaced his inappropriate jackets with fitted three-piece suits but remained poorly dressed. He also lacked the education and knowledge that most of the PSI leaders had.

Mussolini used all his overpowering charm to win over Margherita. He was irresistible. She was seduced. It must have been quite an unusual triangle: Angelica-Margherita-Mussolini. Diego Rivera wrote, "When I first met Margherita, she was a member of the 'salon set,' also frequented by Angelica Balabanova. Around these two beautiful young women clustered such men as Modigliani, Ricciotto Canudo, the brothers Garibaldi....

"The one member of the group who differed politically from the others was Angelica. She was, in fact, a personal friend of Lenin and one of the most eminent social revolutionaries in Paris. Then, one day, Mussolini met and fell in love with Margherita, deserted Angelica, and took Margherita as his mistress. Assuming Angelica's old role, Margherita turned his thinking completely about, nurturing the germ of fascism that had always lain dormant in *Il Duce's* mind."[17]

It is interesting to note how the famous Mexican painter and known womanizer was one of the rare people who depicted Angelica as "beautiful." Just as for Mussolini, for Diego Rivera, physical beauty was not the most important criterion in a woman.

Margherita was supplanting over the Russian revolutionary and her ideas of rescue of humankind. For Mussolini it was time to make his choice between the two women. He hardly gave any importance to any other women in his life. History has left us names like Fernanda Oss, who had a son from Mussolini, and Ida Dalser, whom he knew for some time, who had supported him financially when he could not find work, and who later followed him to Milan. And there were most likely many others seduced by the masculine charm of *Il Duce*. But to him only two women mattered.

Leda Rafanelli, an Italian anarchist journalist, reported how Mussolini confided to her in her Milanese apartment while trying to make her one of his conquests: "'Two women are madly in love with me, but I do not love them. One is really ugly, but she has a noble and generous soul. The other one is beautiful, but she's deceitful, avaricious, even sordid.... The woman who's ugly and good-natured is Angelica Balabanoff.' I gave a start," remembered Leda. "I knew her well, knew her to be a strong and courageous socialist, I had greeted her many times after speeches she had given brimming with revolutionary ardor, and I admired her." Leda felt sorry for her Russian friend: "The thought of her suffering the pains of unreciprocated love grieved me. But immediately another thought struck me: Balabanoff was different from other women: she was a Slav by temperament, used to life's struggle, she was widely traveled and knew socialists in many different countries; she certainly wasn't the sentimental faint-hearted type who'd be plunged into despair because a man didn't care for her."[18]

Mussolini must not have needed much time to choose between Magherita and Angelica, given who would be more useful in his new life. Angelica no longer fit his interests.

Loud, irritating arguments between Angelica and Mussolini became regular events in the *Avanti!* offices and must have seemed strange to the rest of the staff as well as difficult to handle. They could go for days without addressing a single word to each other. They communicated with the help of unflattering notes.

By the end of the summer, Angelica was exhausted by Mussolini's attitude. She was getting tired of her secondary role, something she had never noticed in her relationship with Mussolini before. She did not get along with Anna Kulisciof and Filippo Turati, the leaders of the PSI, and she lost many friends because of her support for Mussolini and his management of the newspaper. She left *Avanti!*

Angelica's dream of their joint work lasted for eight months. She came out of this affair shattered by his cold betrayal, as any woman would have felt after being let down by a lover. She was devastated. However, she was not as lonely as she seemed.

XI

A Well-Hidden Family

Angelica always insisted that she did not have any family. Granted, she did, but she had broken ties with them when she left for Europe in 1897, never to see her "bourgeois, capitalist, and oppressive" relatives again. Remaining rather elusive about her siblings, she wrote once that out of sixteen children, only nine lived to maturity and that the Balabanoff girls outnumbered the boys. In other words, there were at least five sisters and no more than four brothers. So the Balabanoffs did exist somewhere in the Russian Empire.

Angelia's family proved to be difficult to find. The Chernigov archives included no mention of them. There are two possible explanations for this. First is a serious lack of precision on Angelica's part about her relatives, which made the task of submitting more accurate requests to the archives next to impossible. She provided only the first names of her parents, Anna and Isaac, and no dates of birth or death and had never mentioned the names of her (at least) three other sisters or her four brothers. In her memoirs, she devoted a few lines to her elder sister Anna. Anna had lived in Kharkov, and Angelica visited her during her years in school, which created a bond with her elder sister.

In addition, such absence of documentation may easily be due to historical reasons. Few genealogical documents survived in the Ukraine, which during the first half of the 20th century hurtled from one cataclysm to another. It lived through the October Revolution, the Civil War, the famine-genocide, and the two world wars, ending with a massive extermination of Jews in the Ukraine during World War II. The devastating events killed millions of people, while most of the documents were lost in flames during the bombardment, chaos, evacuation, and cold, hungry winters—in order to heat stoves.

Nothing would ever have been known about Angelica's family if not for the astounding correspondence between Angelica and her brothers kept in the RGASPI archives in Moscow, which betrayed an impressively close bond between the Balabanoffs. Back home in Chernigov, she had a loyal and caring family. Her eight siblings loved and supported their revolutionary sister.

The letters showed that her four brothers were called Victor, Samuil, Leon, and Sergei. The most extensive correspondence was between Angelica, her elder brother Victor, and his daughter Lida. Victor was the complete opposite of Angelica. A well-off merchant, he rented a prestigious apartment in one of the richly decorated art-deco landmark buildings in St. Petersburg on *Bolshaya Dvoryanskaya* 21; his family spent their summers in their *dacha* in Pavlovsk, the hip neighborhood of the Russian capital and worlds away from Angelica's tiny rooms and her work for the poor. And yet, he wrote Angelica the most caring and tender letters.

"My dear Anchushka [a diminutive by which Angelica was caringly known in her family]!" Victor wrote as if addressing a child, "I wrote to you end of June.... In this letter I have explained our news in all detail. I would be most happy, and I ask you so, if our personal correspondence could be livelier."

He wanted his baby sister to tell him if she needed anything: Could they send her books? More money? The leftist newspapers?

"I subscribed you to *Birzha*, because it is our only meaningful newspaper at the moment ... *Rech'* and *Den'* are boring," reported Victor on recent developments in the press. "So far I have subscribed to *Rech'* and *Den'* for three months, please let me know if you want them any longer.... Next week I'm going to Kharkov on business and will visit mother.... With best wishes, my dear, and big kisses, I'm waiting with impatience for your letters.... Your Victor."[1]

Just as touching are the letter from Victor's daughter, Lida, who addressed Angelica as *Kumin'ka*, a diminutive from *Kuma*, the Old Russian for godmother, which Angelica might well have become upon Lida's birth in 1891.

"Dear Kuminka," wrote Lida in 1916, "it has been such a long time that I have not received any letters from you! Despite the problems with the post, I'm really worried. I can see that you have not been feeling well recently. I hope that your silence is explained by the postal hitches and that your health is much better. Hope your stay in the mountains did you good as a treatment and as a refreshing elixir for your mood."[2]

Angelica's other brother, Samuil, was a lawyer and took care of the family estate. He was also responsible for sending Angelica her monthly allowance. Every month for 17 years (!) he sent money to his youngest sister. The amount, 50 rubles, or the equivalent of an average worker's salary, had been determined by Angelica. Not once in all that time did he fail to send these funds to his little *Anchushka*, who could freely continue her political activity without worrying about what tomorrow would bring.

The money came from the dividends Angelica was entitled to receive for life from the investment of her share of the family inheritance. According to the family will drawn up on May 20, 1895, Angelica owned a house together with Samuil and her brother Leon, "in the town of Chernigov on the angle of Boguslavskaya street and the Red square," which the three of them decided to put up for sale.[3]

Centrally located, the house quickly sold for 45,000 rubles, approximately $480,000 today. Too busy with her work, Angelica, who then lived in Switzerland, had no intention of spending weeks on travel back home to conclude the sale. She sent her power of attorney to Samuil. While she waited for the sale of the house and her share of 15,000 rubles, Samuil, who adored his audacious sister, continued to send her an advance of 50 rubles per month. Upon the sale, the brothers agreed to invest her share, minus the advance, at four percent annual interest, earning Angelica 760 rubles per year and assuring her a monthly allowance of 60 rubles.[4]

And then there were the scarce, manly, but, nevertheless tenderly written postcards from Leonid, the son of Angelica's brother Leon. "You understand I really need to receive at least some news from you," he insisted.[5]

After reading these letters, one thing came through—upon leaving Chernigov, Angelica broke ties definitively only with her mother, though regular news about Anna Hoffmann's health continued to reach the rebel through her brothers. The revolutionary continued seeing her siblings during their trips to Europe. She preferred to avoid visits to the luxurious resorts in which her family liked to sojourn and gave them appointments in the small coffee shops in the cities.

To this day there is no information about three of Angelica's sisters; their names and fates remain unknown.

In May 1914, to the mutual happiness of Angelica and her niece, 23-year-old Lida came from St. Petersburg to Milan for an extended stay with her adored *Kumin'ka* and to celebrate her aunt's 45th birthday. For days they talked about everything and nothing and walked around Milan. Knowing Angelica, her birthday on May 8 must have been celebrated in a tea-room with hot chocolate and Milanese cannoli.

Young Lida's visit could not have been more timely. Angelica had never imagined that her birthday would taste so sour. After the rupture with

Mussolini, she felt betrayed, deceived, and unfairly treated—all in all, the whole palette of feelings that a woman who has been abandoned and forsaken could experience. She still lived only a few houses away from him, on 9 *Castel Marrone* Street. But she no longer saw Mussolini. By the time she left *Avanti!*, their relationship was over. With Angelica's daily presence not required in the newspaper offices, she resumed her usual life as a nomad, busying herself with traveling and public speaking. Maybe times had changed; maybe the audience felt Angelica's bitterness. This time the reception by the press was much less enthusiastic.

It was not her speeches that were questioned. They were as timely and modern as ever. Addressing working women, Angelica called to those whose "difficult circumstances of life made [them] a factory slave. The times have passed when women were considered inferior to men," she proclaimed, remaining as poignant as ever. "In today's economic situation, she plays a role at least equal to that of her companion. She works as much as he does.... Despite this, her salary is often inferior.... It is not all. After a 10-hour working day ... she does not have a right to rest ... there is house cleaning, children...."[6]

However, for the first time in her speaking career, many criticized her tendency to worsen the truth and found her constant expressions of discontent and calls for revolt unnecessary: "She plays her instrument masterfully," reported *Journal du Jura*. "Unfortunately, her chords are neither always just nor harmonious."[7]

Angelica tried to go to Lausanne for three days, but the authorities had not forgotten the audacious revolutionary and were firm:

"The State board of the canton of Vaud responded negatively to the request for Angelica Balabanoff to stay in the canton of Vaud from 20 to 22 February this year, to give conferences on the professional organization of workers."[8]

So when Lida came for a visit in May 1914, Angelica not only interrupted her travels and lecture tours to spend one month with her niece but showed herself to be a caring and attentive host.

"My dear, when are we going to meet again?" wrote Lida affectionately once she got back home to St. Petersburg from her trip. "Of course both of us cannot know it.

"But think only how wonderful it would be. After such a long separation, it would be especially nice to meet and live again for some time together in Italy. Sometimes I get such a strong desire to see you, with the warmest feelings, I remember the time when we have been together."[9]

If Lida came back from Italy full of ideas about new trips with her aunt, which she hurriedly shared with her, for Angelica the family letters were of little consolation. In the summer of 1914, war was on the way. The Russian revolutionary found herself in total isolation. The PSI, as well as many other socialist parties, declared itself against the war. In reality, most of the socialists supported their respective countries. A true internationalist, Angelica was against any war no matter what the Italian, Russian, or other governments had to say. She was not a Francophile, like many of her French colleagues who, while claiming to be against the war, sided with France. Nor was she a Russophile like some of her countrymen. Neither was she pro–German. But she was for peace. Mortified and confused, she saw her friends and colleagues take different positions.

Just when Angelica thought that relations with her colleagues could not get worse, another revelation came from Mussolini. He suddenly changed his anti-war opinion, announcing his support for Italy to join the war against Germany. On October 18, he published an article in *Avanti!* entitled "From Absolute Neutrality to Active Neutrality," calling for the war and sympathy for the Entente. He claimed that there was a difference between wars. In this case the victory of Germany would mean the end of free Europe. Mussolini called for Italy to side with France. *Avanti!* asked its editor to provide explanations. His point of view did not express that of the paper and of the PSI.

"The man who wrote this article has no place in the Socialist Party. He belongs at the front or in a madhouse," was the official opinion of the PSI about the once-popular editor of the newspaper.

After long debates, Mussolini left the paper and was excluded from the PSI. Quite astounding was Angelica's erratic behavior. One of the first to insist that Mussolini be excluded from the PSI, she suddenly suggested:

"Comrades … I should like to have a temporary allowance made for Mussolini. Until he finds something else to do we should provide for his family."[10]

But Mussolini was too proud to accept it. He was formally expelled from the PSI on November 24, 1914.

Courageously, Angelica continued to maintain her internationalist position. In her effort to "go against the stream," she published an article in *Avanti!*, in which she urged her Italian colleagues not to "make premature judgments about the German socialists" because she did not believe that all of them supported war.[11]

She was immediately accused of being a German spy. In the winter of 1915, she had to move to Berne for fear of being arrested. The separation with her "beautiful adoptive country" would last much longer than she could have expected. With Mussolini coming to power as a fascist Prime Minister, Angelica would become persona non grata in Italy. She would be able to return there only in 1947, more than 30 years later.

Angelica was leaving Italy depressed and disillusioned after the events of the previous two years. To add to her misfortunes, with the beginning of World War I, she stopped receiving her monthly allowance from the family inheritance. Investments in the Russian economy devalued. The Russian ruble was losing its power, and inflation sky-rocketed. The bank investment set up by her brothers no longer yielded any profit. For the first time in her life she had to make her own living. The only problem was that she did not know how.

XII

Back to Russia

The small, quiet city of Berne, built on a hill at the bottom of which flowed the Aare river, struck Angelica with its abundance of trees, peacefulness, and a prosperity she did not expect to see during war time.

After giving it a better look, she realized that in Switzerland, life was just as chaotic as everywhere else. As a neutral country, it provided political asylum. Émigrés were flooding in, looking for jobs. Often the only work available was washing the shop windows at night in exchange for a few francs, which was not enough to pay for a single meal. Communication between the countries had slowed down. There was even a short period during which it was impossible to exchange money. All of these factors added to the feeling of general anxiety and instability that permeated the air.

For the first time in her life, Angelica had no fixed income and could not rely on her family, who had lost much of their investments in the Russian economy. Despite their difficulties, they continued to wire her money whenever they could. From Petrograd, the new name given to the capital of Russia at the beginning of war, Victor sent occasional bank transfers, taken from his own family budget.

"A few days ago I transferred you 190 rubles to the Banque [sic]...," he wrote. "[Unfortunately they gave only 168 Swiss francs], if you have not received it yet, please ask at the bank...."[1]

Angelica managed to secure a few jobs. Before she left Italy, *Avanti!* had confirmed that they would keep her as its foreign correspondent and would pay her 90 Lira (about $400 today) per month. She was occasionally paid as a translator of speeches and proceedings at conferences, bringing her an income of 100 Swiss francs per conference (about $900 today). She also contributed to the Russian newspaper *Nashe Slovo* (Our Word), published in Paris, which united some anti-war Marxists like Leon Trotsky, Julius Martov, and Alexandra Kollontai, and so she might have received a small fee for the articles.

This revenue being insufficient and irregular, Angelica decided to supplement it by translating books. For no particular reason she opted for children's literature, without any prior knowledge of children or the books they read. Having left Russia a long time before, she asked her faithful goddaughter Lida to send her popular publications. But Lida was not much of an expert either.

"I hope you have already received the book sent by registered mail 'The Tales of The Purring Cat,'" she wrote to her aunt. "Maybe this book is not suitable at all, frankly, I'm not at all familiar with children's literature."

Eager to help, Lida needed more guidance: "Please tell me what kind of books you would like to receive, describing more accurately the genre. Would you find it possible to translate a non-fiction literature...? Please ask you publisher what kind of books are more in demand: novels or non-fiction, and write to me. Will send the books to you, otherwise it is difficult to choose, not knowing what you would prefer."[2]

Before long, Angelica abandoned her translation work and concentrated on her anti-war activity. In Berne she joined her old acquaintances, Lenin and his wife, Nadezhda. At that time, Lenin did not have much support even among his comrades. His extreme left, aggressive political views of "revolution at all costs" were not popular. The couple led a secluded, financially strained life. "I highly esteemed his courage," she would say later. Soft-hearted and sympathetic, Angelica often came to visit them on *Distelweg* 11, where they rented two rooms on the second floor of a small two-story yellow-brick town house, sharing with the Lenins a meal of "boiled potatoes" for lunch or "tea and buttered bread" in the evening.[3] The visits did not improve her rapport with Nadezhda, who remained distant and critical of the female Russian revolutionary. Whether or not this attitude had anything to do with Angelica's "more than friendly" relationship with Lenin would remain the mystery of the trio.

Angelica's choice of settling in Berne was not accidental. Her expertise in the organization of international conferences was required more than ever. Her good friend Clara Zetkin decided to gather the prominent socialist women of Europe in Berne to show their unification against the war. She settled on Switzerland because it was a neutral country that could host all European participants and on a female-only event because young women had much greater facility to cross the Swiss border illegally during the war—an almost impossible task for men to accomplish.

The organization of the conference took place in the strictest secret conditions. All preparatory work was disguised in the letters between

XII. Back to Russia

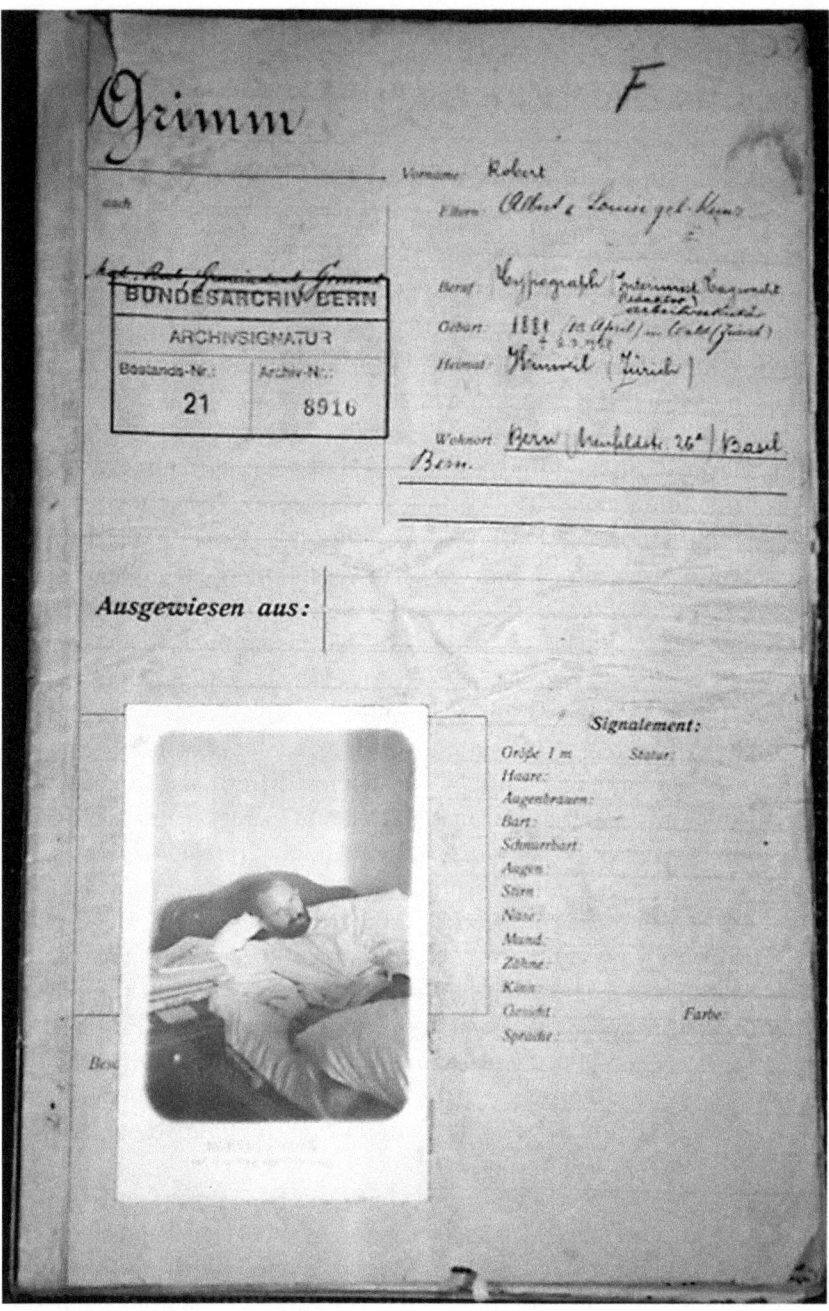

Police file of Robert Grimm, Switzerland, c. 1911 (SFA, CH-Bar#21#1000/131, Nr. 8916. 2012. Photograph by Jean-Loup Lafont).

Angelica, Clara, Rosa Luxemburg, and Lenin's mistress, Inessa Armand, under the discussion of family wedding preparations.[4] Orderly and efficient, Clara continued sending Angelica four-page, 1.5-spaced typed letters with the most precise explanations listed as numbered action items on how, where, and when the conference should be prepared and whom to invite.

After much preparation, the conference was finally held in Berne on March 26–28, 1915. Despite the war, about 30 participants from Germany, the UK, France, Italy, Belgium, and many other countries attended. The event risked causing an inevitable clash between the Russian radical left-wing Bolsheviks, who were for revolutionary seizure of power, and the rest of the participants, most of whom were anti-war pacifists.

In 1961, while writing her book *Impressions of Lenin*, Angelica was still blistering with emotions, remembering Lenin's mischievous doings during the conference. "For natural reasons he could not attend the women's conference," she dryly commented. He stayed in the People's House restaurant, giving orders to Nadezhda and Inessa, who represented Russia. "At the slightest modification ... the meeting was interrupted to allow the Bolshevik delegates hear Lenin,"[5] wrote Angelica, depicting how Nadezhda and Inessa took turns to run to the restaurant to get Lenin's opinion. From Angelica's point of view, Lenin wanted the impossible. He was calling for an irrelevant (for this meeting) resolution which those who were present simply could not sign "for an immediate organizational break with the majorities in the existing Socialist and Labor parties and for the formation of a new international," while the aim of the organizers was to simply show the unity among women against the war and provide some moral support to those who were fighting in the war.[6]

The future leader of the Soviet Union threatened not to sign the conference resolution if his conditions were not accepted. His attitude risked compromising the event, exposing the disagreement to the press, showing that even 30 delegates could not come to an agreement. Running the risk of having a heart attack, the gravely ill Clara Zetkin left the conference room and spent hours persuading Lenin in a tea-room to accept the conference resolution until he agreed.

The same story repeated itself a few weeks later at the youth conference, again co-organized by Angelica in Berne. Russia was represented by Inessa, then 41 years old, but she was the best Lenin could find to represent his ideas. Angelica saw him in the same restaurant: "'Vladimir Il'ich, did you come here for tea or for resolutions?' He answered me with an annoyed glance."[7]

XII. Back to Russia

When the conference was over, Angelica spent a few exhausting days and nights editing and translating the proceedings of the event into German, French, Italian, English, Russian, and Polish. Already in her letter of April 9, Clara tenderly congratulated her: "Hope that you will rest after an excellent translation and work on the Proceedings."[8] Considering the slow wartime postal services, Angelica must have sent out her work on the three-day conference to Clara almost immediately.

As the war went on, the ever-popular anti-war conferences continued. The European socialist internationalists decided to call the first general conference, aiming at stopping the war. The event was to take place in Switzerland. Organization of the event was backed up by well-known member of the Swiss Socialist Party Robert Grimm, with Angelica as an irreplaceable assistant and translator of such meetings. Grimm was 12 years Angelica's junior. The young, handsome, and generous Swiss politician was a dynamic man, with intense, deep-set blue eyes.

His file in the Swiss Federal Archives, a surprisingly slim folder for a prominent underground activist, has on the front a photo showing a dreamy young man with a neat beard, half-lying in bed and wearing a long white nightgown, providing a striking contrast with the majority of the front photos on other folders, usually taken at the police station and depicting the tense-looking faces of the revolutionaries.[9]

For the congress, the organizers chose a small, unknown village—Zimmerwald—in which 21 houses were scattered among the emerald-green valleys and splendid mountain landscapes, not far from Berne. Angelica visited Zimmerwald a few weeks before the conferences and rented the entire hotel and guest house, *Beau Séjour*, an elegant establishment with summer terraces and rooms with magnificent views of the mountains and fields. The place and dates of the conference remained secret, and the delegates were notified by Angelica only a few days in advance by post cards.

September 5, 1915, was the first day of the congress. The owner of the hotel was abashed at the site of the 40 strange-looking occupants of his hotel, who had come from all over Europe to scream and argue in the *Beau Séjour* meeting room. As the event went on, the best press coverage was provided by Angelica for *Avanti!* The name of the small, previously unknown village became widespread. After seeing the name of his hotel in the papers, the owner decided to make a contribution to the International.

Lenin, who radically supported the revolution, compared to other more pacifist groups, organized a clash between factions of the left, centrists and the right wing threatening to undermine the event. He agreed to adopt the manifesto against the war, but announced that in the future he and his faction would work separately. To avoid future disagreements, the conference established the Internationalist Socialist Commission that served to regulate the daily work of the International and solve the eventual conflicts among socialist parties worldwide. This commission consisted of Grimm as the president, two Italian revolutionaries, Charles Naine and Oddino Morgari, and Angelica as secretary and translator. Gossips insinuated that Angelica was nominated because she was the only person who was available to do all this work while everyone else was busy with their actual work and family lives. The position was only seemingly important, as the commission did not have any real authority.

Despite all efforts, the war seemed endless to Angelica. She was not used to staying for so long in the same country and was bored with the repetitive tasks, walks in the mountains, and running into the Lenins. Her centrist position with peace-for-all-at-any-price hardly gained any strength and put her in isolation. She did not support the left-wing group headed by Lenin:

"I have been shocked more than once ... by the fact that their judgment of situations and people would be favorable or not depending on the advantage their faction could gain. This using of two yardsticks I found inadmissible and immoral."[10]

Nor was she for the reformists of the right wing. The revolutionary still believed that a transition would come that would change the world. The unimaginable happened about two years after the conference.

On March 15, 1917, Angelica, at the time ill with influenza in Zurich, received the news of the March Revolution in Russia. Tsar Nicolas II had abdicated. No more Romanovs. The Duma got control of the country and appointed the provisional government. Though a member of the PSI, Angelica could not miss the real revolution. Imagining big opportunities that were ahead of Russia and the revolutionaries, she started to make serious plans to go back home.

"I may have been the only survivor of the twenty or twenty-five Russian émigrés," she wrote later, describing the meeting, which took place in a small, dark hall of the People's house, "who attended the talk Lenin gave, a few days after the February Revolution [according to the Julian calendar, which is two weeks behind the Gregorian calendar, the revolution was in February], in the smallest room in the old People's house in Zurich. The number of those who came to listen to him shows that he had not many followers then," she remembered many years later.[11]

XII. Back to Russia

Within weeks of the event, the Swiss and German governments reached an agreement that permitted the Russian socialists in exile to reach Russia. Such an agreement would allow them to avoid the habitual war problems of crossing Europe, including Germany, as well as getting transit visas—usually unobtainable in such situations. After a modest farewell dinner in the *Zahringerhof* restaurant not far from the *Spiegelgasse strasse*, Lenin left on April 9 with a few close supporters.

Angelica followed in the second train, which held 257 other revolutionaries coming back to Russia, about a month later. The fellow travelers included many future prominent politicians of the yet-to-be-created Soviet State, like Anatoly Lunacharsky, who would become successively the Minister of Education and Ambassador to Spain. The list of passengers divided them into parties to which they belonged. Angelica was listed under "Unidentifiable" or not belonging to any party.

Passengers did not have the right to get off the train during the journey until they reached Sweden. The trains themselves would later create many polemics. Many wanted to know how the agreement to cross the countries could have been reached between the governments at war. Called the Sealed Trains, it is not certain even today whether they were really "sealed" because the Russian citizens crossed countries at war or whether they were protected as diplomatic trains, accompanied by the representatives of the German Ministry of Foreign Affairs, who hoped that the return of the anti-war Bolsheviks would undermine the efforts of the Provisional government to continue the war.

When two weeks later the train passed Sweden and stopped at the Finnish border with Russia, the revolutionaries got off the train to get some fresh air while waiting for the formalities for crossing the border to be completed. As they stood on the platform, happy to be off the train, enjoying the light breeze of the fresh Finnish spring, someone suggested that Angelica makes a speech to mark the event. She refused, using her usual pretext: "I'm too insignificant and too small."

Those who were on the train took her words literally: "Come, we will help you."

"Before I could utter another word," remembered Angelica, "they lifted me up on their shoulders above the crowd. It is from this height that I delivered my first speech in this country."[12]

XIII

De Facto *Ambassador to the Scandinavian Countries*

Upon arrival in Russia, Angelica was unaware that five weeks later she would be accused of being a German spy and be sent to Stockholm on the orders of Lenin to become an image maker for the revolutionaries, and that another three months later she would be nominated a *de facto* ambassador to the Scandinavian countries.

She came back to Russia in May 1917, arriving there only a few weeks after Lenin and Trotsky, thinking about working side by side with Lenin, throwing over the Provisional government, making a Revolution, and establishing the First State of Workers.

However, her arrival in Petrograd was full of surprises, many of which she would have preferred to avoid. First, her brother Sergei had come to meet her at the Finland Station. Unprepared to see any members of her family, whom she had not informed of her arrival, she quickly realized that her arrival had been announced in the newspapers. She did not know that her name was listed in the press among the prominent leaders of the Socialist-Democratic Party or those generally considered by the public as the Bolsheviks, or bandits, and that her family wanted to let her know that this time she had overstepped the limits.

Sergei took Angelica to her older sister Anna who, as the eldest in the family, wanted to verify for herself: "Are you a bandit?" Anna asked her sister as soon as Angelica entered the house after 20 years of absence, greeting her in the entrance of the mansion Anna owned in town, between the marble stairs and white statues of cupids that decorated the hall. The revolutionary thought it was pointless to explain to Anna yet again that she was for peace and helping the poor, and answered positively to her sister's question. To avoid another fight with her sister, Angelica stormed out of Anna's house, which she had visited as a child, into the

XIII. De Facto *Ambassador to the Scandinavian Countries*

street. She thus lost an opportunity to stay with Anna and solve the complicated problem of finding lodgings in Petrograd, which was unfamiliar to her. Sergei was softer-hearted toward his little sister. He took in his *Anchushka,* giving her a room in his apartment—a huge favor in the starved and disordered city, which was in real chaos during the war, with workers participating in daily demonstrations asking for bread and higher wages.

Upon settling in her brother's place, Angelica threw herself into work. She was in charge of two things. She acted as the image generator of the Bolshevik party headed by Lenin. The Bolsheviks were not known abroad. Her responsibilities included informing Western countries about their plans to take over the country. She did so by writing, editing, and disseminating the informative bulletins in all 13 languages she knew, using her impressive network of contacts.

Her other job was to represent the Zimmerwald Executive—anti-war socialist parties to promote peace. She did this together with Robert Grimm, who had arrived in Moscow at about the same time as Angelica. To cover her activities with Robert Grimm, who did not speak Russian, she sometimes presented herself as his translator, and sometimes as his fiancée.

Around mid–July, Grimm was accused of being a German spy. He had sent a telegram from Petrograd to the Ministry of Foreign affairs of Switzerland asking them to contact Germany to see on what conditions the Germans would be prepared to discuss peace with Russia. For everyone in Russia, Grimm became a foreign secret agent and a traitor.

Angelica did not believe these rumors. She thought that Grimm's telegram was explained by his naïve assumption that he could do something to accelerate peace. Nonetheless, Grimm was obliged to leave Russia as a foreign national who had intervened in affairs of the country at war. Angelica, known to many as his wife and translator, was caught together with Grimm in this spiral of accusations, which were multiplying and growing like a snowball.

As Grimm left for Switzerland, Angelica, to avoid dealing with any further misunderstanding, going to prison, or even being executed as a spy, had no other choice than to disappear from Russia.

Lenin suggested he send her to Stockholm as the image maker of the Bolsheviks—in other words, to continue editing and disseminating her pro-revolutionary bulletins, explaining to the entire world the greatness of Lenin's ideas of communism. He elaborated a plan of conquering the world through his ideas, and Angelica was part of this plan. Extreme as ever, Lenin was calling for the creation of the "Third International." He wanted Russia to be at the head of this new communist movement worldwide. If before this time, his militant claims of superiority had provoked and irritated socialists from other nations, they now had some solid foundation. This time, he was the Head of the Party in one of the largest countries in the world, which was about to undergo a revolution.

So the socialists were divided into two factions: those who supported Lenin and those who did not. Those who did not support him, the faction headed by Dutch and Scandinavian socialists, were unsure of the legitimacy of Lenin's proposal for Russia to take over the whole movement. They invited all anti-war Socialist parties to pressure the governments to end the war, but without allowing Russia to take over. Lenin labeled them centrists, warning that parties who sided with the centrists would not be a part of the Russian revolution—a serious threat to all those who aspired to create a new free society.

In deciding whether to go to Stockholm or not, Angelica faced an important dilemma. If she were to go on Lenin's behalf, it would mean that she openly sided with him. The other solution for her was to leave Russia and go back to Berne, remaining a simple anti-war activist and renouncing forever her exceptional relationship with Lenin and the possibility of being an integral part of the revolution in her homeland.

She wondered whom she should support. Lenin and her country? Or the rest of the socialist movement for which she had been working? Lenin did not have right to dictate the will of all socialists and to impose the Bolshevik opinion on the rest of the movement. But the real revolution was so much more important. Angelica decided to side with Lenin.

With Russia still at war, the socialist parties decided to call the Zimmerwald convention (after Zimmerwald congress in 1915) in Stockholm. The only item on the agenda would be who to follow: the Russians or the other Europeans.

Angelica went to Stockholm to organize the convention as a secretary of Zimmerwald, armed with Lenin's special request to sway the parties his way. Before leaving Petrograd, she filed the papers applying to become a member of the Russian Communist Party. She left the papers with her long-term friend Alexandra Kollontai, who was to present them in Angelica's absence.

A few months later, Angelica would be given 25 years of seniority in the party by Lenin, not only acknowledging her work in Switzerland and Italy, but dating her work in Russia back to 1893 and giving her certain

XIII. De Facto *Ambassador to the Scandinavian Countries*

seniority within the movement.[1] She became one of the longest-standing members of a party to which she had never belonged.

Angelica hardly ever saw her brother Sergei during her stay in his apartment and decided to leave him a brief note explaining that she was going to Europe to work for the cause.

She assumed that, knowing his sister, Sergei would not be surprised to find the message and would not need further explanation.

At the beginning of August, she was back on the train to Stockholm. The only way of getting to and from Russia was through Finland and Sweden, on what had previously been express trains that by this time took days to arrive at one's final destination. The trains were insufficient and over-packed. Some were returning to Russia with new hopes; others, on the contrary, tried to escape while it was still possible to do so. The passengers, tired, pale, and lost in their thoughts, were packed into sleeping and dining cars. Those who could not find seats had to stand for hours in the corridors.

Traveling on an official mission, Angelica managed to get a seat, which in itself was a miracle. She thoroughly enjoyed crumbs of stale brown bread and a sip of a dark warm drink that reminded her of coffee, which was distributed by a man with who made his way through the train with his huge basket. What she found most unusual so far was that for the first time in her life, she was going to a country without speaking its native language.

Lenin did not trust the soft-hearted Angelica to go to Stockholm alone to steer the European parties his way. But he desperately needed to assure the workers in Russia that they had international support. To back up Angelica's work, he dispatched Karl Radek to Sweden. Radek was a short, unattractive Polish intellectual with big round glasses and a thick chin-curtain beard that made his face, eyes, and nose look bigger than they were. Angelica, sensing that not much could stop him from executing the worst of Lenin's orders, immediately labeled him as highly immoral.

In Stockholm, things did not go as planned. When the Zimmerwald conference was finally organized and set for the beginning of October, most of the countries invited to participate in it could not attend because of the war. The U.S. socialists did not get their passports in time, while the German, French, and Italians simply could not travel, and so the conference did not have a quorum to take a vote. Most importantly, the October Revolution in Russia was on the way.

Angelica witnessed the revolution on November 7, while sitting in a Stockholm coffee shop with Russian friends and Karl Radek on the phone getting regular news from Russia. This event meant the end of the "life-and-death" struggle for her. She did not mind not being personally present in Petrograd. Angelica enjoyed her supportive role and anonymous activity, finding it just as important as the roles of those who were "at the front."

As soon as the revolution took place and Lenin called for peace "to all nations," she rushed to her office and, together with a few colleagues, printed a document in support of the revolution, assured its translation into 12 languages out of the 13 she spoke, probably not using her Japanese for this occasion, and provided for worldwide distribution.

From that point on, Angelica served as one of the main press centers of the Bolsheviks. Her principal job was the perfection of the image of the Bolsheviks, who continued to be viewed as bandits outside Russia. With the revolution taking over, Lenin sent a new ambassador to Stockholm to represent Russia, Vatslav Vorovsky. Being at the core of the Soviet mission, Angelica moved together with Vorovsky into the Russian Embassy.

Her first serious job as a high-ranked *apparatchik* started with disagreeing with Lenin's orders. Each had a completely different vision of how the Bolsheviks' image could be improved. Lenin thought that by spending money on Bolshevik propaganda he would achieve a revolution in Europe.

"Dear Comrade Balabanoff," wrote Lenin, giving new directions for his colleague to follow, "Excellent, excellent [underlined three times; a habit of Lenin's to lend special emphasis to his words], you are our most capable and deserving collaborator. But I beg you. Do not economize. Spend millions, many many millions."[2]

To support his note, the ships that arrived from Russia every Saturday brought Angelica more letters with directions and hundreds of thousands of Swedish kronas, which she deposited at the bank. She might have had an account opened in her name or managed the Russian State accounts opened in the name of Vorovsky or possibly in those of Lenin and Trotsky.

But Angelica did not believe that worldwide revolution could be achieved by spending millions. As Lenin's insistence on "millions, many many millions" continued, Angelica sent a response by which even Lenin, who had known her naiveté well, was taken aback.[3]

She telegraphed back to him explaining that she was ready to continue issuing the press coverage but did not require money. The revolutionary believed workers should understand the importance of revolution themselves.

Angelica further explained that she could do her work alone, sitting at her small desk in the corner of an office. She did not need staff, a car, or a chauffeur. In any case, the only papers that accepted her articles about Russia were *Avanti!* and the Swedish paper *Politiken*. In addition to that, Angelica tried to save the money of the young Soviet State and often contributed from her meager resources when someone needed help. She helped as many as she could. All impoverished, exhausted people who came to see her, asking for money to help them get back to Russia or for food or clothes, were helped. She kept lists of the amounts she spent, noting meticulously the smallest amounts, which were so insignificant that they caused smiles and confusion among those to whom she reported.

Vorovsky was often traveling on business. Among Angelica's duties was replacing him when he was away. She took over some of the import-export negotiations, during which Russia bought all sorts of machinery from Sweden. When necessary, she represented Russia in Norway and Finland. Without wanting it or being nominated, she became a *de facto* ambassador to the Scandinavian countries.

When Vorovsky came back from his business trips, Angelica would give him a detailed account of her work. "And now tell me," he would say, "how many widows and children did you help?"

In order to prospect the possibility of revolution in other countries as she had promised to Lenin, she maintained correspondence with the Russian Ambassadors in other European countries, such as Maxim Litvinov, the ambassador in the UK, soon to become People's Commissar of Foreign Affairs of the Soviet Union and the Ambassador to the United States. He reported to her that the possibility of the revolution in the UK was dim: "We could not expect the Russian Revolution to take place now in England," he wrote to her, unsure how to convey the bad news to Lenin. "The revolutionary movement starts in other countries and England will join later. Hope to be soon in Stockholm and talk to you in person.... With a cordial handshake."[4]

The only part of the ambassadorial duties that Angelica did not like was giving interviews to journalists. They put her on the spot, which she hated beyond anything else.

"You have probably read the morning papers," she would say to brush off the journalists' attempts to meet with her. "You must excuse me, but I must go."

"What a pity. It would have made a sensational story.... I could have paid you a thousand dollars," one journalist remarked.

"Get out, you miserable rascal. Do you think you can corrupt us?" she later recalled shouting at the confused journalist.[5]

As Angelica's importance within the *apparatchiks* grew, she received a death threat from an anti–Bolshevik League operating in Stockholm, which announced the death sentence to the high-ranking Soviet officials in Sweden. Not only was she on the list, but the League made it official and the threat to Angelica was announced in the media. "Ms. Balabanoff," wrote the French newspaper *Le Matin* on March 6, 1918, "was informed about the death sentence pronounced against her which will be executed at the first possibility."

Not many knew that the *de facto* ambassador to Scandinavian countries celebrated the New Year of 1918 in Stockholm as an utterly unhappy person. She was feeling guilty about her life in Stockholm. It was so much easier compared to those of her countrymen. She found it difficult to look at the grocery and bakery glass windows without thinking of hordes of hungry children who roamed the streets of Petrograd when she had left Russia in August and for whom a cube of sugar was an unattainable dream.

Angelica did not like living in the Embassy and working in the rooms with shining parquets and enormous crystal chandeliers. Nor was she interested in becoming a diplomat or an ambassador. She spoke many languages, she had the necessary upbringing, but her heart was not in it. In the Embassy, she chose the smallest room, furnished with a bed and a table, and maintained a diet of well-infused tea, boiled potatoes, occasional omelets, and brown bread. She considered that it was the only possible way for her to live—as close to the lives of the people in her country as possible. Though from time to time she must have allowed herself a small treat at one of her favorite chocolate shops.

Of course her job had agreeable sides. She enjoyed working with Vorovsky. Thin, tall, elegantly dressed in impeccable stiff-collar white shirts, with his invariable round *pince-nez*, groomed long moustache, and pointed beard, he was a literary critic and an admirer of Anton Chekhov and Ivan Turgenev. They spent evenings together discussing literature and arts. For Angelica it was a welcome break. She did not remember the last time she talked about anything else but politics. She had not yet begun writing her own poems, but these evening talks with Vorovsky, who at times wrote poems, were one of her first introductions into poetry, making her think about starting to compose some poems of her own.

Nonetheless, it was not the kind of life that Angelica had in mind. She was worried for her country. The news coming from Russia—the Civil War; the execution of the Tsarist family in Yekaterinburg and of more members of the Romanov family in July; an attempt to kill Lenin on August 30, 1918, by Fanny Kaplan, who shot him with a revolver; and, finally, the beginning of the Red Terror, aimed at killing all anti-revolutionaries or, in other words, the entire former ruling class, were disturbing to her.

She welcomed some of the new measures in Russia, like the nationalization of private property, banks, and factories, hoping that her 22-room house in the suburbs of Chernigov would finally host poor people and that the peasants would have free access to her family lands and orchards, and she agreed with the strict food ration, which divided the nation into categories according to social class, with workers getting the highest ration.

However, at this point, Angelica's already difficult work to promote Bolshevism worldwide became impossible. Papers published articles about "the Bolsheviks who are the ardent enemies of the tsarist regime who plunge Russia ... into chaos for years to come."[6] No one took into consideration any information provided by Angelica about the greatness of the only state of the workers in the world, which aimed "to create on this earth a real paradise for people."[7]

She was persuaded that Lenin did not even know about the Terror. He would never want to kill innocent people. Angelica knew that she had to get back to Moscow to talk to him. She had to explain to him that only Russia itself could improve its image. She kept asking Lenin to allow her to go back to Russia, but she received negative replies.

In early September, unable to wait any longer, Angelica boarded the train to go back. Upon arrival at the Finnish border, Russian customs refused her the right to enter the country. She was told that she had to go back to Stockholm to wait for official permission to return. She had no choice but to go back and wait. Before the month was over, Lenin finally asked her to travel back to Moscow. She left Stockholm immediately, eager to start working on a real revolution and save her country from chaos. The night after she left Stockholm, a cobblestone was thrown into her room. It landed on her bed near the pillow. The anti–Bolsheviks had executed their promise to kill her. They did not know that she had just left. On the train back to Moscow, Angelica, unaware that she had barely escaped death, had only one thing on her mind: Why did Lenin suddenly need her next to him in the Kremlin?

XIV

Dining with the Lenins

Angelica maintained an extensive correspondence. For some of her friends this was simply a way to exchange casual daily news with the revolutionary. For others, like Ella Wolfe and her husband, the prominent socialist, writer, and historian Bertram Wolfe, knowing all sorts of facts from Angelica's unique past was of the utmost interest for their study of socialist history. Information coming from her letters about Lenin and his mistress Inessa, a daughter they were rumored to have had together, or secret dealings and complex relations between the high-ranking officials of the Soviet state often found a place in the books of Bertram Wolfe.

In her letters, Angelica remained formal and detached when it came to the events of her own life, with one exception. The letter dated December 1959 stands out from the whole lot with its unusually emotional writing. In it, she announced to her friends that she had read an article in the U.S. press announcing that Fanny Kaplan, who had attempted to kill Lenin "died recently and was not killed in 1918," as it had been previously thought.[1] The matter was certainly of much importance to Angelica.

She had been waiting for this moment for so many years that she had lost any hope for it. The Russian revolutionary must have found herself back in early October 1918, when Lenin permitted her to come back to Moscow from Stockholm. At that time, Lenin was still recovering from Fanny Kaplan's attempt on his life a few months prior, in August 1918, during his speech at the Michelson Factory in Moscow. Kaplan fired three shots with a Browning pistol at Lenin as he was getting into his car after the speech, ready to leave the factory. Two bullets struck Lenin: one lodged near his right collarbone and the other in his left shoulder. After a three-week treatment at the Kremlin Hospital, he recuperated near Moscow in a location that was kept secret.

The fate of Fanny Kaplan, a revolutionary who had become disillusioned with Lenin's politics, remained unknown. Many said she had been

XIV. Dining with the Lenins

P. S. Thanks to your intervention, S. Levitas wrote me but of course he forgot not only to give you my greetings but also to send me information about:
what and when have the N.Y. papers published that Dora Kaplan (the S.R. who attempted at Lenin's life in 1918) died recently and has not been executed in 1918.) Since it was always my guess, I would be very grateful if you could let me know. Thanks! once more greetings. Angelica

Letter to Ella Wolfe in which Angelica writes about the death of Dora (Fanny) Kaplan, December 6, 1959 (HIA/BWC, Box 2, Folder 61).

shot without a trial. Angelica found it inadmissible that her comrades-in-arms could kill one of their own. The possibility of such crime made her question the values of the revolution and those whom she had supported all her life, consequently making her wonder if she had made the right choice in coming back to Russia to support the Bolsheviks and Lenin.

The first person who met the stunned Angelica at the train platform upon her arrival in Moscow from Stockholm in early September of 1918 was Lenin's representative, who announced to her that Lenin was expecting to see her the next day. The invitation was unique. Not many entered his private space. Considering the fragility of his physical condition, visitors first had to obtain a note from his physician allowing such a visit. Decisions of whether to allow such visits or not were made by Kremlin officials depending on Lenin's state of health and on the guests themselves, in order to avoid unwanted political influence on the head of the Soviet State. Angelica received such a note personally from Lenin's doctor the minute she arrived in Moscow.

The next day, Lenin's green Rolls-Royce picked her up at her hotel. Driven at high speed by the chauffeur, who had previously driven the Tsar and was now Lenin's driver, the car swiftly took Angelica to the house of the former mayor of Moscow, in *Gorki* (Small Mountains), about 19 miles away from the city. The house was the only building near Moscow to have central heating and water and thus was the most suitable for the ill Lenin and his wife.

In the car, Angelica wondered about the urgency of such a visit. From the minute she had the order to leave Stockholm, she was sure that Lenin had something in mind. The car went through the vast Gorki Park, with maple trees colored by the Indian summer with yellow, orange, and red, before arriving at the two-story ochre-colored mansion with four white ionic columns at the entrance. Angelica, totally oblivious to the charms of a chic suburban neighborhood, would later describe it in one of her interviews as "a small village."[2]

She was welcomed by an unrecognizably frail Lenin and weary Nadezhda, who had gained some weight since Angelica had last seen her. Angelica handed them a gift: a chunk of cheddar cheese she had brought from Sweden, wrapped in greasy paper and then a newspaper. She had remembered Lenin's taste for cheese from their days together in Switzerland. They settled in the Winter Garden—a spacious, bright room, elegantly decorated with mahogany furniture, Bordeaux carpet, and heavy curtains. Barely allowing her to sit down before starting in on her, in his usual brisk manner Lenin wanted to know when one could expect a revolution in Europe. The International Revolutionary movement was one of the most urgent matters for the leader of the Soviet State. Angelica was just back from Europe and was the best person to assess the situation.

She did not want to upset Lenin, but her long stay in Sweden had proved to her that he had overestimated such a possibility. Lenin insisted. He was sure that central Europe was ready. He went on informing her that the workers in Switzerland were preparing their first general strike. But they needed help.

Angelica immediately suggested that she could travel to Germany and Switzerland to see what could be done. She knew most of the party members in both countries. Lenin agreed that Angelica was possibly the only person in Russia suitable for this job, where she could apply her famous linguistic and organizational skills as well as her connections. But the authorities of most of these countries would not welcome her. He seemed to hesitate, though not for long. A few seconds later, Angelica had her next mission. She was to go to Switzerland to sound out the possibilities of a revolution in Germany, Switzerland, and Italy. Her other task was to help manage and fund the first general strike, planned for November 11 in Switzerland. She was to leave Russia immediately. The organizers of the strike needed money, which she could bring with her in cash. It did not even occur to her that this task could have been the main reason for her having been called back from Stockholm and the sudden visit to the Lenins.

The same green Rolls-Royce that had brought her to Gorki Park arrived to take Angelica back to Moscow. Before leaving, she raised the issue of Fanny Kaplan. The foreign press had already announced her execution on September 3. Angelica later recalled her conversation with Lenin:

"'A revolutionary government executes another revolutionary?' I asked him. 'Did we not protest when the Tsar and his police-spies did the same?'"

"I noticed that he became slightly embarrassed, as if ashamed of something. 'The Central Committee will have to decide,' he replied, changing the subject." Angelica came to the swift conclusion that Lenin did not know anything about the execution. He would not have lied to her after all these years of friendship. Moreover, she assumed that "the thought that someone should be executed for having tried to kill him was extremely painful for him."

Lenin suddenly invited Angelica to stay for dinner. The invitation was unexpected. She did not know one single person who had ever been invited to dine with the Lenins. She agreed. Lenin needed to rest. Angelica spent some time in the Winter Garden alone with Nadezhda, with whom she "had never been very close." The surprises of the evening continued.

"Throwing her arms around me," Angelica remembered, astonished, "she sobbed, 'A revolutionist executed in a revolutionary country! Never.'"[3]

A few hours later, Angelica's visit with the head of the Russian State was concluded by a dinner. "On a little converted balcony," she described the dinner in her memoirs, "we ate a bit of bread, a tiny slice of meat, and some cheese—which I had brought from Sweden—and drank a glass of tea with a small piece of sugar." Pointing at the food, Lenin, as if apologizing in front of Angelica for such abundance, explained that it was sent by the workers from all over Russia who wished him a quick recovery and meat had been prescribed by a physician.

Angelica left the domain of Gorki on that day, entirely reassured by her personal friendship with Lenin, the safety of Fanny Kaplan, and by the fact that the Lenins knew nothing about the Red Terror. She had been betrayed once by Mussolini. But Lenin would never do it. More than ever, she was ready to work for the revolution.

The next day, Angelica applied for a visa to go to Switzerland. She was to travel as a representative of the Red Cross mission, which would give her a diplomatic passport and immunity and allow her to transport any amount of money without being searched. Her visa was immediately refused by the Swiss authorities. There was no question of the highly dangerous Bolshevik ever entering the country again. After a short delay, both sides, Russian and Swiss, found a solution. In exchange for her visa, the Russian authorities agreed to allow a group of Swiss citizens who were refused exit visas by the Russians to return to Switzerland. Angelica described this impressive exchange of civil war hostages against a visa for a tiny woman in her memoirs in a rather matter-of-fact way. "The Swiss authorities agreed for me to enter if a group of Swiss citizens ... were allowed to return to their homeland. This was arranged and I received a diplomatic pass."[4] She also made a promise not to participate in any revolutionary activities. Angelica left Moscow within a few days, carrying with her, according to some reports, 10 million Swiss francs, estimated as millions and millions of dollars today according to the inflation rate currency converters.

At that time she completely forgot the issue of Fanny Kaplan and only remembered it much later in her life. It was regularly discussed in the press. Rumors multiplied. Some said that Kaplan had been killed, others that she was imprisoned for life or sent to the labor camps in Siberia.

For years, Angelica had asked herself whether that visit, prolonged by a dinner at Lenin's house and Nadezhda Krupskaya crying on her shoulder, was a show to persuade her that no one was being killed, or at least that the Lenins were not aware of it, so that she would go ahead with her mission in Switzerland. She could not bring herself to believe, no matter how much her friends tried to persuade her, that friendship and sentiments did not exist for Lenin—but that if with Angelica it was the only possible approach, he was ready to do so in order to keep her in his net.

"When you spoke with Lenin and Krupskaya," wrote to Angelica in 1961 her long-term friend and revolutionary Raphael Abramovitch, "at least Lenin was aware of the execution by shooting, but he kept putting all blame on the *TzK* [Central Committee]. As for Krupskaya who cried on your shoulder, they might have hidden it from her. Regardless, Lenin did not show any humanity or any generosity. It was not in his nature."[5]

Angelica's other friend, a historian, Boris Nikolaevsky, who accumulated over the years an impressive personal collection of archives on Soviet history that the Bolsheviks tried successively to buy and steal from him, was just as firm. In his letter to Angelica dated July 4, 1959, he wrote: "As for Kaplan, she was executed by shooting by the commandant of the Kremlin...."[6]

Despite what her friends said, until the end of her life, Angelica remained persuaded of her unique friendship with Lenin and that Fanny Kaplan was never actually executed. The above-mentioned article that appeared in the U.S. press in 1959 was the best confirmation of her convictions.

XV

Post-Mortem Research

Not only did certain events in Angelica's life prove at times to be puzzling, but the documents related to her existence are sometimes just as odd. Among them is Angelica's file, created by the Department of Police and Justice in Berne in 1903 and kept in the Swiss Federal Archives. The folder opens with a thick, greenish from time, cover page that has her name, place and date of birth written in the Gothic ink-pen handwriting, and with Angelica's photo on the front. Taken at the police station, it showed a tired, tense-looking woman in her thirties with badly brushed curly hair and large shadows under her eyes, wearing a dark, buttoned wool cardigan.

Consisting of numerous boxes, the file contains information that was collected on Angelica all throughout her life and for years after her death. The Swiss police continued to be interested in the revolutionary even after she had passed away. What interested the federal archivists in Berne the most was her involvement in the first and only general strike that took place in Switzerland in November 1918 and her possible intention of fomenting a revolution in Switzerland on the orders of Lenin. They hoped that Angelica left behind archives or correspondence that could shed more light on these events and decided to put this task in the hands of the ambassador of the Swiss Embassy in Italy, expecting to get hold of any documents in Angelica's possession.

9 December 1965 G/ah
The Honorable
Philippe Zutter
Ambassador
Swiss Embassy in Italy
<u>Rome</u>
Via Barnaba Oriani 61

Your Excellency,

The recent death of Angelica Balabanoff in Rome did not pass unnoticed in Switzerland. Many journalists remembered that this Russian, whose life stretched from the Tsarist Court to the Secretary of the 3rd International, had played a relatively important role in our country during the time of the general strike in 1918. For the record, amongst others things, Ms. Balabanoff was accused of bringing 10 million [Swiss] Francs into Switzerland, destined for financing revolutionary propaganda.

The deceased, whom Lenin, after the Zimmerwald conference, named "the most advanced member of international communism," but who afterward worked for the American Socialist Party with Norman Thomas and even later in that of the actual Italian President, certainly left behind letters and documents. It would be interesting to know if among these papers, some could be of use for the history of the Swiss Worker's movement in 1917 and 1918! As I do not know whom to address to clarify this problem, I allowed myself to contact you...

Even though the general strike of 1918 is only of historical interest, it would be important to do the utmost possible to try and solve the enigma which still surrounds this event. The papers of Angelica Balabanoff might help to do so.

Thank you for your help in advance.
Yours faithfully,
(L. Haas)
Confederation Archivist[1]

The reply that followed showed that the ambassador took the question more than seriously.

> Swiss Embassy in Italy
> Rome, 21 February 1966
> Ref. A. 57.—5
> Your ref.: G/ah
> Federal Archives
> Archivstrasse 24
> Berne

Dear Mr. Federal Archivist,

Referring to your letter of 9 December 1965 and my further communication of 26 January 1966, I would like to let you know that I was finally able to get in touch with the executors of the will of Ms. Angelica Balabanoff. Through the intermediary of the cultural section of the Italian Socialist-Democratic Party, I received the addresses of Ms. Gabriella Majer (Via Ruggero Fauro 63, Rome) and of Mr. Giorgio Giannelli, the Chief of the Press Bureau of the Ministry of Public Health, both friends and executors of Ms. Balabanoff's will.

According to the information provided by Mr. Giannelli in the documents left by Ms. Balabanoff, there are only recent letters and notes, containing no relation to Switzerland. In addition, these few letters—of no interest to us—are now in the Austrian Embassy, which claimed them, given the fact that the deceased was an Austrian citizen.

>
> ...
> The Swiss Ambassador
> Signature[2]

In response, the archivist proved to be yet one more person who deplored the lack of documents related to Angelica's life and expressed the following opinion:

> 28 February 1966
> G/ah
> Swiss Embassy in Italy
> Via Barnabariani 61
> V/Ref.: A. 57.–5
> <u>Rome</u>
>
> Your Excellency,
> Thank you very much for your letter of 21 February this year, regarding the papers of Angelica Balabanoff. The information you provided seems to confirm a hypothesis according to which Ms. Balabanoff destroyed the greater part of her archives. If one thinks about the political role played by this Russian revolutionary, we can only deplore this loss.
> ...
> (L. Haas)
> Confederation Archivist[3]

So what did Angelica do in Switzerland on the orders of Lenin that many years later continued to stir the curiosity of the Swiss authorities?

XVI

Organizing the First and Only General Strike in Switzerland

Though Angelica left no documents that recount her participation in the strike in Switzerland, her involvement was partially described by the Russian and Swiss authorities of the time. The correspondence between the representatives of the Ministries of Foreign Affairs of both countries, published in *Suisse-Russie. Contacts et ruptures* (Switzerland-Russia. Contacts and Ruptures), cites the events of the 1918 strike, as well as giving us record of Angelica and her stay in the country during this time.[1] These letters, completed by a few articles published in the Swiss newspapers, revealed an astounding picture of the Russian revolutionary's whirlwind two-week trip.

On October 24, Angelica took a train to Zurich armed with her Red Cross passport and a substantial amount of cash to supervise the strike and look into the opportunities of having a revolution in Switzerland, Germany, and Italy. The exact amount of money she transported remains unknown. She always denied having brought any money with her: "The Russians could have done a wire transfer through a bank," was her standard reply when the issue came up in the interviews and in her discussions with friends. The Soviet authorities for obvious reasons have never confirmed the amount. However, no one doubted that the arms purchased for the strike in Germany were paid for with funds that had come directly from Russia and that the need for more funds was the main reason for Angelica's precipitous trip.

The strike, led by Angelica's long-term friend Robert Grimm, was to begin on November 11. The primary demands of the participants were a 48-hour work week and retirement pensions. Preparations had begun months in advance. The strikers, workers from different industries, were

Police file of Rosa Bloch, Switzerland, c. 1920 (SFA, CH-BAR#E21#1000/131, Nr. 8670. 2012. Photograph by Jean-Loup Lafont).

XVI. Organizing the First and Only Strike in Switzerland

divided into small groups, according to their place of work, and met weekly to prepare the event.[2]

Angelica had arrived about 10 days prior to the planned date. When the train reached the border of Germany and Switzerland, she bought newspapers to look at the headlines and see if there were articles about the upcoming event, only to realize that two of the papers carried articles about her. *Gazette de Lausanne*, in the section "The Undesired," announced: "Madam Angelica Balabanoff, the Russian Bolshevik of importance, has arrived in Switzerland for a short visit," "with many millions," stated another paper that claimed that she had arrived "for the purpose of provoking a revolution here and in Italy."[3]

Angelica understood that the Swiss secret services had monitored her every move since the moment she received her entry visa. She had no doubt that, knowing that she was engaged in politics, they would want to expel her as quickly as possible. These articles served to alert the population and attract attention she did not need, considering the delicacy of her mission. The media exposure served its purpose. When she arrived at her hotel in Zurich, she saw that it was under a kind of siege by various strangers who solicited Angelica for money. "I have heard how generous you are," said her visitors, who waited outside of the hotel. "If you lend me some money, you will never regret it," insisted the others.[4]

Needless to say, the unwanted visitors left with nothing. But the harm had been done. Her work, to reassure the maximum participation in and efficiency of the strike, while keeping it strictly confidential, was difficult to accomplish with so many eyes turned on her and her money. The agitation around her visit quickly mounted, to the point that the day after her arrival, the director of the police department in Geneva, from whom Angelica was 170 miles away, demanded to know:

"The Swiss authorities of what country authorized the entrance of this person into Switzerland? We would like to know more about her activities, what exactly is she doing, does she travel and where."[5]

So chased by the opportunists who wanted money and by the secret agents who tried to get as many details concerning her work for the strike as possible, she tried to escape from the hotel unnoticed to attend the last preparatory meetings with the organizers and deliver a few speeches to attract more participation. Some of her activities were disguised as shopping trips and meetings with old-time friends. Her main interlocutor with the strikers, aside from Grimm, was Rosa Bloch, whom Angelica had known since her first days in Switzerland.

If Rosa had not had long curved eyebrows, hair put up in a bun, and a preference for white, starched-collar blouses, she would have looked like a man. She was a small, corpulent woman with a potato-like nose, long, thin, firmly pressed lips, and a large square jaw. Rosa was a jewelry trader in Geneva. But her heart was in underground politics. An anarchist who later became a communist, she was one of the most trusted contacts of the Bolsheviks in Switzerland. The two women made regular tours to the jewelry shops and cafés while discussing the last-minute arrangements.[6] To accomplish Angelica's other objectives—studying the likelihood of revolutions in Italy and Germany—she was in close touch with the Russian Embassies in both countries by telegrams.

Angelica's work came to an abrupt end when, a week after her arrival, she received a telegram from the Soviet Embassy in Berne asking her to come to meet the representative of Russia. Since the Revolution in Russia, the Swiss authorities had not accepted the new Soviet State. The mission was represented in the country by an emissary and a few diplomats and was not involved in any diplomatic activity. Thinking that there must have been news related to the strike coming from Lenin, she traveled immediately to Berne and presented herself at the grey-stone Embassy building on *Schwanengasse*, familiar to her since the time of her first propaganda activities in St. Gall and her recurring problems with her passport renewal. She was brought into the office of the emissary and her good friend, the stylish, thin-faced, and serious-looking Yan Berzin. Instead of a telegram from Lenin as she had expected, Yan Berzin handed her an official note from the Swiss Foreign Office, which read: "The Allies and especially Italy have requested the expulsion of Dr. Balabanoff."

But Angelica had no intention of leaving until the strike was over. After a short discussion with Berzin, the reply that she provided to the Foreign Office asserted: "I refuse to leave, unless the Labor unions in Switzerland decide that I should leave."[7]

So the strike started as planned on November 11. The Federal Council deployed part of the army to calm down the strikers. The event went on for three days without much success. Most of the demands were rejected, though the working week was eventually reduced to 48 hours.

The authorities, seeing Angelica's resistance and suspecting that she was supported by the Soviet mission, accused both parties of espionage and preparing a revolution. On the same day that the strike began, the Red Cross and the Soviet Embassy were given 24 hours to leave—barely enough time to prepare the luggage and burn all papers, political letters, and encoded telegrams. Diplomatic relations between the two countries came to a halt. The circulation of letters and exchange of diplomatic couri-

XVI. Organizing the First and Only Strike in Switzerland

ers as well as accordance of entry visas had stopped on both sides. Angelica, who traveled with a Red Cross passport, lost her diplomatic immunity.

On November 12 at 6 a.m., a messenger came to see Angelica at her hotel in Berne with a request that she immediately present herself at the Soviet Embassy. She knew only too well that it meant expulsion. In vain, she tried to contact the Swiss Labor Union Executives to let them know that she was leaving, while the messenger waited for her outside her room, allowing her some time to get dressed. But the telephone in her room had been cut off. In her distress she left without taking any of her belongings, remembering at the last minute to put on her coat.

The same morning, *La Gazette de Lausanne* carried the articles: "Never should Angelica Balabanoff have been tolerated in our country," singling her out as the main foreign national responsible for the strike.[8]

"As I drove to the Embassy with the messenger," Angelica recounted her last hours in Berne, "I saw that the streets were filled with soldiers and that trucks mounted with machine guns were patrolling the city.... As the embassy staff was gathered on the street in front of the building, the staff from the neighboring French Embassy and onlookers gathered to watch the expulsion."[9]

The members of the Embassy staff, headed by Yan Berzin, who seemed slimmer than ever, with a peering look in his deep-set eyes and pursed, turned-down lips, waited on the street with their luggage. The lights in the Embassy were off.

"Government trucks, flanked by soldiers on horseback," she described the strange night in her memoirs, "were sent to fetch our luggage, but we were ordered to walk.... As we started the French surged forward and began to shout insults...."

Angelica, who out of the whole staff of the mission had been the most exposed by the media, heard her name screamed.

"Fearing for the children in the group," she recalled, "I detached myself from the other Russians and faced them.

"'*Oui, c'est moi, Angelica Balabanoff,*' I announced. '*Que voulez-vous?*' I do not know what happened then. In a pandemonium of shouting and horses' hoofs I lost consciousness."[10]

When Angelica opened her eyes, she was at the train station, half-lying on a cold grey-stone bench. The station being a good thirty-minute walk from the Embassy, she had to have been taken there by the soldiers. She saw blood stains all over her clothes and a sleeve of her dress torn apart. Only then did she realize that her arm was bleeding. She shouted to one of the soldiers to help her with a bandage, but no help came. The commander brusquely explained to her that the rest of the staff was assembled in the next hall. As railways were not working because of the strike, the refugees would be taken by cars to Konstanz, a German town on the border with Switzerland, where they would board the trains. The Germans agreed to grant the mission passage through the country to Poland. As soon as the cars arrived, Angelica would join the rest of the staff and would be provided help.

Eight cars, probably Piccard-Pictet, dispatched by the Swiss army to transport the mission, traveling at a speed of 12 miles per hour, took nearly nine hours to reach Kreuzlingen, a small industrial community just across the border with Konstanz, getting the mission there by the end of the day. However, instead of heading through to Germany, the cars suddenly stopped in town. It was getting dark, and Angelica could not see where they were. With no explanation, the mission was invited to get out with their luggage in front of a three-story sky-blue building.

"We are staying in Switzerland overnight," Angelica hypothesized, hoping that the decision for their expulsion had been overturned. All she needed was a phone or a telegraph to get in touch with Rosa Bloch and Robert Grimm.

Instead, however, the man who accompanied them into the building announced to Yan Berzin, who headed the mission, that there had been a delay in negotiations with Germany. They were to stay in the building until the negotiations were complete. They were not allowed to leave this place or have any contact with the local population.

The building was a local school. To welcome the visitors, the tables in two rooms on the first floor had been moved along the wall and the floor covered with bundles of hay. A few oil lamps provided little light. The Swiss representative explained to the tired and worried-looking members of the Soviet mission that they would receive some food provisions. The water supply and washing bowls were available down the corridor.

The high-ceiling rooms were clean but cold and humid. Angelica was anxious and exhausted. She slept with her coat on. Her arm, wounded in the recent clash with the soldiers, was well-bandaged, but it hurt. Considering the accident was the fault of the Swiss authorities and her advanced age—she was 49—they offered her a room in a hotel, but she decided to remain with the staff of the Embassy and to sleep on the floor. The mission was provided with bread and cheese. But they had to remain on school grounds guarded by the police and were given no information as to how long they would sleep on the bundles of hay.

XVI. Organizing the First and Only Strike in Switzerland

The ordeal continued for 72 hours. On the foggy morning of the third day, it was announced that negotiations had been completed. Eight Piccard-Pictet cars picked up the mission. Fifteen minutes later they crossed the German border, where the cars simply slowed down; the orders came not to search the passengers and their luggage. They headed directly to the Konstanz railway station, boarded the train, and went toward Poland, where they would catch a direct train to Moscow.

The expulsion of the Soviet mission worsened the already poor relations between the two countries. The Swiss insisted later that "everything possible was done by the Federal Government for the Russian Mission's safety, and they profited from the immunity generally reserved for the missions officially recognized; in particular the members of the Mission took their luggage without any sort of custom revision."[11] However, that was not the opinion of Angelica and Berzin. Judging from the letters that flew from Moscow to Berne with the official Swiss couriers, the revolutionaries did not soon forget the three-night stay on the school floor. For

View of the Kremlin Towers from the lobby of the Hotel National, Moscow, where Angelica lived during her four-year stay in the capital, 1918–1922 (author's photograph).

them, their staff had been treated as wrongdoers and not as a diplomatic mission. As such, they did everything in their power to delay the return of the Swiss citizens remaining in Russia back to their country. In 1923 diplomatic relations between the countries would come to a complete stop for over 20 years.

On her way back to Moscow, Angelica was depressed. She could not imagine such a sad end for what could have been the most beautiful trip. With more courage than ever, she was ready to pursue her goal of fighting for the oppressed. For the moment, it seemed that she could do more in Russia than in other countries, and she hoped to remain there for some time.

Only after crossing the Polish border did Angelica remember how cold it could be in the East in winter. With all the events of the past days, she had forgotten that she had left her clothes in the hotel in Berne. She would need to find something to wear upon arrival. On the train she tried to warm herself up with hot water that she managed to get in the stations when the train stopped. Some of the water she drank, and some she poured into the empty wine bottles she had recovered along the way, placing them under her arms and between her thighs.

After a week-long trip, the train finally reached Moscow. It was early in the evening, but it seemed like midnight. Angelica, who was watching the snowy landscape outside the window, suddenly saw a reflection of her face and for the first time realized that some of her hair had turned white.

"Comrade Balabanoff," a man dressed in a plain black military uniform appeared in the doorframe of her train compartment. "I'm here on behalf of the Ministry of Internal Affairs." He wanted to know if Angelica preferred to be lodged in a private apartment or a hotel.

Angelica had completely forgotten that she needed to look for a place to stay.

"I'll live like everyone else," she said.

"We will assign you a room in the National Hotel. Most of the government officials stay there." The man left abruptly.

A few hours later, Angelica was back in her homeland to work for the revolution. Or so she thought.

XVII

Vice President of Foreign Affairs to the Ukraine

The Hotel National where Angelica spent four years during her stay in Moscow, between 1918 and 1922, has always been considered one of the landmarks of the city. If during Angelica's times it had been reserved uniquely for government officials, today it is a luxury five-star hotel with room prices starting at 250€ per night. Constructed in 1903, it has marble halls, crystal chandeliers, elevators with art-deco, iron-forged doors, and white statues of Greek gods as the bearers of the heavens on each side of the elevator.

The reception area of the hotel and rooms offer a majestic view of Red Square and the Kremlin's red towers and walls. One cannot help but feel a part of the heartbeat of Moscow.

Upon settling in the hotel, Angelica felt far from happy. She would have preferred to get a room in the workers' neighborhood to live like ordinary people. However, as incredible as it may be, with her functions as elite member of the party, it was not easy to arrange.

"I had returned to Moscow," she wrote later, "prepared to live like an average citizen or at least like the humblest of party members, prepared that those who had led or instigated the Revolution ... should expect to make even greater sacrifices than those who followed them.... I felt a sense of shame even in my comfortable room at the National when I knew that others—both workers and intellectuals—had to wait for months, to beg, insist, and scheme to get any shelter at all.... And yet what could I do? If I refused to accept these privileges, it would seem like ... an implied criticism to those who had already accepted these conditions."[1]

Angelica asked for the smallest room and was assigned a "cell-like" space in what used to be the quarters reserved for the servants of the guests of the hotel. The elegance of the once glorious Tsarist times was slowly fading out, and the lack of maintenance during the last few years had begun to show. The walls in her room were covered with stained, stripped, light beige wallpaper and a few tilted framed pictures of Moscow.

The room was equipped with mismatched oak and mahogany furniture—a bed, a table, two chairs, an oil lamp in case the electricity would be cut off, an armoire with a long oval mirror, where Angelica kept her sparse clothes, along with the indispensable fruit jelly which she used to sweeten her tea, and heavy olive-green curtains with Bordeaux-colored ornaments on the windows. Hot water for tea was provided in the *samovars* by the concierges on every floor. The hotel had a restaurant on the ground floor that served coffee made of beans and roasted corn, black bread, cheese, and occasionally pressed beef.

Angelica had been away from Russia since practically the beginning of the revolution in October 1917. She knew that the infrastructure of the city was down. Most of the water and heating facilities were broken. So staying at the hotel had its advantages, like the absence of fleas and other insects that ravaged Moscow, beds made up with thick linen pillows and sheets, and a constant supply of wood and electricity. Stacks of wood provisioned for the hotel—difficult to find in town during winter—were kept outdoors. Day and night, they were guarded by the police from the hordes of women who roamed around the hotel looking for any opportunity to find something to heat their apartments. Most importantly for Angelica was the constant supply of electricity, guaranteed by the electric power generator of the hotel, allowing her to read and work until late at night. The regular blackouts in the rest of the city forced most of the citizens to use oil lamps, which were insufficient in the evening.

The reality of daily life took her by surprise. The "ration dictatorship" introduced by Lenin divided the population into 33 different categories, from workers to intellectuals. The latter received the smallest portion of bread, made of a terrible mixture of kidney bean flour and ground straw, hardly a human meal, while the high-rank of government members to which she now belonged were entitled to special categories of food. Not only she could order as much bread as she wanted, and often white bread, but she also discovered that, as with all of the Kremlin staff, she could place special orders. Lenin, known for simple daily habits, asked for sardines and confectionary, Stalin for pepper, while many received cigars, and approximately 240 pounds of caviar were distributed every month.[2]

She also had access to the Kremlin facilities, which included shops, hairdressers, a sauna, a pharmacy with a sufficient stock of medication, and a hospital, all of which were run by nearly 2000 people. And if she was in no mood to eat in her room, she could go to one of the large Kremlin restaurants, reserved for the party members, with the food served by cooks trained in France who had worked previously for aristocratic families. Angelica intensely disliked the privileged treatment she was entitled to when the lives of ordinary people were so drastically different. She opted for the mid-range ration allocated to female factory workers.

"Privileges had always been a torture for me," she wrote later, remembering her childhood nightmares. "My whole life I enjoyed privileges and my whole life I fought against them."[3]

The revolutionary was also entitled to a salary, but with skyrocketing inflation, money meant little, and it was impossible to buy anything with it. Margaret Grace Bondfield, a British Labor Politician who visited Russia together with the British delegation and met Angelica, described in her memoirs how during her stay in the city she had tried to get hold of a pan to make omelets without going through her Kremlin connections. She discovered that a pan cost three rubles in a shop, but to buy it, one needed to spend a week queuing and filling out administrative forms, asking for permission to get a pan assigned to one's household, "have passes to take out parcels and passes to enter public buildings."[4] The same pan was available on the black market without any queues for the disproportionate amount of 2500 rubles— an average salary was around 3000 rubles per month. Besides, getting eggs meant going to the black market and risking being caught by the police.

Like most of the *apparatchiks*, Angelica rarely used money. In emergency cases she placed orders in the Kremlin for anything she required, from clothes and toiletries to furniture or a car with a chauffeur.

Angelica was one of the rare women who enjoyed the status of a high-ranking official, together with Lenin's wife, Nadezhda, his mistress, Inessa, and very few others. She was also one of the few to have direct access to Lenin's study in the Kremlin Senate and his private phone number.

As a newly arrived official, Angelica had to find an activity. One of the astounding revelations that she faced once back home was the Red Terror. Before coming to Moscow, she refused to believe the stories of mass murders of what the Bolsheviks called counter-revolutionaries, or in other words the entire former ruling class, which had started after an attempt on Lenin's life. She judged the killings, imprisonment, and deportation of innocent people that she had heard about from friends or read in the foreign press as temporary measures for the sake of the revolution. Her own family did not avoid this fate. One of her brothers in Chernigov was killed by the peasants, who wanted to take over his land and estate, and cut into pieces. His wife was gravely wounded and died in the hospital without learning the terrible fate of her husband. Angelica, refusing to believe that this could be a policy of her government, considered it an accident, possibly ignoring so many other similar "accidents" that took place all over the country.

"I went to Moscow, where my doubts and apprehensions grew," wrote the revolutionary, who, once back in the capital, learnt the real figures of the victims of the Terror. They were estimated to be in the thousands, while the rumors that circulated among the *apparatchiks* quoted six-digit figures. Those who were not killed were put into prisons that were crammed with noblemen, Tsarist officers, or people who simply owned an apartment and were thus considered anti–Bolsheviks.

Angelica decided to work with prisoners. She was sure that most of them were innocent. She did not think that being anti–Bolshevik was a crime comparable to that of being a thief or a murderer. She went to see Lenin in his study in the Kremlin Senate, a triangular-shaped yellow building easily identifiable from Red Square by a red State flag on its green dome. During a short meeting she asked him to let her work in the prisons, to "save the prisoners ... from shame, maledictions and responsibility."

Her old-time Berlin friend immediately told his secretary to telegraph an order to Cheka (The All-Russian Emergency Commission for Combating Counter-Revolution and Sabotage) with the necessary instructions for Angelica's instant nomination to the prison governance.

She began spending her days in the prisons. She visited shabby, stiff, large rooms that housed a sizeable number of beds, or at times nothing at all, with prisoners sitting on the floors, often ill with typhoid, suffering from undernourishment, with rations reduced to a half a kilo of bread per day and hot baths allowed once per week. "The repressions had become extremely severe, the prisons were jammed," she remembered. "Some prisoners, in tears, insisted they were innocent, others did not even know why they had been arrested." An additional and quite unexpected surprise was that "among the guardians of order" were individuals who had exercised the same function under Tsarism.[5]

To be liberated, the prisoners had to stand in front of the tribunal of counter-revolutionaries, which more often than not was already set against them. So to be more efficient, she asked to be admitted as a judge. After weeks with no answer, she went to the tribunal to see why she had not yet received a positive response: "These are instructions of Comrade Lenin," said one of the judges. "Apparently you are too kind to be a judge."

As Angelica struggled to accept the reality of prisons in Russia and her incapacity to help the innocent, she continued to do what she did best—public speech. She remained one of the most popular female speakers in town and was often called to address female audiences and workers in the factories who called for bread and getting paid. Her public appearances always had the desired effect:

"It was evident that they were bored," remembered Marguerite Harrison, an enigmatic American journalist and spy who came to Moscow from the United States to spy on Russia and assist American prisoners, only to be imprisoned herself for 10 months and liberated later in exchange for food and other aid to the Soviet State. Before being imprisoned, she had been introduced to Angelica, who had been about to speak at a factory. "Many were half asleep," continued Marguerite Harrison, describing the audience, "others staring at the walls and ceiling, still others trying to quiet their restless babies. The instant Balabanova stepped on the stage there was slight rustle as everyone leaned forward to get a close look, for hers is a personality that compels attention."[6]

Angelica spent entire days on her feet, often forgetting to take meals, devastated by the people's suffering that she was seeing every day and worn out by the work. In such stressful situations, her temperature was frequently below normal. The main food staple of the capital was black bread baked with straw, which caused stomach pain. She started to lose weight. "My body aged prematurely," she wrote.[7]

Fatigued and undernourished, she fell ill. For days her temperature remained below 96.44 F. She received a visit in her hotel room from Doctor Vladimir Vinogradov, a mid-height man with a little moustache and a serious though sarcastic look in his eyes, who a few years later would become the private doctor of Stalin, remaining in this capacity for nearly 30 years throughout Stalin's stay in power. Vinogradov prescribed her white bread, which was much tenderer on the stomach and a rarity in the starving Russia.

"I cannot accept it," said Angelica. "None of the workers I see every day eat white bread."

"Does your party really prohibit eating white bread?" asked the apolitical and sardonic Vinogradov.

"What?" burst out Angelica, jumping on her bed. "Do you believe special regulations are necessary to make us understand that one does not eat white bread when the people have not even dark bread?"[8]

Vinogradov left her room having failed to persuade her to consume any staple or medication that was not available to the general population—in other words she had refused to allow him to give her any treatment at all.

The above dialogue was reported to Lenin: "I bet you do not even take the ration you are entitled to," he accused her the next time he saw Angelica when she got better.

Only after being pushed around and screamed at by Lenin, which was his usual way of showing concern for his colleagues, did Angelica agree to get glasses adjusted for her eyes and choose a fur coat from a collection of nationalized coats. For years she remembered her trip to the room where heaps of furs in all shapes and colors, taken away from their previous owners, were piled up in one of the offices. Unable to bear the sight of the scene, refusing to hear the requests of the fur-keeper to look at the luxurious mink and sable items of the "collection," she chose the first from the pile. Too big, made of brown beaver, it was a man's coat. Even though Angelica rose to a high position in the otherwise all-male Bolshevik hierarchy and was often obliged to attend important functions, she paid little attention to her appearance. The beaver coat covered her from head to toe and kept her warm. The observant Marguerite Harrison reported on seeing Angelica after the trip to the fur room: "a dumpy little woman, slightly bent, wearing a man's coat, many sizes too large, a big fur collar touching the edges of an astrakhan cap pulled far down over her ears...."[9]

By the end of January 1919, Angelica had heard about Karl Radek, organizing the "foreign sections of the communist party." The German war prisoners, many of whom were not socialists, were liberated and sent back home with money on condition that they create propaganda for the Russian revolution. How could the government entrust large sums to them to promote the Revolution abroad?

Angelica rushed to Lenin:

"I advise you to get back your money and your credentials. These men are merely profiteers of the Revolution," she told Lenin, explaining that he had chosen the wrong people.

"Why get excited over so little?" he told her, sending her away.

About two weeks later, Lenin asked her to come to his office. Thinking that he had finally realized that she was right, Angelica contentedly went to the Senate building. However, upon her arrival, Lenin ordered her to leave Moscow. The party nominated her to take over the position of Christian Rakovsky as Commissar of Foreign Affairs of the Ukraine. She had to leave at once.

An order from Lenin was not to be debated. Angelica packed her luggage and hopped on the train the next day. She had spent barely four months in the city. Not suspecting that there might have been reasons why Lenin did not want her in Moscow, she still found it strange to be

XVII. Vice President of Foreign Affairs to the Ukraine

nominated in charge of foreign affairs of the Ukraine, which was a part of Russia and did not have foreign affairs of its own. She thought at that time that one of her new tasks would be to improve the image of Russia in Europe, and the Ukraine, being geographically closer to Europe, presented a better location for that.

She went to Kiev on the "government express train." In other words a train that had enough coal and hot tea to take her to her final destination without being stopped in the middle of a forest and asked to cut wood for the locomotive or to help repair the broken rails. Even so, it took the new Commissar of Foreign Affairs of the Ukraine one week to get to Kiev instead of the usual three days.

Her new assignment was good from two points of view. Firstly, she got along well her new superior and the head of the Ukrainian government, Christian Rakovsky. She had known the old Bulgarian commissar in the early days of her career in Switzerland and was more than happy to work with him again. Tall, with a trivial, mouse-like face, dressed in an indispensable bow tie and fitted striped suits, he was a physician and a great admirer of French literature, which was also his language of communication with Angelica. Secondly, she could do what she called "real work"—being in touch with people and helping them.

Angelica's mission to Kiev lasted two days. She was summoned back to Moscow by a telegram received from Lenin. She was to travel back immediately. Lenin had finally been able to achieve his long-term dream, that of creating the Third International and uniting all communist parties under the banner of Russia to impose the power of his party and revolution worldwide. The time was as good as any.

To prepare the event, in mid–February, the Commissar of Foreign Affairs of Russia, Georgy Chicherin, announced on the radio the meeting of the International on March 2 in Moscow, calling for communists from all over the world to come to the city. The only problem was traveling to Russia. Soviet Russia was unpopular; most countries did not renew their diplomatic relations, interrupted after the revolution, and it was technically impossible to get into the country. The railway connection, slow and insufficient, was through Finland. As Angelica put it, one "needed to be a hero to get to Russia at this time."

Coming from Kiev, Angelica was one day late for the congress. Upon her arrival, Lenin's Rolls-Royce summoned her to the Kremlin. "Entering the Small Hall of the Kremlin, where the meeting was supposed to take place," wrote Angelica, describing one of the Kremlin parade rooms with high-arched, gilded, light-colored walls, "I saw about 30 people. To represent the party, not only did you need to have a mandate but also at least to be in contact with the country you represent and this was impossible. Only one of them was a legitimate representative, Hugo Eberlin from Germany. Others were either the expats who had been living in Russia for some time or war prisoners, like the French communist Jacques Sadoul, who came to Russia during the war and decided to remain there."[10]

She understood why she had been sent to Kiev for the duration of the conference preparations. Lenin knew that she would have realized right away that the attendees had no right to be there and that her frankness could sabotage the event.

Lenin called upon Angelica to come to Moscow when the event was already in full swing, to represent Italy and the PSI, the party of which she was still a member. She was the only representative of the PSI at the meeting and, in Lenin's view, the legitimate one to act for them. As the meeting went on, he started to send Angelica messages. That was how participants exchanged their thoughts during the meetings:

"Please take the floor and announce the affiliation of the Italian Socialist Party and the whole Zimmerwald movement to the Third International." Angelica did the unthinkable. She looked at him in disbelief and shook her head. She actually said "no" to Lenin.

"I cannot do it. I'm not in touch with them," she wrote on the same paper.[11]

However, as the meeting went on, the combination of general enthusiasm and speeches had a profound effect on her, and she felt drawn into the event. Moved, together with other participants, she started to demand the creation of the International. Lenin and Trotsky kept bombarding Angelica with notes asking her to make a speech, and Angelica did not resist. After all, she faced the two greatest politicians, Lenin and Trotsky, who were used to handling much more complex issues than a tiny stubborn woman. She went to the podium:

"Without underestimating the great responsibility that I take upon myself," she said finally taking the floor, "I declare that the majority of the Zimmerwald parties approve the immediate creation of the 3rd International."[12]

Angelica decided not to attend the last day of the meeting. She wanted to go back to the Ukraine to continue her work. While saying good-bye to some of her friends after the meeting, she met Trotsky.

"Good-bye, Lev Davidovich," she said.

"Good-bye? What do you mean?" he asked. "Don't you know that you are to be Secretary of the International?"

XVII. Vice President of Foreign Affairs to the Ukraine 137

She rushed to Lenin. "You have just nominated me to work in the Ukraine."

Lenin replied: "Comrade Balabanoff, you have one quality, or maybe it is your drawback, you have a lot of connections and you are the only person who can do this job...."

Closing one of his eyes, as usual when he wished to speak categorically, he added: "Party discipline exists for you too, dear Comrade. The Central Committee has decided."[13]

It was pointless to argue with Lenin. Angelica felt that she was at home in Chernigov, with her mother telling her: "Your father and I have decided." Once again, her inner feelings told her that it was time to leave Russia and go back to Europe, and yet once more she brushed these thoughts aside, thinking that the big revolution and liberation the revolution gave to the working class was more important than her feelings.

"We will inform Comrade Rakovsky that we need you here," Lenin told her before she left his office. "Your belongings will be sent back to Moscow."

The same evening, both Angelica and Lenin went to the theater to see Anton Chekhov's *Three Sisters*, the play popular with the *apparatchiks*, who interpreted it as the story of the decay of the privileged class. Most of the tickets were distributed to the workers, many of whom were in a theater for the first time. Angelica and Lenin decided to give away their tickets to those who needed them more and were about to leave when one of the organizers shouted: "What? Comrades Lenin and Balabanoff are leaving? We can add two chairs." Embarrassed, they proceeded to their seats. As the performance started, Lenin showed Angelica

At the First Congress of the Comintern, 1919. From left to right, Grigory Zinoviev, Vladimir Lenin, Vatslav Vorovsky, Angelica Balabanoff (collection of Giorgio Giannelli).

a man dressed in a leather jacket seated next to them. Angelica thought that he looked like someone who worked in the *Cheka,* the recently created secret police agency known for its repression.

"Do you know this Comrade?" he asked.

"I am not sure; perhaps I have seen him somewhere."

"His name is Stalin," Lenin said.

The next day was the last day of the Congress and the first day for Angelica in her duties as Secretary of the International. She had no choice but to attend. She was also the only person at the event able to translate speeches and debates between French, German, English, and Russian. One of her rare photos taken in Russia is the underexposed image showing her seated next to Lenin in front of the members of the International at the long, rectangular, draped table that served as a tribune, lit by a tripod lamp, wearing a three-quarter-length-sleeve dress with her hair braided at the back of her head.

The translation was consecutive. One of the participants later remembered with laughter that the newly appointed secretary adjusted her translations. She could take 10 minutes to translate a four-minute speech because she thought that the subject was of interest to the audience and was badly presented by a speaker or a few minutes to summarize a long one if she found it boring and dogmatic. During the pause, Trotsky came to see her:

"Comrade Balabanoff, what are these creative translations?" Angelica said nothing but decided never to translate official speeches in Russia again.

At the end of the meeting, the creation of the Third International was approved. The decision went largely unnoticed in the world. Without any legitimate party representatives, such an organization was illegal. Neither Angelica nor anyone else realized that they had just witnessed the creation of the largest propaganda unit in the history of socialism, the aim of which would be world revolution. That evening, Angelica did not think about any of it. Touched to tears by the celebrations organized in the impressive Large Kremlin Hall with white ceilings, silver moiré walls bordered with scarlet ribbon, elaborate metalwork doors with branches of gilded laurel and crystal torches, followed by the fireworks seen by crowds of people from Red Square, she was certain that she had been present at a true union of people.

> So comrades, come rally
> And the last fight let us face
> The Internationale unites the human race.

The next day, Angelica, who thought that this time she was back in Moscow for good, settled into her old room in the Hotel National and started her new job. The International, called Comintern by the Russians,

XVII. Vice President of Foreign Affairs to the Ukraine 139

had its offices in the center of Moscow on *Mohovaya* Street. She was presented a list of offices, furniture, and staff that she would need as Secretary of the International.

"I should like my office to remain as it is—in my own two rooms," she said. "I do not need a separate building."

Angelica's new boss was Grigory Zinoviev, whom she described later as "the most despicable" and "low-grade individual" she had ever met "after Mussolini."[14] An ambitious, canny, unattractive, corpulent man with a large, crooked nose and unruly, curly black hair, Zinoviev was disliked by most of the people who knew him. Angelica loathed his demands for everyone to rise when he entered the room and his luxurious lifestyle, which he did not try to hide. "Zinoviev typifies Bolshevism as far as its methods are concerned," she wrote in her memoirs. He traveled between Moscow and Petrograd by a car accompanied by servants, a cook, and a secretary. During his trips to Europe, he occupied suites of 14 rooms with one or two cars waiting at the entrance of the hotel at the perpetual disposal of his "Red Excellency."[15] However, his qualities were difficult to ignore. A speaker of exceptional strength, he had an unusually high tenor voice, which captivated the crowd, capable of persuading even his opponents with the first few words of his speech.

Zinoviev chose to have his headquarters apart from the Comintern, in the building that had formerly been the German Embassy. It was one of the few buildings in Moscow that remained intact after the Revolution and was richly decorated with Rococo furniture, gilt wood mirrors, and 19th-century German paintings of snow-covered mountains and green-valley landscapes. Angelica did not mind. The less she saw of him, the happier she was.

The work of the new First Secretary of the Comintern was to unite, promote, and solidify the socialist parties in the world around Russia. She welcomed foreign guests in Moscow and St. Petersburg, briefed them on Russia, and provided them with the manuals prepared for such visits. She quickly discovered that Zinoviev's task was what Angelica would later call "red fascism"—to conquer the rest of the world through any means including blackmail. He recruited all sorts of people proficient in illegal work, provocation, murder, organizing strikes and anti-governmental meetings, capable of changing their physical appearances and escaping from the police, to go to Europe, carrying large sums of money, with one aim: worldwide revolution.[16]

Such operations were financed through the sales of the imperial treasures from the Kremlin. Diamonds up to 64 karats, Fabergé eggs, and paintings confiscated from the private collections of their formerly well-off owners served the "urgent needs" of the Comintern. The lists of the objects sold were discovered in the archives in Russia in 1992 but have never been published. One of these lists attested that the portion of the money from the personal items of Tsarina Alexandra amounted to 475 million golden rubles, which would be a few hundred million U.S. dollars today.

Angelica did not need long to openly show her disapproval of Zinoviev, his recruiting methods, and sales of jewelry. She quickly found out that all meetings of the Comintern during which decisions were made were held without her. She started seeing documents with her forged signature. She went to complain to Lenin and stopped signing any documents at all. At the end of March, Zinoviev came to see her:

"Since our movement is spreading so rapidly, we should create another office of the International in the Ukraine," he told her, announcing that she was in charge of it.

"Why should I leave Moscow again?" Angelica could not understand. She had just been ordered to stay in the city, and her clothes had finally arrived from Kiev.

"We need to spread out our forces," said Zinoviev. "Why should we keep our best people in one place?"

Angelica, who stilled believed in her unique relationship with Lenin, thought later that Zinoviev did not want her in Moscow because she refused to participate in his illegal dealings and because he was jealous of her close relationship with Lenin. Never did she entertain the thought that Lenin had agreed to "send Balabanoff out of town."

Despite being pushed away from the center of activities, her new job was nonetheless rather important. The International was spreading its wings. Offices were created in Amsterdam, Berlin, and Stockholm with the aim of propagating socialism and revolution. Together with Christian Rakovsky, Angelica was responsible for the creation of the most important of them all, the so-called Southern Bureau in Kiev and Odessa, the location chosen because of its greater proximity to Western Europe than Moscow.[17]

"You will be responsible," Zinoviev specified, "for recruiting the propaganda agents who would be dispatched to the Comintern offices in Europe. After your first stop in Kiev, you are to go to Odessa."

When Angelica heard about Odessa, her heart sank. She had known that her radically anti–Bolshevik family had moved from Petrograd and Chernigov to Odessa. The supporters of the Tsar wanted to get closer to Constantinople in case they might need to escape from Russia to avoid the death penalty vowed by the Reds. The port of Odessa became a strategic escape location. She did not doubt that her family was in need of help, money, and exit visas from Russia. Meeting them would be unavoidable.

XVIII

Governor of Odessa

Angelica's new job in the Ukraine consisted of three different parts. As Vice Minister of Foreign affairs, her main task was to deliver propaganda speeches among the local population, to explain the role of the Bolsheviks and the Revolution. The Ukrainian citizens were confused as to which side they were on. Between the beginning of the Revolution in October 1917 and 1919, the Ukraine had been through 17 evacuations and witnessed unending military conflicts. It had been occupied, destroyed, and plundered in turn by the Russian Provisional Government, the Austro-German and French armies, the White Volunteer Army, and twice by the Soviets.

As a Secretary of the Comintern, Angelica was responsible for the creation of what later would be called the Southern bureau. Her task was to find, train, and send agents abroad, mostly foreign nationals, who would be equipped with money or jewelry destined for sale and dispatched to France, Germany, Italy, Bulgaria, Greece, Turkey, and the United States in order to promote communism, open new offices, stir up workers, and publish propaganda magazines subsidized by the Bolsheviks.

Her final objective was to increase the anti-war propaganda within the French Army in Odessa. By the time Angelica arrived in the Ukraine, Odessa, one of the largest ports in Russia, was again occupied by the French army under the command of the General d'Anselme, who had received an order to create a *cordon sanitaire* between Russia and the West and liberate Odessa from the Bolsheviks.

To achieve the dissolution of the army and an end to war activities, Angelica was joined in Kiev by an intelligent French communist, Jacques Sadoul, about 10 years her junior, who, besides propaganda work, might have played an important role in negotiations between the Soviets and the French Army. Known for his sarcastic humor, he must have gotten along well with the revolutionary. Once back in France, he would become a well-known reporter for the French socialist paper *L'Humanité*.

At the beginning of April 1919, the militants published two issues of the French review *Drapeau Rouge* (*Red Flag*). The publication was created to dissuade French soldiers from continuing their military action in the Ukraine. About 5,000 copies of each review were sent to Odessa.[1] The result was eminent. Already in April, the first soldiers started to join the Bolsheviks, who, among other things, promised food, knowing that the French campaign had been badly organized and that there were problems with the food supply.

No matter how much Angelica tried to delay the long-dreaded trip to Odessa and meeting her family, in July she received an order to go there. Though she remained rather vague in her memoirs about the real objective of her trip, her importance within the *apparatchiks* seemed to have grown. Her new tasks included the organization of the compulsory draft into the Red Army.

The government train took her to the once popular and picturesque upper-class resort dubbed the "Black Sea Babylon," bringing her into the city early in the evening. Angelica had not been to Odessa since she was a child. With the summer heat gone, the air was filled with the sounds of cicadas and the scent of acacia. Instead of taking the car that came to pick her up, she opted for a short walk. She was assigned a room in the building reserved for government officials, situated on the city's main street, Primorsky Boulevard, and not far from the City Council where she would have her office. Following the scenic streets with French- and Italian-style architecture, she headed to Primorsky Boulevard with its maple, lime, and chestnut trees, making a detour to the Potemkin Stairs, which provided a splendid panoramic view of the port and the sea and which a few years later would be made famous by Sergei Eisenstein in his film *The Battleship Potemkin.*

With Jacques Sadoul in Odessa, 1920 (collection of Giorgio Giannelli).

Angelica's overall impression of Odessa was drastically different from that of her first steps in the city. She later remembered the once popular seaside resort as the saddest and worst place she had ever seen. The building in which she lived had unkempt rooms equipped with an old bed, a table, a chair, and a small, cracked bowl that allowed some water in the room to wash her face. To keep away the fleas, which crawled around by the hundreds at night and prevented her from sleeping, she found four more bowls and put each leg of her bed into a bowl with water.

The severe shortages of food meant that supplies were first distributed to the marines and soldiers, then to those who supported the communists. The rest of the population was left to die.

"Why did Dante," wrote Angelica, "the immortal creator of the Inferno, not see what I was seeing? If he had, he would probably have depicted a less mystic, less symbolic image of hell, a more realistic and a more horrifying one...."[2]

The black market of Odessa, though officially forbidden, was larger than elsewhere in Russia. One of Angelica's missions during her stay in town was to investigate its origins and possible elimination. The investigation did not take long. She quickly found out that the market was managed by the head of the communist party in Odessa "as a part of policy of tempting out of hiding the steadily dwindling supply of consumer goods," she recalled years later. Those who were caught selling goods at the market were killed or sent to prisons. Profits from the market dealings went personally to the head of the communist party. A very abashed Angelica went to meet with the leaders of the Odessa communist party.

"I'll report to Lenin," she said angrily.

Her protest was greeted with laughter: "Don't you think he knows?"[3]

Angelica had traveled to Odessa with Jacques Sadoul. A photo of the two of them taken on the stairs of one of the administrative buildings depicts Angelica standing two stairs higher than Sadoul and still barely reaching to his shoulder. Both are dressed in black, Angelica wearing a long skirt pleated at the waist and Sadoul, thin and tall with a little moustache, in a plain military uniform. There is something in the photo, in the way they stood next to each other, that implies a trusting relationship between them and probably even more than friendship.

For the first time in her life Angelica had a personal secretary, Suzanne Girault. Born in Switzerland and an ardent communist, Suzanne had fled to Russia before the Revolution. After working as a French governess in a well-off family in St. Petersburg, she married and moved with her husband, Nicolas de Frenkel, and two children, Jeanne and Leon, to Odessa. When the Revolution came to the city, she entered her son Leon into the French unit of the Soviet army and offered her services to the Bolsheviks. As Angelica's personal secretary, Girault would follow her to Moscow to work for the Comintern.[4]

The meeting that Angelica had dreaded most since she learned that Lenin had ordered her to Odessa took place a few days after her arrival. She was making a speech in one of the halls when she heard that a woman was asking to see her. Angelica, thinking that it was yet another person who would need clothes or demanding the release of a wrongly accused family member from prison, went to see her. It took Angelica a few seconds to realize that the weeping beggar with trembling hands was her elder sister Anna—the one Angelica had called "Mama" during her youth in Chernigov.

Angelica had not seen her sister for two years. As the revolutionary stared at her sibling, who continued to stand bent down with her face half-hidden under her worn-out, light-grey shawl and with her body covered with a long, smudged, brown hemp robe, she finally realized that the most uncomfortable encounter of her stay in Odessa had just occurred. Anna had aged. It was difficult for Angelica to accept that this elderly woman was the same person who, 30 years prior, had been admired in Kharkov for having built over time the richest scientific library in town in her house; the same person with whom, as a child, Angelica had discovered the most beautiful landscapes in Europe from the window of the first-class train compartment; sojourned in the top-end hotels of Montreux and Baden-Baden; enjoyed lavish meals and musical evenings on the open terraces of those trendy resorts.

On that summer day in Odessa, Angelica was afraid. The five-foot-tall Governor, as she had already been dubbed by the Swiss secret police, had no doubt that her sister had not come just to embrace her.[5] What could she need? Food, extra baby milk, or the release of wrongly accused prisoners, like dozens of pro-communist petitioners who queued for hours in front of her office?

Distressed, Anna pleaded for help. *Cheka* (Extraordinary Committee Combatting Counter-Revolutionaries) had announced a compulsory draft in Odessa. Anna's only son, an ardent anti-communist, risked execution by firing squad if he did not join the Reds. She begged Angelica, who was responsible for conscription, to find someone in the Extraordinary Committee who could exempt him from the army on any grounds.

The few words she exchanged with Anna felt like a dreadful eternity to Angelica. Lenin's protégé was at a loss. She knew only too well what she risked in helping anti–Bolsheviks, even if they were her relatives. It was not only her reputation that was at a stake. In the eyes of the new Soviet regime, the Balabanoffs were traitors. And yet, how could she refuse Anna—the only person who had provided love to fill the empty space in her heart, emptiness that had arisen from years of misunderstandings with her mother? Angelica told Anna to return the next day.

What could Angelica do? She had just told off one of her cousins who had come to her office to ask for shoes. This conversation was later reported by Suzanne Girault, who had been in the adjoining office.

"Anchushka," Suzanne heard one of Angelica's visitors call her by an unusual name, "we need shoes, at least one pair for the family. We have nothing to wear."

Shoes were one of the first necessities sent in help packs to Russia from abroad.

"We have no more shoes. Shoes are for those who work." Susanne suddenly heard Angelica raising her voice. "If you work, you might get a pair of shoes, but not from me. On what grounds do you want shoes?"[6]

Angelica felt no guilt in telling her cousin off. Refusing Anna was a different matter. Anna had been like her mother, the mother she had never had. If only Anna had asked for food or clothes. But how could Angelica help to liberate anyone's son from joining the Red Army on false grounds when she was responsible for mandatory conscription?

As agreed with Angelica, Anna was the first in line of petitioners who waited for the Governor of Odessa to arrive at her office in the City Council at six the next morning. She patiently waited for the doors to open in front of the majestic white columns of the entrance and the two statues of Ceres and Mercury in the front. Overloaded with work, Angelica could not see her. She asked her sister not to come back again. She would go to Anna's place to meet her husband and son whenever she could find five minutes in her busy schedule. Angelica came to see Anna the following day. Anna lived in a dark, humid basement. The long narrow window allowed a glimpse of light only on a sunny day. Anna's son was losing his sight and had had to stop his scientific work. He was nearly the same age as Angelica, and they had often played together as children when Angelica had vacationed with her sister in Kharkov.

Angelica's visit to Anna's home in Odessa was brief. She promised to see what she could do. Angelica had to make what would end up being the most difficult decision of her 65-year career. She attempted to continue with her daily routine. She thought that the best solution would be asking Lenin to send her back to Moscow. However, she did not need to call anyone. The same morning, she received a telegram order from Lenin:

"The White Army is approaching Odessa. Immediately travel back to Kiev to take responsibility over the treasury of the Soviet State."

The revolutionary left Odessa before the end of the day, on the train that had been sent with the express purpose of bringing the vice minister back to Kiev. She had no means of contacting Anna. The two sisters would never see one other again.

In her memoirs she wrote that she did not help her nephew, considering it inappropriate in view of her role in Odessa. However, he never did go into the Red Army. Anna's family miraculously escaped to Constantinople, from where her nephew got to Paris, where he would continue to see his aunt in the 1920s. Was she the one who had helped him out of the army and provided the family with the necessary documents to get to Constantinople? Or was it someone else? The most difficult episode in Angelica's life thus remains a mystery.

Back in Kiev, Angelica took responsibility over the treasury of the Soviet State and resumed her propaganda speeches. Shortly after her arrival, she began to hear rumors about the disappearances of innocent people. Many of them were Jews, often the families that Angelica had known during her adulthood. It became quickly apparent that these disappearances were linked to a certain Count Pirro, the ambassador of Brazil settled in one of the private mansions in Kiev, who promised to provide foreign passports and permits to leave Russia in exchange for money to all those who wanted to go to Europe or the United States. After people got in touch with him and gave him money, they were never called to get their passports. Instead they were mysteriously killed or simply made to disappear while Count Pirro continued his flourishing activities undisturbed, attracting more people into his nets.

By the end of November 1919, Angelica was certain that this was a serious matter and not a singular case. At about the same time, she received the order to leave Kiev with the treasury of the Soviet State to go back to Moscow. The White Army approached Kiev, and she had to leave immediately. Responsible for "great sums of money in foreign currencies," she forgot about Count Pirro. It took her two employees and a few days to count and prepare the hefty bundles of British pounds, German marks, and French francs for transportation before putting the bills, wrapped with paper marked "Treasury of the RSFSR (Russian Soviet Federative Socialist Republic)," into the suitcases. She said good-bye to Jacques Sadoul and Suzanne Girault, who were to join her in Moscow a few weeks later. On a dreary December morning, protected by the guards who helped her to carry the suitcases with money, Angelica boarded the unheated train in which she had a compartment of her own guarded by soldiers.

Upon arrival in the capital of Russia a week later, she was picked up by Lenin's familiar Rolls-Royce. The car took her directly to the Headquarters of the Comintern on Mohovaya Street, where she was prepared to attend to a tedious procedure of verifying the amounts of money she had carried with her and making a financial report to the treasurer.

Instead of settling her into one of the offices, as Angelica had expected, the clerk who had met her at the reception did not even look at the reports she had with her or the suitcases with money and simply ordered them to be taken away. Seeing Angelica's astonishment, he laughed: "A statement of assets? From you? It would be like checking up on Comrade Lenin."[7]

Angelica knew where she would go next. She asked the driver to take her to the Lubyanka building, the headquarters of the *Cheka*, the Soviet State security organization and its director, Felix Dzerzhinsky, dubbed "Bloody Felix" for his drastically severe measures during the Red Terror. After arriving at the massive building with three-band cornices marking each floor and with a clock in the uppermost band of the façade, she asked to be taken to see Felix. She wanted to talk to him about Count Pirro. She had no doubt he would be in. She had heard legends about his 20-hour work shifts. He was also known as "a fanatic and a sadist."

Without getting up from his desk, Felix thin, long-faced, and cold-eyed, dressed as usual in a plain military coat to keep himself warm, explained to her that Count Pirro was one of his agents. He helped to find and kill the traitors to the Revolution.

Barely saying good-bye, Angelica hopped into the same car, asking the chauffer to deposit her this time at the Kremlin Senate, and then sent her luggage to the Hotel National, where her room was prepared for her. She went to see Lenin, to whom she continued to have immediate access. But her meeting with the head of the Soviet State did not go as she had expected.

She later reported how, "looking at me squint-eyed as was his habit when he wanted to study a person's innermost thoughts, he said to me in the tone of a father who, with affectionate pity, realizes the son's inadaptability to the exigencies of life: 'Comrade Balabanoff, what use can life find for you? Is Count Pirro our Agent Provocateur? If it were possible, I would even send some into Kornilov's army,'" referring to one of the generals of the anti–Bolshevik movement, obviously seeing nothing wrong with having Count Pirro's reports kill innocent civilians.[8]

Angelica later thought that, together with violence and dishonesty, disrespect toward human beings was one of Lenin's main errors in directing the country.

Lenin had no intention of letting Angelica go back to her hotel to rest. He had thought of new, unexpected responsibilities for her, the most mysterious and inexplicable of her whole existence, which would last for the next two years.

XIX

Lenin's Most Trusted Agent

The years of 1920–1921 are the most difficult to describe in Angelica's life, so great a gap is there between what she wrote about herself and the information coming from third sources.

Angelica always insisted that, hardly back from the Ukraine, and disagreeing with Lenin's politics of the Red Terror, which she had been witnessing since the beginning of the Revolution—the story of Count Pirro being the last drop she could endure—she entered into a long two-year conflict with Lenin, Zinoviev, Dzerzhinsky, and the rest of the Communist officials. She was banned from official functions and had no new responsibilities, though she was allowed to keep her room in the Hotel National. She was also unable to leave Russia. Lenin refused to provide her with an exit visa. She knew too much. He did not want any of his dealings with the Comintern, recruiting secret agents and mass killings of innocent people, to be known outside Russia.

The problem was that not only is it difficult to imagine Angelica unoccupied, but there are masses of reports about her continued work in Europe as Lenin's agent. And for the first time in her life, the reports came not only from German and Swiss secret services but also from their French, British, and American colleagues.

On January 1, 1920, less than two weeks after her supposed return to Moscow from Kiev, the police forces of at least half of the countries in Europe were alarmed:

"Balabanoff has just left Berlin to go to Zurich," the German police hurriedly informed their Swiss colleagues. "She is traveling with four fake passports and important sums of money."

The French helped by immediately providing the names under which she was traveling: "A dangerous communist, ... Balabanoff, also called Balabanowa, Balaban, Delafontaine, Lafontaine...."[1]

As soon as the police of the canton of Zurich received this information from their European colleagues, they immediately forwarded it to the rest of the cantons: "All borders were alerted to the presence of a woman, Balabanoff, in possession four different passports. To facilitate search for Angelica within the country, in case she manages to cross the border, we are again publishing an official announcement for search, this time with the photo, for her arrest."[2]

Germany and Switzerland issued a warrant for her arrest and, to ensure more efficiency, provided her physical description, getting her age wrong.

"REPORT ON BALABANOFF: 35, brunette, strong corpulence, oval figure, small eyes, medium height ... her traveling made easier thanks to her fictive marriage ... a means much employed at present, with papers issued at the government office...."[3]

Alas, to no avail. The police arrived too late every time. "The German authorities even helped her to travel from Stettin to Frankfort," their French colleagues sarcastically noted.[4]

A few days later, the French added even more confusion to the already complicated hunt for the revolutionary by stating that she had been seen "leaving Odessa before the end of January to go to Italy through Constantinople" apparently "in charge of propaganda in Italy...."[5]

As more reports confirmed her "traveling through Riga, Stockholm, Copenhagen and Christiania" in the company of an ardent communist, agent Varnetzky, additional details about her work surfaced.

"Both delegates," reported the Swiss, "are currently in Holland where they have transported large quantities of gold and jewelry. With the help of this money they have the intention of founding other propaganda bureaus in Western Europe."[6]

Angelica traveled disguised sometimes as a worker and other times as the wife of a merchant, in second- or third-class trains or a sleeping coach. The letters with orders from Lenin and Zinoviev on how to instill revolution worldwide were hidden in the double lining of her coat.

Upon remitting the letters and jewelry to various Comintern offices in Paris, Brussels, Cologne, Berlin, and Amsterdam, she shared her experience with novice agents on how to publish and distribute communist papers and literature and become a skillful courier able to cross borders unnoticed by the police. Then she dashed off to another destination while the letters and money received from the sales of jewelry brought by Angelica were redistributed to other places with more couriers.[7]

She might have disagreed with Lenin's politics in Russia, but her devotion to the cause and the revolution remained unchanged. She continued her work, hoping for another revolution in Europe that would not take

XIX. Lenin's Most Trusted Agent

the same gruesome and blood-stained turn of events as the one in her homeland had.

The efforts of the European police to stop the revolutionary yielded no results:

"She has not been seen anywhere," stated one of their reports.

"Balabanoff is in Turkestan," insisted the paper *Le Domokrati*, N 11 of January 14, 1920, referring to Turkestan Republic created after the Revolution that was eventually split into Kazakhstan, Kyrgyzstan, Tajikistan, Turkmenistan, and Uzbekistan. The paper further affirmed that Balabanoff had never been to Europe and informed its readers:

"London—*The Times* reproduced the news from *Izvestia*, the official newspaper of the Bolsheviks, concerning an important mission which sends her to Turkestan, called the Red Orient. The mission will include a large number of Muslim communists as well as the famous Miss Balabanoff."[8,9]

The Red Orient mission was a project developed by Lenin. At a time when most people did not know how to read or write, and paper printing was an expensive business, the Soviet government came up with the idea of propaganda trains. Masterfully painted in bright colors with propaganda themes, they were kitsch, impressive, and equipped with modern bathrooms, restaurants, and meeting rooms. These trains were sent to address the population in the most remote areas of the Turkmen region in Central Asia.

"Balabanoff never came to Europe," reported one of the offices, adding even more uncertainty to Angelica's whereabouts. "She left Russia three weeks ago with a propaganda train to go to Iran," placing her at least 500 miles farther south of the Turkmen region. So what was Angelica doing while all these reports kept pouring in? She was in Geneva. She received the news about her purported trip to Central Asia while sitting in her favorite café—The Landolt—treating herself to a cup of Assam tea and a chocolate. The news made her flinch.

Indeed, before leaving Russia as Lenin's courier, on January 1, she was called into the Kremlin office of the Secretary of the Party, Nikolay Krestinsky. Krestinsky was a tedious man whom Angelica considered a phony bureaucrat, a man possessed of an unwavering facial expression, pursed lips, round glasses, a short mustache, and a small square beard.

"Comrade Balabanoff," he said in a dull, monotonous voice without getting up from his chair, which confirmed Angelica's opinion of him as a pen-pushing bureaucrat.

"We have a piece of work here which will certainly satisfy you and which is extremely important to us. We would like you to take charge of the propaganda train which we are preparing to send to Turkestan."

The proposal was unexpected. Going to Turkestan presented multiple problems. Not only were first-time visitors prone to coming down with illnesses such as typhoid and cholera, but a woman in charge of a mission to Muslim countries and without speaking the language was an unusual combination.

"We need a popular name," explained Krestinsky, "A prima donna."[10]

By the time the "Prima Donna" left Krestinsky's office, she had officially refused to go to Turkestan. Angelica went to Europe, thinking that the matter was closed, only to find out there from the papers while in Switzerland about her planned departure.

So after reading about her trip in the Swiss newspapers, she decided to head back to Moscow to see what was going on and bring Lenin the return letters reporting on the situation among the parties in Europe.

Angelica arrived in Moscow to find out that the European journalists were well informed. The preparations for her trip to Central Asia were in full swing. Her previous refusal had not been accepted. All people in Russia were expected to be dedicated to the building of the regime and to the sacrifice of their personal lives. "In the 1930s," she wrote later, "a similar breach of discipline would probably have resulted in my imprisonment or worse."[11]

And this was not to be the last of Angelica's surprises. She sensed that the Kremlin was hiding many things from her. Whom could she trust to find out what was going on? Sudden help came from John Reed, who lived in Moscow. Angelica had met the well-known American journalist for the first time in Stockholm. They had gotten along right away. John Reed was the first person to persuade her to come with him to watch Charlie Chaplin movies, *The Vagabond* and *Police.* As a rule Angelica considered watching films a waste of time, usually opting for the news program at the cinema. He also suggested that she should write her memoirs because her life was so interesting. At first an ardent supporter of the communists, John Reed came to live in Russia to report to the U.S. newspapers about the progress in the Soviet State. A victim of his own naiveté, by the winter of 1919, he was disillusioned with the Soviets. Suspecting his disappointment, with Trotsky in charge of the famous journalist, they did everything they could to prevent him from leaving Russia, afraid that he would talk about it in the United States. Trapped by those whom he once considered his friends, Reed understood only too well that Angelica, who was just as naive, needed help and advice.

XIX. Lenin's Most Trusted Agent

In the spring of 1920, John Reed came to visit Angelica in her room at the Hotel National to tell her that a socialist delegation from Italy was expected in the country. The leftist visitors from Europe wanted to see the young Soviet state in evolution. The delegation was to arrive in May. The date of the train departure to Turkestan was scheduled for the same time. There was a plot against her in the Kremlin.

"They are trying to get rid of you," John Reed explained her situation. "They do not want you to meet the delegates; you know too much."

Angelica was aghast. After all, it was her job as Secretary of the Comintern to receive foreign guests, especially from Italy, because she was a member of the PSI and "nearly an Italian herself."

"Do not they trust my loyalty?" she asked.

"Yes, but they are also afraid of your honesty."[12]

Angelica's mission to Central Asia would become a common joke for years to come. Those who were out of favor with the party and were sent to work in the south of Russia, away from the center of activities, were said to be "banished to eat peaches like Balabanoff," referring to a fruit available only in the southern part of Russia and a rarity in the capital.[13]

Angelica's mind was set. She would meet the Italian delegation no matter what she had to do. There was no way she was leaving Moscow. She spent the next few months busying herself with redistributing the beneficial aid which came to Russia. Clothes, food, and daily necessities flew into the country from all over the world and needed to be distributed and transported to remote areas. She organized unloading, managed the sorting procedure, the renting of wagons, the distribution and shipment of all materials. In February, when she was again invited to Lenin's house for dinner, she brought Krupskaya "a warm blanket and dresses received from a co-operative in Italy, which subsequently tried to establish business relations with Soviet Russia.[14]

A few weeks later she ran into John Reed again:

"There is a meeting of the Comintern going on in the Kremlin, aren't you invited as a Secretary?" he asked.[15]

Angelica immediately went to see why she had not been invited. The Kremlin guards, who were used to seeing her frequently entering the Kremlin offices without any prior arrangements, let her in. No one even thought of asking her for an authorization or a passport. She went straight into Zinoviev's office, a spacious room with high molded ceilings, sparsely furnished with a bureau and another mahogany table with six chairs for the meetings.

"Angelica Isaakovna," Zinoviev explained as he rose to greet her, "because of your refusal to go to Turkestan, the party has decided that you are no longer Secretary of the International."

That was more than Angelica could take. On her way back to the hotel, she suddenly felt how drained and weak she was. She had not had one day of rest since her arrival in Russia. For months, she had ignored that her temperature was again lower than normal. It was as though her body could not take the pressure any longer. She could not remember how she got to her room. All she wanted was to lie down and close her eyes. The next day she did not get out of bed. Angelica spent the whole month of April 1920 bedridden in her hotel room in the Hotel National and receiving a string of guests who included both friends and enemies.

The notorious American anarchist Emma Goldman arrived in Moscow after being expelled from the United States and having her passport revoked. The unattractive, well-built, and extremely intelligent Emma was the victim of a personal vendetta of the FBI director, J. Edgar Hoover. Like many leftists, she thought that by coming to Russia she was coming to a "promised land." And as with many foreigners who arrived in Moscow to witness the revolution, Emma met Angelica:

"I soon discovered that Balabanova—or Balabanoff, as she preferred to be called—was at the beck and call of everybody," wrote Emma Goldman shortly after her arrival in Moscow. "Though poor in health and engaged in many functions, she yet found time to assist to the needs of her legion callers. Often she went without necessities herself, giving her own rations, always busy trying to secure medicine or some little delicacy for the sick and suffering.... Almost everyone ... was the concern of this remarkable little woman: no one needed a Communist membership card to Angelica's heart. No wonder some of her comrades considered her a 'sentimentalist' who wasted her precious time in philanthropy."[16]

The two women immediately became friends. Emma would need Angelica and her connections to be introduced to Lenin, to obtain a Russian passport, and get medication when ill from the Kremlin pharmacy, the only place that received a decent supply of pills. When she found out that Angelica was ill, she rushed to see her new friend:

"I found Balabanova in a small cheerless room, lying huddled on the sofa. She was not prepossessing but for her eyes, large and mutinous, radiating sympathy and kindness. She received me most graciously, like an old friend, and immediately ordered the inevitable samovar. I walked to her couch and stroked her thick braided black hair, already streaked with grey.... She had some *varenye* (fruit jelly) and Swedish comrades had given her some biscuits and butter. She felt very guilty to enjoy [sic] such luxuries when the people did not have enough bread. But her stomach was bad; she could digest nothing, and so perhaps she was not as inconsistent as she might appear."[17]

Besides the friends who visited, Angelica's high-ranking comrades were also worried. A phone call from the reception of the hotel announced a visit from Zinoviev and his wife to Angelica. Before she could say anything, they were standing at the doors of her room.

"Comrade Balabanoff," he said "you are reinstated in your duties as the Secretary of the International."[18]

No matter how naïve Angelica was, even she understood what was going on this time. She was one of the most known and respected socialist figures outside Russia. The news that she was no longer the Secretary had created an uproar among the Western European parties.

Angelica refused Zinoviev's invitation, only to receive it the next day again from Trotsky. Angelica had always gotten along well with Lev Davidovich, but her refusal was firm. For her it was over; there was no going back.

"I saw many things which have opened my eyes," she wrote to Emma Goldman in 1933. "If I could only admit that that grown-up people and revolutionaries were capable of such intrigues and gossip and secret diplomacy instead of speaking openly, I wouldn't be able to help laughing and thinking how easy it would have been to tell me openly that they do not consider me ... for this work. But they preferred to have my name [attached] to ... methods which I would never have agreed to—this is the key of the situation."[19]

No longer in her duty as Secretary of the Comintern, Angelica agreed to take care of Italian delegation, with the aid of Suzanne Girault, who lived in Moscow with her two children and worked for the Comintern, serving at times as Angelica's secretary. The Russian revolutionary personally knew most of the delegates. Her spirits lifted with the arrival of her friends from Milan, whom she had not seen for a few years. She left aside her usual black dresses. Elegant in a white blouse and beige tailored suit, with a matching round hat she had picked up while sorting some of the clothes shipped by Italian workers to Russia, she took her old acquaintances around Petrograd and Moscow to show the first achievements of Soviet Russia in the factories, prisons, army barracks, and schools.

With Angelica, one is never lacking in new mysteries and hidden corners of her life. Another of her secrets was revealed during the visit of the Italian delegation.

XX

Freemason Without an Apron

In July 1920, Zinoviev used the presence of the Italian delegation and called for the Second International Congress in the Kremlin, choosing the breathtaking Vladimirsky Throne Room, with its pink marble arched walls and a unique window in the center of the ceiling, as the main venue for the event. It was attended by participants from Europe, Asia, and the United States. Angelica, in her function as irreplaceable translator, opted for a simple black dress with slim sleeves up to her elbows, showing her full hands, with her hair braided around her head as usual. She arrived just in time to see the throne pushed aside to serve as a coat hanger and replaced by a tribune. The rooms around the hall—a smoking room, a reading room, a cafeteria—were used to accommodate the delegates. She poked into the Tsar's bedroom to see how they had changed it and saw about five people resting on the Tsar's bed.

As the congress started, Zinoviev announced the policy of dictatorship of the proletariat. He read out "21 conditions," or prerequisites, which specified the rules to be followed by all communist parties who wanted to remain in the Third International. Among others, the conditions imposed a break with the reformists, the publication of propaganda journals, and the fighting of counter-revolutionaries.

Most of the party representatives insisted that these conditions would split and weaken the positions of their parties within their respective countries. But the Russians were not accepting any exceptions to their new rules. All parties were given four months to accept and implement the 21 points. Angelica later thought that for the PSI, accepting the 21 points had resulted in the split of the party into Communists and Socialists and loss of popular support in Italy, which Mussolini used to his advantage by creating his party, winning a majority of votes, and establishing fascism. "The party starts to devour its own children," Angelica wrote after the congress.

Zinoviev's famous "21 conditions" were in fact 22. The last one, rarely mentioned today, prohibited communists from being freemasons. The freemasons were given a year to choose which of the memberships they wished to maintain. All of a sudden Angelica, who in her role of a translator had no right to vote or express herself at the meeting, stood up and openly disagreed with Zinoviev on this point.

"It reduces the right to personal freedom and democracy," she insisted, deciding at that same moment to leave Russia with the Italian delegation after the congress.[1]

Angelica's unexpected participation in the congress on the issue of the freemasons and her immediate decision to leave Russia were not as surprising as they seemed. Throughout her life, she had been closely linked with the brotherhood. Though the revolutionary never mentioned belonging to any lodge, she had more than a passing interest in the fraternity. The events in her life that linked her to the freemasons, whether it be people she had met, pivotal events in her life, or even historical personalities, were too numerous to be coincidental.

Her favorite historical figure was Giordano Bruno, and her favorite historical event was the Paris Commune, were both highly valued by the freemasons. Practically all names cited in her memoirs, whether those of her professors in the University of Brussels, or those she would meet later in her life, are the names of freemasons. It is possible that she was first introduced to the brotherhood and its rituals by Célestin Demblon at the Grande Lodge of Brussels.

Another example of her curious connections with freemasons was her odd meeting and conversation about poetry with Rabindranath Tagore, whom Angelica would meet in Vienna in 1922. The unusual part of this meeting was that she usually did not attend social events with celebrities and was not interested in meeting bohemian and fashionable poets or writers. They would have been unlikely to have met in the same room unless the event had been organized by a Viennese Masonic Lodge.

It would be difficult to say with certitude today what Angelica's connections were to freemasons. None of the lodges in Brussels, France, Switzerland or Italy, which were open to contacts with women who were friends or family members of their members, had her listed in their archives. Today Angelica would be called a "mason without an apron," or a "good layman," a person who was not initiated but shared the same views as masons. She might have decided not to join the brotherhood, which at the time was not as admissive of women as it is now.

So at the end of the Second International congress, without telling anyone in Moscow, Angelica accompanied the Italian delegation to Tallinn, where she planned to obtain a visa to get to Italy. No archives contain information about this trip. All that is known is that she was stopped on the border by Russian customs, who sent her back to Moscow. She was officially banned from leaving Russia without getting official permission first from Lenin and Zinoviev.

With a heavy heart, Angelica had to go back to Moscow, where this time she launched a formal procedure to acquire an exit visa. She expected it to be a matter of days. But October, November, and December passed by and no papers arrived. Not only did Angelica know too much about what was going on in Russia, but her departure would have shown an open split within the Russian party membership.

During these sad days of sequestration, she often met with John Reed and his wife Louise Bryant. John Reed had recently tried to escape Russia by crossing the border to Finland, using sledges on wheels as his main mean of transportation, but was caught before he managed to reach Finland and returned to Russia by force after a short imprisonment. The author of the bestseller *Ten Days that Shook the World* no longer had control over his own life. He often came to Angelica's place. She made her habitual strongly infused tea. They talked about the possibilities of the revolution in the future, losing hope of it becoming a democratic event. "Jack spoke bitterly of the demagogy and display which it had," and they made "no effort to hide from each other what was on their minds," Louise Bryant remembered later.[2] Angelica became one of the few people with whom he could speak freely during his last days before dying of typhus on October 20, 1920.

Reed, the only American to be buried near the Kremlin Necropolis had a pompous state funeral organized for him by government officials. Angelica was asked to make a speech. But she decided not to go, finding it all too hypocritical, and instead stayed alone in her room in the Hotel National, as she had often done in the last few months, unable to cope with all the duplicity and violence she was witnessing. She probably wondered whether she would ever leave her country alive. For the first time in many years she remembered her final meeting with Anna Hoffmann, her mother's curse and the Chernigov legend of the young Motrya Kochubeevna, who was cursed by her mother for escaping from home and suffered an unfortunate early death, becoming a restless soul.

As 1920 came to an end and Angelica lost hope of getting any exit papers out of her country, Lenin made a sudden proposal. He suggested that she could be appointed the ambassador to Italy. The Soviet Union was reestablishing its diplomatic relations with many countries, interrupted after the revolution. There was one condition—Angelica would have to agree to follow the rules of work of the Soviet regime. A few years ago it would have been a dream job for the revolutionary. But this time she declined the offer. She also confirmed later that she was not sure whether Lenin had really meant to give her such an important post.[3]

However, this proposal gave her a new idea. One of the first countries to open a Soviet Embassy was Norway. Alexandra Kollontai, Angelica's long-time friend, had been appointed as ambassador, becoming the first woman in the world to hold such position. Angelica had always gotten along with Alexandra. Early in 1921 she applied to go to Norway as a member of the staff.

Emma Goldman remembered meeting both revolutionaries in Moscow: "The two leading communist women of Russia proved the greatest contrast. Angelica Balabanoff lacked what Alexandra Kollontai possessed in abundance: the latter's fine figure, good looks, and youthful litheness, as well as her worldly polish and sophistication. But Angelica had something that far outweighed the external attributes of her handsome comrade. In her large sad eyes there shone profoundly compassion, and tenderness. The tribulations of her people; the birth pangs of her native land; the suffering of the downtrodden she has served her whole life were deeply graven on her pallid face."[4]

In addition to sharing socialist ideas, Angelica and Alexandra both supported free love, thinking that being devoted to ideas was more important than having a family. Alexandra had a string of lovers who became younger as she aged, and more than one ended his life because Alexandra refused his advances.

Angelica honestly believed that with Alexandra in charge of the Soviet mission in Norway, she would be able to work according to her convictions and without being pushed around by the *apparatchiks*. Lenin agreed to let her go to Norway if she would write an article against Filippo Turati. Turati remained a popular leader of the Italian socialists but refused to join the communist movement. Despite Angelica's recurrent problems with Turati and Anna Kuliscioff since her management of *Avanti!* in Milan, betraying Turati was something she couldn't do. The photo of Filippo Turati with his thick moustache, long beard, and fearless look in his black, radiant eyes was one of the few remaining pictures Angelica continued to keep on her famous altar next to her bed. Writing an article against him was out of the question.

Six months went by. At the beginning of November, Angelica finally heard that the Swedish prime minister, a socialist, Hjalmar Branting, would grant her a visa to stay in Sweden. The favorable decision for an entry

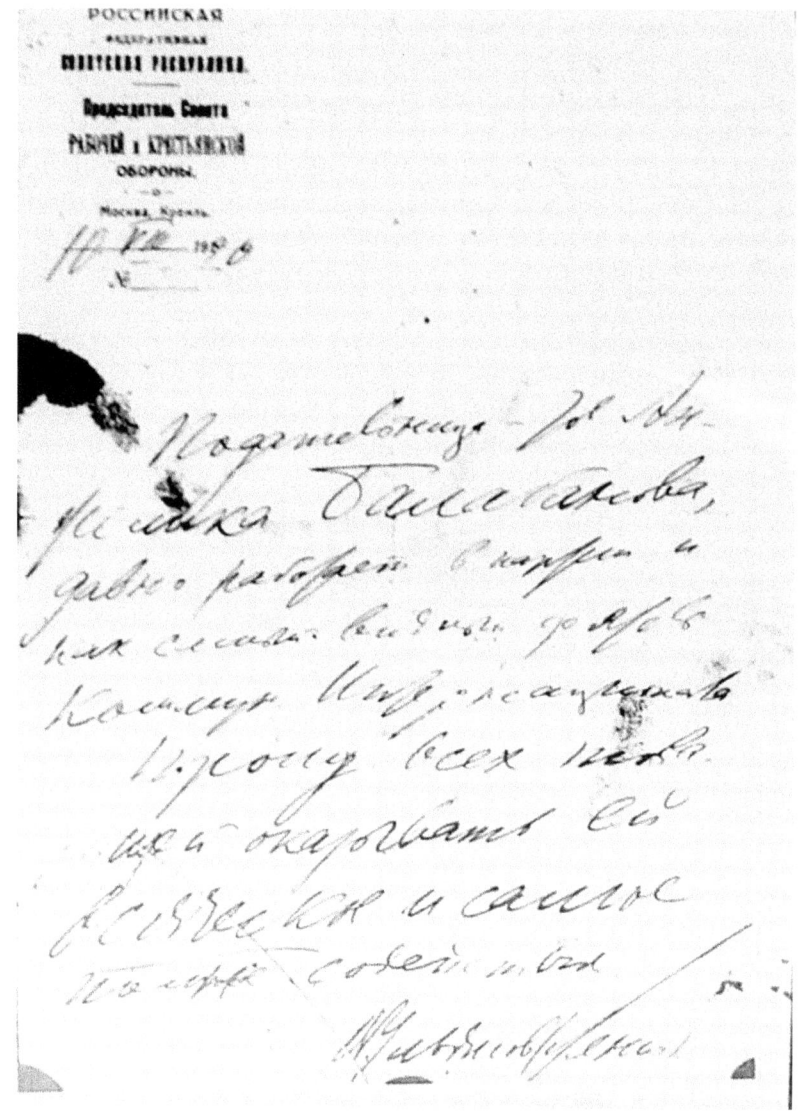

An official note written by Lenin to replace Angelica's identification papers, 1920 (HIA/BWC, Box 2, Folder 9).

permit was based on her health conditions which required a specific treatment. Coincidentally, Hjalmar Branting was a freemason. Not only did he provide her with an entry visa to Sweden, but he also sent a personal escort to take her out of Russia. The Swedish socialist politicians Frederik Ström and Karl Kilbom came to Moscow with the express purpose of taking her with them to Stockholm.

Needless to say, the secret services in Europe were immediately informed and alarmed by such news. "I also hear from a good source that Angelica Balabanoff, a notorious Bolshevik," reported the UK diplomatic services in Stockholm, "is expected here within the next few days.... Madame Balabanoff has to come to Sweden for sanatorium treatment," confirmed the UK secret agents, affirming that she was not traveling as Lenin's agent. Nonetheless, Angelica was quickly becoming a *persona non grata* in many countries.[5]

The Russian revolutionary had no problems obtaining a letter and the necessary papers from a physician demanding her long-term treatment abroad. After years of exhausting work in the starved and deprived Soviet State, it was not difficult to prove that her health needed to be taken care of. The matter was quickly finalized. By the beginning of December, she had her papers and was ready to go.

"I returned the documents and credentials issued to me by the government and asked for simple identification papers," Angelica reported in her last conversation with Lenin.

"What?" Lenin said. "Identification papers? You are better known than I! ... But if you desire I shall give them to you with all my heart."

"You know ... perhaps Russia does not need people like me..." added Angelica before leaving his study at the Kremlin Senate.

"'She needs them, but she does not have them,' Lenin said in a sad, grave, voice. ... These were the last words I heard him say."[6] Shortly before her departure from Russia, Angelica moved out of her room in the Hotel National. Her friend David Riazanov offered her a place to stay in his apartment. Riazanov was the founder of the Institute of Marx and Engels in Russia. In the 1920s and '30s, he traveled in Europe to assemble a unique collection of communist-related documents for his institute, which he bought or received as a gift from Russian immigrants, European socialists, and people who had personally known Lenin or Marx. Despite remaining faithful to the Soviet regime, in his heart David was unmistakably Angelica's friend. Out of favor with Stalin as of 1931, exiled in Saratov, when any move was interpreted as being against Stalin, David tried to obtain food for children of other "enemies of the state" and would be executed by Stalin in 1937.

Report issued by the UK Secret Police upon Angelica's arrival in Sweden, 1921 (The National Archives of the UK, London).

XX. Freemason Without an Apron

The note Lenin promised to Angelica was delivered by a messenger to Raizanov's house the same evening. It read:

"The President of the People's Commissars of the socialist Soviet Republics asks all institutions and individuals to give Comrade Angelica Balabanoff <u>every assistance</u> required."

Before Angelica left Russia, her comrades made another attempt to persuade her to stay. Leon Trotsky invited her to his office for a private meeting:

"Staying here," explained Angelica, "I'll become a demagogue, never say to the masses what I do not believe, and what I cannot give them."

"On what condition would you stay?" he asked.

"I want to be able to tell the masses the truth."[7]

Years later, Angelica proudly summarized, "I was the first and perhaps only militant Socialist, who, without suffering any persecution whatsoever, left the fatherland of the revolution for reasons of principle only."[8]

The day of Angelica's departure, she returned to Riazanov's place from running early-morning errands. She was told that Lenin had called three times. She returned his call by dialing the direct number of Lenin's reception:

"Vladimir Il'ich," the secretary said, "wanted to know if you need anything. He wanted to make your travel as comfortable as possible."

"Thank Comrade Lenin for me.... I shall need nothing."[9]

Angelica arrived in Stockholm on December 17 "with Frederik Ström [and] Karl Kilbom ... who were returning from Moscow."[10] The Swedish comrades provided an escort and official protection on behalf of their prime minister that Angelica needed in both countries—with Russians displeased with her departure and the Swedish ditto about her arrival. She left Russia forever four and a half years after she had arrived to foment the revolution.

"It gives me immense joy," Angelica wrote one year before her death "to be able to appear as I am, with a clear conscience; it is a piece of luck for which I envy myself."[11]

In this new chapter in Angelica's life, things were to become yet again more complicated than expected. After entering Sweden, she spent a few months there, and then she disappeared. All traces of her were lost. It was as though she no longer existed.

XXI

An Adolescent Armenian Boy

Up through 1922 every year of Angelica's life had been filled with so many events that at times she was difficult to follow. All of a sudden there was a dearth of information about her throughout 1923 and the beginning of 1924. There were no lecture tours or meetings to attend in Prague, Vienna or Berlin, no letters to write or language lessons to give.

The first published document about Angelica after she left Russia appeared in April 1924. The document was rather gruesome. It was an article reproduced in the Swiss newspaper *Le Journal de Genève*, from the *Pravda* newspaper, the main tabloid of Communist Russia, which announced that her Soviet nationality and passport had been revoked. The article was swiftly reproduced in the Swiss, German, French, Italian, and English press in the "Russia" section.

> Balabanoff Excommunicated
> The famous Russian revolutionary, Angelica Balabanoff, is well known in Italy and in Switzerland, where she had lived during the war and from where she had been expelled along with the Soviet mission.
> According to the information received from Russia in Italy via Berlin, the Pravda edition of 8 April published the news that the Control Communist Party Commission had excluded Balabanoff from the party.
> "It is with shame," concluded the article signed by the Secretary of the Central Control Commission, Emelian Jaroslavksy, "that we think about Angelica Balabanoff who for years had been a member of the communist party."[1]

The excommunication must not have been a surprise for Angelica. A few months prior, she had lost her main protector, Lenin. He had died in January 1924, having succumbed to complications from three strokes. Stalin came to power. She must have realized that her future would be precarious.

XXI. An Adolescent Armenian Boy

The name of Jaroslavsky at the end of the article was probably no surprise either. Dubbed the Soviet Pope for promoting moral values, he was an ardent Stalinist, responsible among other things for falsifying and changing Soviet history under Stalin's guidance, and he would soon be writing similar articles on Trotsky and Zinoviev, who would become enemies of the Stalin regime.

So in April 1924, Angelica had no identity papers, no means of traveling, and no country with which to identify. In addition to Russia, she was denied the right to enter the UK, Switzerland, and Italy, since Mussolini had come to power in 1922. But there is still an 18-month gap of ignorance as to her whereabouts between the moment she left Russia and the time when her passport was revoked. Angelica's first moves after leaving Russia were easy to trace. She came to Stockholm in December 1921. In Sweden things did not go for her as she had planned. The Swedish government had benevolently granted her an entrance visa to enable her to leave Russia; however, by accepting it, she agreed not to participate in any political activities. Such an agreement interested quite a few countries who did not want to see her in Europe under any circumstances.

To reassure its Foreign Ministry, the UK secret services reported on her presence on Swedish soil: "Madame Balabanoff is ill and in urgent need of sanatorium treatment and it is in order to endeavor to obtain effective remedy for her illness that she is now preceding to Sweden. It scarcely needs to be mentioned that such conditions have been laid down for her admission to Sweden as will entirely prevent her engaging in any kind of political activity."[2]

For four weeks following Angelica's arrival in Stockholm, she kept her word. This was not because she gave up on politics as she had promised, but because she was ill. "My organism has been so weakened by work and undernourishment," she commented in her notes, "that I feel like an old woman."[3]

The revolutionary left Moscow "aged and depressed." She remembered later that the doctor, after ordering her to stay in bed, asked:

"What did you live on during those four years to reduce yourself to such a state of fatigue?"

To make her feel better, and if possible smile, her friends and acquaintances brought her food, delicacies, and the chocolate that Angelica was so fond of, but she "found it hard to look at the food on the table or in the stores without recalling how the children in Russia had crowded about the doors of the bakeries, hoping to get a few crumbs...."[4]

While she was ill, the Swedish prime minister, Branting, was verbally attacked for hosting a dangerous communist in the country. She was still a member of the Russian Communist Party and as such dangerous to security in most countries. "After 1921," reported the French police, "she was sent for propaganda purposes to Western Europe...."[5] Few knew or believed that Angelica was openly anti-communist at this point.

As soon as she was well enough, she rushed to participate in anti-fascist and anti-communist meetings. But the rioter did not want to put Branting's career in danger and decided to leave Sweden. Where to go? Her long-time friend with whom she had been through many campaigns and propaganda tours, Valentino Pittoni, a well-known Socialist Deputy in Trieste, who has had a bronze bust erected for him on one of the squares of Trieste, asked Friedrich Adler, a member of the National Council of Austria, if anything could be done for Angelica. Adler, just as Angelica, was against Lenin's politics of communist dictatorship and thought that with her knowledge of internal Russian affairs of state, she would be a useful tool for Austria to fight Russia. Rather quickly, he obtained permission from the Ministry of Foreign Affairs in Vienna to issue her a visa. Angelica moved to Vienna, where she must have spent some time.

"She lives now sometimes in Vienna, sometimes in its outskirts," testified Victor Serge, a socialist who came from Moscow and must have met with the Russian revolutionary, "[carting] her possessions, those of an eternally poor student, from one furnished room to another: the spirit-stove for tea, the small pan for omelets, and three cups for her guests.... Small, dark, and beginning to age...."[6]

It is at that moment that she disappeared from public view. It is difficult to believe that this committed, always-on-the-move woman did nothing noteworthy for nearly two years. However, during this time period the U.K., Swedish, Czech, French, and Austrian secret services, usually rather fond of news about the revolutionary, remained silent. Unexpectedly, the only document which might shed some light on her whereabouts turned up in the U.S. in Angelica's FBI file. The report dated, August 1923, stated:

> Case Originated N.Y.   N.Y. File R-61-E
> Instructions of Special Agent in Charge, Edw. J. Brennan
> 8-9-23
> In Re: Angelica Balabanov, alias Balabosnov: Alleged Communist Activities
> alias Sophia Rosenthal : Alleged Communist ActivitiesAt New York, N.Y.:
> In reference to Agent HAAS' report on this case, dated May 28th, 1923, I have to report that on SS. Madonna, that arrived today, August 1st, from Constantinople and Mediterranean ports and was boarded by

XXI. An Adolescent Armenian Boy

agent, a passenger by the name of HOVANNES BALABANIAN arrived as an immigrant. He embarked in Constantinople and is manifested as 23 years old, Armenian by race and chauffeur by trade. He was born in Constantinople and was in this country from 1918 to 1922. The manifests do not show to whom he intends to go, although he intends to remain in New York, if permitted to land.

In view of the fact, according to report received from the Police Department of New York City, that subject is supposed to be a woman "who makes up as a boy," and who is a courier in the service of NICOLAS LENIN, agent marked the manifest (No. 2, line 8), so that subject's sex can be determined in the Medical Department of the local Immigration Service on Ellis Island.

In case subject should be found to be "feminine generis," this investigation will be continued.

Acting under instructions, I today called on Lieut. J . Gegan at Police Headquarters, this city, and received the following information which he had received from a reliable confidential source to wit:

That subject, who is said to be Lenin's most active and co

Confidential agent, having terminated a successful mission in Berlin, has started for the United States, protected by a German passport; that she is forty years of age, has dark brown hair and gray or dark blue eyes; is not a Jewess and travels disguised as a boy of twenty years; it is presumed she will attempt to enter the United States in this disguise.[7]

The valuable report does at least one thing—it suggests Constantinople (Istanbul) as her possible whereabouts in 1923. What about the rest of the information it contains? Angelica surely did not come to the United States before 1935 and did not work for Lenin again once she left Russia.

The FBI had also most likely exaggerated her capacities of passing unnoticed as a young man. In 1923 she was 54, so to pass for someone half her age and to persuade the Medical Department of Ellis Island that she was a man was too much even for Angelica.

Yet the notorious globetrotter *was* quite capable of dashing off to Turkey without telling anyone, as well as dressing up as an Armenian chauffeur to facilitate her travel through Europe. After all, she had already had experience in touring Europe on Lenin's orders, presenting herself each time as a different person.

So why would she have traveled to Constantinople? Why did she not board the U.S. ship as she had obviously planned to do? Why did the FBI follow her from Vienna through Yugoslavia and Bulgaria all the way to the Bosporus?

There was one subject on which Angelica was never loquacious, and that was her family. It is highly possible that this voyage was related to her elder sister Anna. Angelica probably found out that Anna had fled with her husband and son to Constantinople from Odessa to escape the Bolsheviks and was having difficulties getting from there to Europe. That was the situation of thousands of refugees who did not want to accept the Soviet regime and came to Turkey with one thing on their minds: to get from there to Europe or the United States. Once in Constantinople, things got much more complicated for most of them. The infrastructure of the small city was not prepared for such a sudden influx of refugees. Prices escalated.

Anna must have carried some jewelry and cash with her. But the Russian currency was devalued. The once strong Tsarist money had been long replaced by Soviet rubles, which were unrecognized outside Russia. The main item of exchange was diamonds, but with so much jewelry brought into Constantinople by the refugees, diamond prices went down. Anna must have found herself on the street with no money, neither any work nor a place to sleep, totally unprepared by life for such a situation. The visas and tickets to Europe were accessible only for those who were lucky enough to get them or who had brought enough money with them.

Angelica, with her dream of a revolution brutally destroyed by the very people she trusted so much, might have decided to help Anna—"the only family she cared for"—and left for Constantinople to look for them. Searching for her sibling in an overpopulated and unknown city must have gone on for months. The mission would have been close to impossible. Angelica would have visited as many cheap hotels, pension houses, immigrant restaurants, clubs, and humanitarian missions as she could, in the unbearable heat, dirt, and chaos, until she would unavoidably find out through the grapevine that she had arrived too late. Her sister and brother-in-law had died of starvation. The only survivor was her nephew, who by then had left for France.

Devastated, Angelica decided to go to the United States to start a new life, which put the FBI on alert. She may have changed her mind at the last moment, deciding to remain in Europe, where she could be more useful in fighting against Stalin's Red fascism and, with Mussolini coming to power in October 1922, Mussolini's Black fascism. The newly created Armenian chauffeur might have boarded the steam ship *Madonna*, disembarked at one of the Mediterranean ports in the South of France, and gone back to Vienna.

Going to Constantinople was a grueling and emotionally intensive experience, which demanded much physical and emotional strength to get through in one piece. By the time Angelica got back to Vienna, she had decided not mention her experience even to her closest friends. She may not even have needed to excuse her absence. She traveled on average every two weeks for lectures, and her close friends were used to her regular escapades.

Return to Vienna was by no means easy, though Angelica's passport problems were quickly resolved by her Austrian socialist friends. Two months after her Soviet nationality was revoked, with the help of Friedrich Adler, she received Austrian nationality and a passport by naturalization, which she would keep until the end of her life. Adler thought that she would be one of the best people to help Austrian socialists to fight Stalinism and fascism.

Between Angelica and the Austrian socialists began what would grow to be a mutual, long-term relationship of love and respect. In the 1950s the Socialist president of Austria and mayor of Vienna would personally invite her to the socialist congresses and lovingly call her "the Grandmother of Socialism" and "the old First Lady of Socialism."[8] They would regularly offer her cold water treatments and sojourns in Winterberg, Westfalien, where the doctor was a socialist and she could "feel at home" and stay there for weeks; it was a place of which she would become very fond in her later years.

Back in Vienna, the imminent problem to resolve after procuring a new passport was how to make a living. Angelica must have lost some of her youthful vigor. Years of deprivation added to the grief over her family and the loss of her country and did not pass unnoticed on her physique. But she did not change her lifestyle. She settled in a maid's room on the sixth floor of Beatrixgasse 3, in the center of Vienna. The location of her lodgings allowed her to walk around the city and avoid spending much on public transport. "When I came back to Europe and took up the struggle for life," she confessed later to Emma Goldman, "I felt so happy it was just a honeymoon with socialism, to be what I am and not what my name says, to get up early in the morning, sick, to run to give lessons to come back hungry and get pains and ... give me so much moral strength that I was able to survive a terrible blow."[9]

Besides giving language lessons, Angelica took on freelance journalism for the Swedish newspaper *Socialdemokraten* and the Oslo newspaper *Arbeiderbladet*. Both newspapers had asked her to give them an interview about Mussolini. The interview was so successful that it was reprinted in other papers, and she was invited to write articles for both publications.

Having a passport and some money to get by was reassuring, but the realities of daily life must have been stark. She observed with fright how Stalin and Trotsky fought for power in Russia, Trotsky losing to Stalin and being deported. "He has no courage to fight till the end," she hastily concluded regarding Trotsky's ethics of conduct, still unable to grasp Stalin's true personality—that of an atrocious dictator he was becoming.

Hoping to win over Stalin's politics, she participated in the organization set up by Friedrich Adler, the so-called 2½ International. It was organized in response to the Comintern, and it united socialist parties that were not members of the Comintern. The idea was short-lived. The organizers could not compete with their already powerful Big Brother.

One can only guess Angelica's feelings when she watched the news about her ever-popular ex-vagabond Italian protégé in the cinemas. Mussolini thrived, successfully conquering Europe though image and propaganda. He paraded in front of the cameras on horse, dressed in a riding suit and derby hat, gaily playing with a lion cub called "Italia" and proposing agricultural reforms to get Italy out of economic crisis.

Emma Goldman would later summarize Angelica's feelings: "She is one of the very last great idealists left in this rotten world and so gifted in languages ... in fact in every way; and over and above is her great loving heart.... She is indeed a rare spirit. She suffers deeply under two disappointments—her pupil Mussolini and the Communist Party in Russia to which she had belonged. This is her great tragedy."[10]

Thinking that Mussolini's position should not be that stable in the government, unable to sit and watch his accession to power, Angelica decided to fight against him. "The eternal protester focused on combating her Italian pupil whose career was as promising as she had imagined but unfortunately in the direction opposite Angelica's," commented one of her friends. She became a one-woman reception and job committee in Vienna for numerous Italian immigrants who left Italy to look for work. With her amazing capacity for creating entire networks of contacts, she was always aware of job openings, cheap places to sleep, and means of finding news about the loved ones back at home.

She started to write again for *Avanti!*, hoping to remind Mussolini of so many events of the past. Her efforts did not pass unnoticed. "Living in Vienna," reported the newspaper *Sentinelle*, "she writes again for *Avanti!* Such collaboration must evoke strange souvenirs for Mussolini...."[11] However, the main person to whom Angelica's articles were dedicated was oblivious to her efforts.

Every grief needs a remedy. "I began to write poetry," she admitted to Emma Goldman, "and how much, if you only knew. Mostly in French...."[12] The first ideas of poetry-writing came to her during her first discussions with Vorovsky, which both enjoyed during the long winter evenings in the

Russian Embassy in Stockholm throughout the winter of 1917. She remembered later that another person who had suggested to her, even if halfjokingly, that she should write poems was a great literary personality whose advice was not to be judged lightly—Maxim Gorky. Once they had met in Moscow on the occasion of the arrival of the Italian delegation in the city, and when she took half an hour to translate a few words he had addressed to Italian comrades, he said, "Angelica, you should be a poet."

She composed in five languages, translating her own poems in all five of them. In the poem "There is no Sunshine, no Happiness at all in my Bereaved Soul," she confessed:

> My Soul
> Is burning into thirst of liberty for all;
> My Soul
> Is longing for a slice of bread for all;
> My Soul
> Is striving for the happiness for all;
> My Soul
> Is tortured by the pain for all;
> My Soul
> Is crying with tears for all;
> My Soul
> Is dying of the frailty and the sadness of the whole.[13]

By the end of 1925, the center of antifascism had been formed in Paris. The city attracted many Italians who had escaped there to get out of Mussolini's clutches and who were getting organized to fight him. Angelica's old-time friend Filippo Turati was about to move to Paris (after the death of his long-term partner, Anna Kuliscioff, who had passed away in Milan in December 1925) to become the leader of the PSI in exile. They got in touch with Angelica, suggesting that she come: "My Italian Socialist comrades insisted that I join them, which I did," she later explained regarding her departure.[14]

She could not know that Mussolini's feeling of revenge was reciprocal when it came to his Russian muse. He established a well-organized network of spies in Europe and received regular information about his enemies. Angelica topped the list.

XXII

Persona Non Grata

Angelica's memoirs, *My Life as a Rebel,* in which she told her life-story, ended in Vienna. She decided not to describe neither her 10-year stay in Paris, from 1925 to 1935, nor her long stay in the United States, which followed afterwards, commenting that her "activity was very limited" and that she did not "participate in the political life of the countries whose hospitality I enjoyed."[1] It is true that Angelica's involvement in political activities had been slowing down since she had left Russia. However, one thing was sure: Angelica, being Angelica, continued her existence as a remarkable human being.

Her stay in France was well "documented" by the French police. The files are kept in the Remembrance and Cultural Affairs Section of the *Préfecture de Police*, where her name shows under code BA 1986, labeled as Bolshevik Propaganda Activist, a label that seemed to have stuck with her for life, even though when she moved to Paris she was no longer a Bolshevik.

The masses of reports depict a dramatic and morose existence for the Russian revolutionary in Paris.

"The militant named Balabanoff, Angelique, called 'Balabanova,' called 'Balabanov,' called 'Delafontaine,' called 'Lafontaine' ... is lodging ... at the family boarding house on 46 *avenue du Roule in Neuilly* at 35 francs per day," stated one of the early reports, demonstrating the knowledge the French police had about the dangerous communist and that they were ready to expel her at a moment's notice. A few pages later, the report stated that her rent had gone up to 44 francs, and Angelica was forced to move to *10 rue de la Tour d'Auvergne*, where she was lodged for a few weeks at the house of Italian socialist Georges Salvi while looking for another suitable location.[2]

She no longer had money to pay for her room. She carried her possessions from one apartment to another, spending a few months in each place. "My own living conditions are worse and worse," she confessed to Emma Goldman. "I was even without a room for a while," she added, allowing one only to guess where she may have spent the nights.³

A rare photo of the time showed Angelica wearing a worn-out dress, sitting on a couch in a room that could not have exceeded two square meters, with a table and a lamp beside the couch. She looked tired, hunched over, and depressed, with flat, dull, unwashed grey hair twisted into braids around her head and enormous dark shadows under her eyes from constant undernourishment and frequent bronchitis.

She tried to get by using her usual rescue incomes—as a language teacher and translator. Robert Grimm, who kept in touch with his faithful comrade-in-arms, even procured a few opportunities for her in Switzerland. She was invited to translate at the textile conference in Zurich. But there was no way that the Swiss were going to let her in. No matter how much her friends insisted that it was "hard to find a competent translator aware of technical textile terms," bombarding the authorities with reference letters, the answer was firm and negative.⁴

Avanti! in Vienna, 1925. With Mussolini coming to power in Italy, publication of *Avanti!* was moved from Milan to Vienna and Paris, often reduced to a small impromptu exhibition in a coffee shop or a place of socialist gathering (collection of Albert Tosoni-Pittoni).

Mussolini's spies gladly reported to *Il Duce* that, unable to find sufficient jobs, "she lives in absolute misery."[5]

In an effort to establish herself as an author and make some money, she published her book *Memories and Experiences* in German, Swedish, Norwegian, Hebrew, and Italian, but in small editions and with little success. Not only was her style of writing a bit demagogical, but she was impractical when it came to the business end of things, unable to take care of marketing or negotiate with the publishing houses. She confused the royalties that were due to her from the books with the money she owed to the translators, thinking that it was their fee. Instead of giving them 10 percent of the amount, she would give them the entire amount of her advance. So the book writing hardly provided any additional income.

Only a few miles away from the fancy shops of the *Rue de la Paix*, Lalique crystals, Coty's perfumes, and the *Ledoyen* restaurant behind the *Petit Palais* with its dinner at 40 francs, she lived "on 5 francs per day," agents reported to Mussolini, "reads daily newspapers, including *Pravda* given to her by journalist friends as she cannot afford to buy any.... At her place she has a small library which is the main part of her small luggage...."[6]

Five francs a day is the equivalent of $0.30 at that time (about $4 today). When a dozen eggs cost $0.55 and 1 kg of bread $0.24, Angelica's budget reduced her diet to almost nothing. An omelet of two eggs beaten with a bit of bread soaked in milk was a royal and rare meal. "My standard of life," she wrote in another letter to Emma Goldman "went down to such a level that it was hardly human."[7]

Between Angelica and Mussolini, it was a war without mercy. But it was not on unequal terms. Angelica continued to do what she did best. Using her extraordinary networking capacities to bring together Italian immigrants in France, she helped them settle and find jobs and lodging. With *Avanti!* banned in Italy, she became the editor of the paper in Paris. Editions were published on a small scale. At times an issue was simply put together by Angelica and exposed

A political cartoon targeting Mussolini, created by Italian socialists in exile in Paris, 1929 (collection of Albert Tosoni-Pittoni).

for a few weeks on the walls on the second floor of one of the "friendly" Parisian coffee shops whose owner was a socialist.

Much to Mussolini's annoyance, she was often invited as the main speaker to conferences like "Mussolini and Fascism" and was seen in Berlin, Dresden, Duisburg, Bratislava, and Vienna, her main condition being for the organizers to pay her traveling fees. "Fascism is a temporary phenomenon and is destined to die," she said as the Italian spies summarized the subject of her speeches in reports for their prime minister, tracking Angelica down all over Europe.[8] Afraid to anger their powerful boss, they worsened the reality: "The conference finished for Balabanoff as a fiasco, everyone laughed."[9]

Together with friends from the PSI, Angelica helped to open a cafeteria for Italian socialists in Paris, *Popote*, "A Mess." They rented a large, bright room with cooking facilities in the center of Paris. Equipped with long rectangular tables covered with traditional French red-and-white checked cloths, the cafeteria could fit up to a hundred people. It served simple Italian food on thick white faience plates decorated with flowers and rooster and house red wine in dark green, solid glass bottles. For a small fee, Italians could get together, exchange news, and have a good meal.[10]

But what could Angelica do against an entire State machine that worked for Mussolini? Her place next to him has been occupied by Margherita Sarfatti, by then a sworn enemy of Angelica. Just as with Angelica, Mussolini's relationship with Margherita surprised many people, who wondered how a beautiful, wealthy, and sophisticated woman could be attracted to her social and cultural opposite. But she was totally in love with him. They stayed together for more than 20 years, with silent agreement from her husband and Rachele's violent scenes of jealousy notwithstanding. Margherita would go as far as to convert to Catholicism when Mussolini put forward anti–Zionist and anti–Semitic policies in Italy.

In 1926 Margherita published a biography of Mussolini, *Dux*. The book remained on the bestseller list until 1938, went through 17 editions, was translated into 18 languages, and was followed by another publication: *Mussolini: L'Homme et le Chef*.[11]

As Mussolini's image-maker, while writing his biography, Margherita did not spare Angelica's persona. Her Russian rival was no longer dangerous, but she wanted to take revenge on the once powerful enemy who with her "tame Kalmouk ugliness" had once been so important to *Il Duce* and who had refused to publish Margherita's articles in *Avanti!* The "Russian fury" was "deprived of any sense of humor," triumphed Margherita in her books, "as well as all sense of beauty, in fact, [this was] for her own good, otherwise she would have drowned herself in the nearest well, or perhaps not, as water was unfamiliar to her," wrote Margherita to make sure that her words would be heard worldwide.[12]

Mussolini had sworn that Angelica's name would never be mentioned in Italy. "The woman who made Mussolini" was not cited in his biography, which mentioned his wife, Donna Rachele, only once. However, when in February 1927 the Russian press published an article announcing the death of Angelica in Leningrad (new name of Petrograd since the death of Lenin in 1924), Mussolini broke his promise, immediately reproducing the article, as did the majority of the European press. But she was not dead—she had probably been confused with another Balabanoff. Triumphing, Angelica gave an interview to *L'Ere Nouvelle* confirming, "The news of my death is premature. I'm safe, working with you for the triumph of our cause."[13]

On 25 October 1932, Mussolini celebrated 10 years in power. A lavish ceremony in Milan staged for this event was widely transmitted in the cinemas. Anxious and fretting, Angelica watched her ex-protégé on a large screen in the cinema on the *Grande Boulevards*, wearing a black shirt, giving his speech standing on the impressive elevated tribune draped with long, dark red cloth, upon which his personal symbol was embossed in gold.

"More beautiful will be the 10 years to come," he said.

Angelica felt helplessness, worthlessness, and guilt, "suffering terribly of what is going on in the world...." Her hopes of social revolution were disappearing forever.[14]

> Life's cup I have drained
> And found no joy therein
> The Mountains of sufferings I have climbed
> And for myself no comfort thought...
> > Now I am at life's end
> > Rejoicing that not turn
> > And no way back
> > And no deceitful happiness
> > Call and tempt me

She signed her poems Zaira, a pseudonym she had taken for her poems and correspondence a few years prior, knowing that she was being followed.[15]

Just before New Year's Eve of 1932, she decided to commit suicide by taking an overdose of sleeping pills. Luckily, she shared her distress with an Italian couple she knew. They took her into their house and nurtured her for a few weeks, providing warm meals and a welcoming home. According to one of the reports from the Italian police who tracked Angelica down, she was staying temporarily with friends in *Montreuil-sous-bois*, a quiet residential area in the suburbs of Paris. No matter who her saviors were, staying with them made her change her mind.

After celebrating New Year's Eve with her rescuers, Angelica was well enough to live on her own again and moved to 78 rue Bloomet in the 15th *arrondissement*. The beautiful building with art-deco iron entrance and balconies had maid's rooms on the top floor available for as little as 350 francs per month. To get the money to pay for a real room of her own, she decided to sell the handwritten note that Lenin had given her before she left Russia. Russians were interested in buying any memorabilia related to their main revolutionary. Angelica sold the letter for half of its worth.

She watched the grey gloomy year of 1933 pass by as Hitler came to power, the first boycotts of Jewish magazines occurred in Germany, and Mussolini was praised by the American press for his leadership. The next year did not promise to be any more optimistic. More and more of her friends were prosecuted and killed in Germany and Italy. Knowing what Angelica was like, she must have suffered just from breathing the air freely while others were dying, when she suddenly fell in love.

Her passion was Vittorio Terracini, a thin, elegant, sun-tanned Jewish tradesman from Turin. He was also a homosexual, 30 years her junior, and a spy for Mussolini.

XXIII

The Spy Whom I Loved

With so many Italian leftists moving to France, Mussolini created a sophisticated network of spies who sent regular reports back to Italy. Angelica did not realize that many of her new friends were in fact spies, like the Consani couple. Angelica was so close with them that their children even called her "aunty." This relationship allowed *Il Duce* to follow his ex-muse even in the most delicate situations. He knew what she ate, what she read, the people she met, the places she had been to, and the subjects of her conversations.

It is in February 1934 in the home of one such "friend" she was visiting—somewhere between Nice and Golf Juano in the South of France—that she was presented to a young, sun-tanned, slender stranger whose name was Vittorio Terracini and who was rather attentive to her. With all her naiveté, Angelica failed to realize that the new object of her passion was not interested in women, much less that he was a spy. She felt that there was something different in the way this man, who was 30 years her junior, looked at her.

As a spy, Terracini reported on other homosexuals. He was persecuted for his homosexuality by the fascist regime, and becoming a spy gave him the possibility of escaping Italy with the silent agreement of the authorities and continuing the life that suited him in France in exchange for reports on Italian homosexuals. He immediately showed himself caring and slightly flirtatious with Angelica, hoping, no doubt, to find out about her antifascist activities and draft a few extra reports to *Il Duce,* scoring points with the Italian secret services. He could not know that a few moments after their first encounter, the revolutionary would be burning with an all-consuming passion for him.

As for Angelica, she probably needed to fall in love. This great eternal feeling added light to her life and helped her to find the strength to deal with her family and political dramas.

The newfound love of Mussolini's ex-muse was immediately conveyed to *Il Duce*. Rejoicing at the flow of information on the anti-fascist movement that Angelica would be eager to deliver to her lover, Mussolini could not miss the opportunity to learn more about her activities. The prime minister added duties to Terracini's work. He was now to report on Angelica as much as he could, not refuse any dates, and to show himself as a zealous lover. Terracini had no other choice but to obey. Refusing to comply with the orders was practically impossible, considering the number of people who counter-spied on the improbable couple.

Angelica, imagining a beautiful romance that could be so much better than her horrid daily life, decided not to pay any attention to the fact that the stranger never talked about his family and often disappeared without any explanations. Beaming with love, she looked "for any pretext to be with him," reported the informers. Dates, set mainly in the houses of friends, multiplied. Unfortunately for Terracini, she did not mean to talk to him about politics. She talked about love and quoted Byron and Arthur Rimbaud in French and Italian. After a few dates, one of the reports indicated, she "confessed her intimacy." She explained that she was looking for someone to get married to. She might "lose her Austrian nationality" and would "need to obtain another passport by getting married."[1]

That was more than Terracini could handle. He ran away to Italy. Unable to follow him there, Angelica waited for her hero.

"She dedicated a poem to him," testified one of their "mutual friends," "awaits his arrival in a few days like mad, to walk with him in the woods. Terracini will need to be provided with a chastity belt to avoid attacks."[2]

Terrified, on the way back from Italy, Terracini made only a brief stop in Paris and hurried from there to Barcelona, where he hoped to join his gay friends and resume his normal life. But he had underestimated Angelica.

"Balabanoff is to join a conference of Freethinkers in Barcelona," was the warning telegraphed to Terracini by one of the other spies. No one told him that she had not been invited to this event but had decided to go on her own.[3] Her main reasons for her trip were to join her love and to work on the book she was writing about Mussolini. After a short stopover in Barcelona, she planned to spend a few weeks in Palma di Majorca, choosing this location "because of the cheap fare and cheap life," she explained in a letter to Emma Goldman.[4]

The Spanish had never refused Angelica a visa. After paying the hefty amount of $2.95 (about $50 today) she quickly obtained one. On June 23, 1934, she took the 7:20 p.m. express train to Barcelona. Terracini had no other choice than to meet his Russian companion the next day at noon at the train station and help to carry her luggage: two suitcases with books and the draft of the book on Mussolini. He had already received orders to read the book and report on it. Her stay in Barcelona for the congress was short. To her regret "she saw little of Terracini," who disappeared into the gay Spanish scene, unable to endure the *tête-a-tête* regardless of what the punishment might have been. Angelica repacked her suitcases and went to Palma di Majorca, demanding that the object of her affection accompany her. He had no other choice. Besides, this trip gave him an opportunity to look for a chance to read the draft of the book about *Il Duce*.

Saving from her meager budget, Angelica had thoroughly prepared for the journey. Despite her lack of money, she bought tickets for a boat and in a cabin for two. To Terracini's horror, he found himself shut up with her for the duration of the voyage. "Under the rain and cold wind," he later reported, "Angelica cited poems until she got sea sick."[5] Terracini, afraid that she might get too sick, did his best to animate the conversation. He suddenly "remembered that Chopin and Georges Sand came to live on the island for a year," reviving Angelica's spirits with the romanticism of the story.[6]

Upon their arrival in Valldemossa, after "a short taxi ride from the port, she was settled in the Casa Bibiloni Pension," a six-story building with arched balconies, which, considering that it was the low season, had only five pensioners. Terracini's efforts to get a sight of the book were in vain. At this stage, it consisted of sporadically written, difficult-to-decipher short notes and was of no interest. As there was no book to read, to his relief, he could go back to Barcelona without any delay. Wishing that Angelica enjoy the quiet and finish her book, he promised to be back soon. He kept his promise. This sole visitor returned in a few weeks, at the beginning of August. However, disturbed by her sentiments, or perhaps in need of rest, her writing had not progressed.

After six weeks she decided it was time to go home.

"I would be very glad to stay here, but my duty calls me [back] to Paris," confessed Angelica, whose anti-fascist work was of not much use in Palma di Majorca. Her Italian friends in Paris even accused her of trying "to stop her fight for the cause."[7]

In the middle of August, Angelica, after a short stop in Madrid and Barcelona, went back to Paris. Before leaving Spain, she suffered a terrible shock. She learned the truth about Terracini. One of the reports to Mussolini stated that she had "found out through the grapevine that many of people she considered friends in Paris were in fact Mussolini's spies, including Terracini." She was marked for life and in the future would avoid befriending unknown people, assuming they were spies sent by Stalin or Mussolini.

She was back in Paris as a frightened, lonely, and lost woman who trusted no one.

> Et je veux lorsque l'heure arrive
> Où je dois passer sur l'autre rive
> Je sois tranquille et calme
> Et ne verse point de larmes,
> Et que ce qui me verront mourir
> De ma mort n'emporte qu'un souvenir :
> MON SOURIRE...[8]

She started carrying poison with her. The news of Angelica's state of mind became quickly known. Worried about her, Robert Grimm obtained permission from the Swiss authorities for Angelica to stay in Brissago, near Lake Maggiore, in the *Albergo Brenscino* pension house.[9] It is difficult to imagine how he managed to do it, but thanks to her friend, she spent what were for her an indispensable few weeks in a small town near the azure lake. She devoted her time to walks along the hilly streets and mountainous paths under the shades of closely planted palms and small trees and to writing poems.

Angelica missed her family. For the first time in Brissago, she explored the mother-child relationship. In her poem "Mothers," she wrote:

> Wind is blowing. Waves are roaring.
> I'm a sick child and full of fear;
> But the voice of my mother I hear
>   "Oh, my child, my dear
>   I have not gone,
>   I'm near,
>   You are not alone."[10]

But Angelica knew only too well that most of her siblings and cousins had died in Russia. She hoped that some had managed to escape, but she had no news of them, nor did she expect to have any. The only person with whom she was in contact was her nephew, Anna's son, whom she had seen a few years prior in Paris, the one she had been looking for in Constantinople. For 15 years she had not heard a single word of him. But this meeting brought back so many painful memories, reminding them both how different their priorities in life were, that they did not resume contact.[11]

Back to Paris after a short stay near Lake Maggiore, with her faith restored, Angelica decided it was time to move to the United States. Her first attempts to go there dated back a few years. Her visa had been denied twice in the late 1920s on the grounds of being a Bolshevik and friend of Emma Goldman. She was still suspected of being a "dangerous" revolutionary who was refused entry into many countries. Even the French authorities were wondering whether her presence was welcome on French soil: "Angelica Balabanoff … after being expelled from Switzerland and Italy (not without reason) after interdiction to stay in UK and the U.S. is settled here under pretext of doing journalism," they reported, "but in reality she is doing the same thing here she has been doing in the countries mentioned above, which is anarchist propaganda…."[12]

In 1931 Emma Goldman advised her to apply for a visa again, this time as a foreign correspondent of the Swedish newspaper *Socialdemokraten* and the Norwegian newspaper *Arbeiderbladet* paper she had been working for: "They [the U.S. authorities] usually do not ask questions from correspondents," she reassured her friend.[13] To help Angelica, Emma demanded that her partner and the well-known anarchist Alexander Berkman (whom Angelica had also met in Moscow) coach her inexperienced friend for an interview at the Embassy. Without any delay, Berkman started coaching: "Say to the Council ONLY that your Norwegian paper has asked you to go there," instructed Alexander in his letters from Nice, afraid that the Russian rebel would launch into one of her socialist fights with the Embassy staff, trying to prove to them the importance of social revolution, and that her visa would be refused yet again. "He will ask you for what purpose," continued Berkman from Nice. "As the representative of the paper, of course (you will answer); namely, to write on financial or other (social) conditions."

Imagined dialogue with the Embassy staff learned by heart, Angelica passed her interviews with flying colors and received her visa, at which point she realized that this time she did not have enough money for the trip. She needed to pay for a ticket and travel insurance and have money for the first few months. The U.S. comrades "sent her 400 dollars anticipating her trip," in July 1931, which would be sufficient to start her life in New York.[14] But she could not afford to pay for her ticket and insurance.

Emma Goldman offered help from St. Tropez:

"My own, unworldly Angelica, if I were not sure that you will have success in the States I would not have said I should love to lend you the amount necessary. I know that you are hopelessly impractical, you are like my beloved Louise Michel who never could make a step without running into someone who stripped her of what little she so badly needed for herself. Of course you need a manager and I am certain one could be found once you are in New York."[15]

"I will not even try to tell you what a relief you letters are for me," responded Angelica. "Dearest friend, even if you had the money I would not accept it, first of all because I have no possibility to give it back, even if the sum was a much smaller one."[16]

So in the summer of 1935, Angelica went back to the U.S. Embassy to find out that her visa was still valid. The only remaining question was the money. And luck suddenly smiled on her. She was offered a one-month translation job in Brussels, lodging included, allowing her to put money aside for the ticket and travel insurance.

"After years of unemployment and practical starvation," she described her stay in Brussels to Emma, "I have the possibility—owing to the ... very low price of food here—to 'enjoy' a few weeks of 'rest,' and I was able to buy the most necessary 'toilette' [items]."[17]

Once the work was done, Angelica headed back to Paris, where she still needed to work to avoid spending the money she had earned in Brussels and set aside for the trip. Her luck continued. She found a short-term job "translating and typewriting" in one of the typewriting agencies in Paris. The job was boring and monotonous but Angelica was beyond happy: "the lady has so much work ... '[I will] exploit you' was the explanation and I was very grateful for her sincerity. Besides, I prefer to be exploited than to exploit myself."

Angelica even left the "dirty" rooms of the rue Bloomet and moved into the "Paris Home" boarding house for a few months. At 400 francs per month, it was expensive, but at least the rooms were clean and had "a small kitchen" and "a cheap restaurant." With her hopes of going to the United States renewed, she wrote to her friend: "Dear Emma ... I am much happier than I was when I had 22 rooms at my disposal or the Kremlin with its apartment."[18]

In November 1935, while Mussolini, more famous than ever, announced a collection of gold, including the wedding rings of his admirers, to financially support the party and paraded in front of journalists and cameramen doing all sorts of sports activities bare-chested, Angelica had her ticket to New York on the Steam Ship *Exeter*, which was to sail on December 13 from Marseille.

Not only was she going to America as a journalist, but American publishers were interested in her book about Mussolini, promising her an advance of as much as U.S. $1,000 (about $17,000 today), and Emma was helping her to secure her first lectures and new publications, providing Angelica with useful addresses and advice: "I am certain that ALL my friends will be happy to assist you," Emma reassured her.[19]

Until her final days in Europe, Angelica continued traveling for her propaganda work, which also allowed her to avoid spending money on a room in Paris. "I'm going from place to place ... addressing the starving German workers," she wrote to Emma from Berlin only twenty days before her departure to New York. "I cannot afford to come to Paris.... From here I'm going to Vienna; you may imagine how exhausted I am both physically and mentally. If I find something to live by, I shall come back to France before I go over to the U.S. I feel very lonely."

She came to Paris just in time to attend a farewell banquet on December 7 organized at *Popote* by about forty of her friends, mostly the PSI representatives in exile, and left for Marseille the next day to arrive in time for the departure of the ship.

The S.S. *Exeter*, one of "The Four Aces," belonged to American Export Lines. It was the first comfortable place Angelica had been in years—she had her own cabin, equipped with an elegant single oak-wood bed, two mirrors, a wash basin, and a private bathroom.

Like a child taken on a merry-go-round, she spent hours on the promenade deck, outfitted with palm trees and deck chairs, covered with cozy blankets; she played cards occasionally in the Country Club Veranda Café, which was decorated as a Winter Garden with palms, rattan chairs, tables with tablecloths, and comfortable sofas with deep cushions in red that overlooked the decks and the sea. Even more imposing was the dining room, with round tables for eight people, each set with fine crystal, silver, bone china, and fresh linen, which Angelica tried to avoid, remaining faithful to her habit of sandwiches and apples.[20]

At the age of 66, she was going toward a new adventure. She had no savings and no pension, and she was about to become famous all over the world.

XXIV

The Foundation of Angelica Balabanoff

Angelica's stay in the U.S. between 1935 and 1947 is most richly documented by information from at least 15 different universities and archives, not to mention the FBI. Despite Angelica's decreased activity in politics, there remains a most interesting correspondence between her and Leon Trotsky, who, by then exiled in Mexico, developed strategies on fighting Stalin and wanted Angelica as an ally. Angelica also made remarkable new pen pals, including Norman Thomas, the charismatic six-time presidential candidate from the Socialist Party of America, who was looking forward to Angelica's anti-fascist lecture tours in the United States; the German psychologist Erich Fromm, with whom she wrote articles; the founder of the American Civil Liberties Union, Roger Baldwin, who helped her to obtain her U.S. visa; the American philosopher Sidney Hook, with whom Angelica discussed the "weight of psychological responsibility" that she felt for many events in her life[1]; a diplomat, Lane Lyle, the first chief of the mission of the U.S. Interests Section in Havana, and many others with whom she exchanged beautiful letters about her life.

When Angelica arrived in New York at the end of December 1935, she settled in the Hotel Park Plaza, on 55–58 West 77th Street, advertised in the publicity brochure of the time as agreeable establishment "facing lawns and trees of Central Park" and "away from the large buildings of Midtown" while the guidebook, *New York, City of Cities*, referred to her neighborhood as a "...depressed area ... with cheap flats."[2,3]

She had aged. The years of her deprived lifestyle and deep sorrows had not passed unnoticed on her body.

"Balabanoff is short, fat, shapeless—brown gray hair tightly wound about her head," reported journalist Alma Lutz, a writer and editor on national women's rights, who came to interview the revolutionary at the

Park Plaza and was taken aback by Angelica's looks. "She wore a loose brown dress, rather soiled, too large for her—many of her teeth were gone. She apparently cared nothing for her appearance. With a little care, she would have been fine looking."[4]

The apartment at the Hotel Park Plaza was the first place the Russian revolutionary occupied that could be called "an apartment" since she had left her family house in Chernigov that could be rated as an apartment. It was equipped with a real kitchen in one of the corners of the apartment, sufficient space to pile up her books, an electric fan for the hot New York summers, and even a radio and a gramophone. To outsiders, however, the place still looked scruffy:

> I sat in [the] lobby for 15–20 minutes and looked about what appeared to be a home for refugees," reported Alma Lutz, who had come to interview Angelica. "I heard almost no English…. She arrived—[a] short round ball of a woman—carrying a bunch of violets—poorly dressed—carrying those violets as if they were a real joy.
>
> We went up to her room—a back room on a small Court—you could see only gray walls. The halls en route were dirty…. Her room—couch, book case—round table covered with blue table cloth, a kitchen cabinet, an electric grill—both adjoining."[5]

But Angelica considered it to be so natural that she lived a plentiful and ample life that she immediately drew other people into her world:

"She made me feel almost ashamed of my good clothes and comfort," Alma Lutz finally confessed, as her first uncomfortable feelings about her hostess swiftly evaporated. "I liked immediately [sic] and admired her devotion. She was warm, friendly, great-hearted and intensely tragic. She made me feel as if I had never tasted or faced life."[6]

Angelica arrived in New York with her usual two suitcases filled with books and a bit of clothing as her only property. When Lola Maverick Lloyd, the head of the Women's International League for Peace, asked her to give to the League's archives a handwritten autographed paper, a draft article or a letter, Angelica wrote back to her saying that she had "no papers" in her possession and "kept nothing related to work." Most of what she had written she "did not sign"; moreover, she never "had personal archives or a regular home." The "only personal paper" she had, a note signed by Lenin, she "gave to Russians for money."[7]

Despite her relatively easy life in the United States, as compared to her past experiences, Angelica had problems adjusting to the American lifestyle. The giant skyscrapers and agitated midtown life differed so drastically from the slower and more leisurely European style she was used to.

XXIV. The Foundation of Angelica Balabanoff

"I suspect that the rush and hurry of American life, its materialism and callousness are not much your taste," Norman Thomas wrote to Angelica as soon as she had arrived to welcome her onto American soil. "But I hope," he continued, hoping Angelica would start her anti-fascist lectures as soon as possible, convincing the public why joining World War II would be important for the United States, "that you have also found other features of that life—the comparatively free, generous spirit of it, the new interest in social problems, particularly among our Italian elements there."[8]

Angelica would need nearly a year to get accustomed to such seemingly simple things as food. Grocery shopping trips turned out to be difficult expeditions with most of the staples unfamiliar to

Angelica's bank savings account book, 1930s (IISH, Folder 2016, author's photograph).

her. "American food does not [have any] taste [for] me at all," she reported to Emma. The selection of affordable Italian, Russian, Greek, Chinese, and the newly popular Japanese cuisine with fashionable suki-yaki restaurants seemed to be made for Angelica, with their low prices and modest settings, but she was lost in the abundance of unusual choices. Even finding her favorite sandwiches was not as easy as it once was. She was not tempted by a five-cent sandwich at a hot dog counter or in a hamburger shop. Angelica finally made a small exception for "a thick spread of cream cheese between two slices of raisin bread," easily available in the street shops.[9]

Emma, worried for her aging friend, sounded the alarm. A solution to Angelica's problems was immediately found in the form of a "secretary," Kitty Crowe. Angelica helped the young woman, who would rapidly become a friend and a "dear child," to pay her rent in exchange for an "introduction" into the U.S. way of life.

"As far as Kate is concerned," Angelica continued to report to Emma Goldman, "she is a real friend and helps me a great deal.... I cannot pay her as I would like, I just help her pay her room [costs].... She comes for an hour in the morning, has her breakfast with me and helps [with] cooking."[10]

Despite Angelica's hopes to make a good living in the United States and being graciously paid as a talented speaker, helped by a manager who would obtain her lecture engagements, her financial conditions remained as strained as they had been in France. "Here too [I] spent very little," she confessed to Emma Goldman. "I'm living ... off my lectures (mostly Italian).... Sometimes I take 15 percent of the having, after having covered all the expenses by my work."[11]

She maintained in her account at the Central Savings Bank at approximately $1,000 USD (worth about $17,000 today) that she received as an advance for her book about Mussolini, making weekly withdrawals of $20-$50 and just as regular deposits.[12] Careful with money, she listed her daily expenses on bits of paper in accurate columns, regrouping them by week and by month. But her financial situation had quickly deteriorated.

"You know how I used to live in Paris," Angelica wrote to Emma Goldman. "Here I live much worse because the number of those I have to help is much greater. I make debts to be able to fulfill my most elementary duty to save human beings from something which is worth than death."[13]

Lola Marverick Lloyd came up with an ingenious idea for Angelica to make extra money. She suggested that her Russian friend ask the Soviet authorities to give her back the note written by Lenin in exchange for money and resell it in the United States with the help of Lola, for much more money than she had in Paris.

But the moment chosen to make this transaction could not have been worse. It was the end of 1936, the beginning of Stalin's purges, when the most innocent people were arrested for treason, tortured, killed, or sent to the Gulag camps. Angelica must have heard about the trials of the leaders of the party, which were well-publicized in the international press, like the well-known trial and execution of the hateful Zinoviev, but the deaths of tens of thousands of others were not reported. She did not understand what the actual scale of the purges was. Only much later, after Stalin's death, did she find out about the similar fates of her dear friends, David Riazanov, her nephew Leonid, Christian Rakovsky, and so many others among her colleagues who had been executed in the Lubyanka and gulag.

Angelica could not know that by asking her friends in Russia to obtain her letter from Lenin, she was putting their lives in danger. Accused of being in touch with an enemy in exile, they would in turn be branded enemies of the nation. Thinking that Lola had an excellent idea, Angelica had

XXIV. The Foundation of Angelica Balabanoff

"cabled to Oslo" to Alexandra Kollontai, with whom Angelica had maintained contact throughout all those years and who was still the ambassador to Norway. The revolutionary then reported back to Lola that she "was expecting a response rather quickly," asking her to start looking for potential buyers of the note.[14] For some reason Angelica thought that Stalin, solicited by Kollontai, would send Lenin's note back to her.

However, January and March passed by without news from Alexandra. She most likely did not even tell Stalin about Angelica's request and hurriedly destroyed her friend's telegrams before they could be intercepted by too many people in the Embassy who might report Alexandra to Stalin. Angelica cabled repeatedly to Oslo. Then she stopped. Someone must have educated her on the real turn of events. "For the first time I'm ashamed of what is happening in my country," she wrote to Trotsky.[15]

Lenin's note forgotten, she decided to establish herself as an author and share her boisterous past with the whole world. Her book proposals were met by publishers with initial excitement that quickly faded. An excellent speaker who could add so many spicy stories to her narratives about Lenin and Mussolini, she was stale and demagogical as a writer. In her books, she skipped all scandalous facts, sticking to dry narratives about her beliefs, rendering her books hard to sell.

Columbia University holds the digitalized recordings of the interviews she gave in 1956 to Radio Liberty in Munich, Germany, with her slow and agreeable voice and her formal and outmoded but witty and humorous way of expressing herself. Whenever she thought that the interviewer asked a question that was too intimate, she would abruptly stop him: "You know what,

Cartoon featuring Angelica and her poems, New York, 1930s (IISH, author's photograph).

let's not go into details," she would comment dryly and move on to another question, like that of a socialist conference she obviously considered much more interesting.[16]

So when Angelica's memoirs, titled *My Life as a Rebel*, came out, the critics were at first ecstatic. "Her story is absorbing throughout," reported *The New York Times*.[17] "Of the many Russian revolutionary exiles, Angelica Balabanoff is next to Trotsky," continued *The New York Herald Tribune*.[18] Getting ready for public success, Angelica had her first posed photos taken. Her white hair was arranged by a hairdresser—she had probably not been to one since Chernigov—a little make-up to help stamp out the shadows under her eyes, and a bit of natural-colored lipstick, Angelica looked ready to go out. But the book did not sell. Angelica blamed the high price: $3.75 (about $60 today). "My book is not read by those for whom I wrote it," she complained. "I understand that the price of the book is far too high ... to allow labor to buy it—a circumstance quite independent of my will—over which I have no control."[19] However, among the real reasons for the book's failure was her pedagogical style of writing, which inevitably failed to please. Sales did not exceed 3,000 copies, much less than expected and hardly providing her any income.

Angelica reading *Avanti!*, 1939 (collection of Giorgio Giannelli).

"Angelica is like Father Time in *Jude the Obscure* by Thomas Hardy," wrote Emma Goldman. "She was born before her time—a tragic figure, and she sees through tragic eyes. That is of course her misfortune and the regret of many of her friends. Isn't it just like Angelica's 'business ability' to actually believe that any scenario that she might write would bring her fifty thousand dollars.... I had hoped that she would establish herself in America as a speaker, which would have enabled her to do her work and to earn enough to make ends meet. I am sorry this is not the case."[20]

Despite the book's lack of success, Angelica never gave up her writing attempts. She decided to raise money "to print poetry and a second volume of Italian memoirs," waiting for nearly 10 years to collect enough funds to produce her main poetry book *Tears*, which reunited her best poems written in five languages.[21]

Remaining as active as usual, the revolutionary traveled widely to give her anti-fascist and anti-communist lectures to promote awareness in U.S. citizens of the danger of fascism and communism. She went to Illinois, California, New Hampshire, Connecticut, Minneapolis, and other places, thoroughly avoiding Brooklyn, where she was reportedly afraid to set foot to visit her friends, Emma and Bertram Wolfe, who instead came to visit her in Manhattan.

Angelica continued to help war refugees, was a member of the New York anti-communist Ukrainian group, and also traveled to Mexico and Buenos Aires as a journalist to touch base with local Russian and Italian anti-fascist and anti–Stalinist refugees who had settled in these countries.

However, there was one person whom Angelica did not help. It was Margherita Sarfatti. In 1938, Sarfatti was forced to leave Italy because of anti–Semitic laws, and she attempted to emigrate to America. Angelica did everything in her power to block Margherita's entry into the United States. In the end, she would end up going to Argentina.

On July 27, 1943, when Angelica least expected it, her photos and interviews were all over the American press. This sudden fame of the revolutionary was preceded by important historical events. Two days prior, the Italian radio had broadcast the news at 11 p.m. that Mussolini had been voted out of power and arrested. The next day the papers all over the world came out with articles announcing the end of Mussolini. The following day, the *New York Post* and *Herald Tribune* published the revelations of a witness that the press called "Mussolini's Dearest," "Former Friend," and "The Woman Who Helped Get Mussolini Started."

The interviews followed one after another. At that time, Angelica moved out of Hotel Park Plaza and into one of the big apartment houses on quiet West End Avenue, living on the edge between the poor and the well-to-do side of the avenue. "It should have happened sooner," she said to *The New York Post* journalist, which came to her apartment, confirming that she "rejoiced at his finish."[22]

Angelica's sudden fame in America carried on even after Mussolini's fall. The announcement that the person "she got started" was executed on April 28, 1945, brought real disarray into her life. On that day she called a friend and went to watch a movie, unable to think about anything else apart from the day when, more than forty years before, she had been young, willing to help, and attracted to a man who showed so much potential.

From now on, Angelica faced verbal persecution from journalists and bystanders, which followed her on and off until her death. She was forced to provide an explanation for this unusual relationship, as to why and when they had met, and how she could have spent so much time with the infamous dictator, and who would trust her now?

Hounded by the press, which published articles with titles such as, "She tried to give Him a Soul ... but Created a Monster," Angelica made a few unconvincing attempts to elucidate her role in creating one of the most infamous dictators of all time:

"I diminished his mistrust of himself, his sense of inferiority, and in our work together, encouraged him not to feel dependent on me ... at this time he also began to speak. As he had no means of livelihood [sic], the local comrades would pay him seven francs [sic] for each speech. This was the beginning of his career."[23]

Nonetheless, one of the most devoted socialists of the 20th century had yet to explain why she spent over 10 years of her life with the future dictator, educating him, polishing him, forming him, and having a long-lasting relationship with him. Angelica denied any close relationship between them: "As a matter of fact there is absolutely no evidence to support such an assumption," she said in one of her interviews in 1943.[24]

The only words that sound remotely like an explanation, and not a terribly convincing one, can be found in her unpublished memoirs. Referring to Mussolini as a "coward" who "was afraid of his own shadow," she wrote: "Why then, should I remember particularly my encounter with certain Mr. Mussolini? Yes, I do. The reason is that he is one of the beings I met for whom I had only a feeling of pity. All that I did for him was dictated by his feeling, provoked by his extreme weakness, by the way he depended upon me and appealed to my aid."[25]

Exhausted by the years of pain she inflicted upon herself after she broke with Mussolini in 1914, Angelica found it easier to express her torments in the poems she often composed in Central Park, which was only a 10-minute walk from her apartment, while walking down its alleys and feeding squirrels:

"Life's talons hard and cruel
They throttle me and fetter me;
I yield not—I march on—"[26]

In the end, Angelica was just a human being, with a passionate and idealistic nature. She certainly sensed that this man had some outstanding qualities that could turn him into a brilliant politician. She could not imagine that they would be so gruesomely used against her and her beloved Italy.

The rumor that Angelica was the mother of Edda, the eldest daughter of Mussolini who was born in 1910, caused considerable trouble to just about everyone who was involved in the story. At the end of World War II, Angelica and Edda were even questioned by the representative of the American authorities in Italy and followed physically by journalists. The issue was publicly addressed by the majority of Mussolini's family. A "stupid insinuation, that Benito had her [Edda] with the agitator Angelica Balabanoff," is how Rachele referred to the rumor in her book *My Life with Benito*.[27]

Edda, while describing the rumor as "a mysterious story" and "pure invention," confirmed that her father and Angelica did have a sexual relationship.[28] However, to some, the story seems rather credible even today. Edda was provocative and avant-garde—the first woman in Italy to wear trousers and drive a car, who openly declared her weakness for Russia and Russian culture. She was the opposite of her traditional mother, Rachele, who never did anything that was not expected of a traditional Italian housewife or that would be considered outside the norms. Needless to say, mother and daughter did not get along, which for onlookers seemed only to confirm the rumors that circulated about Edda and Angelica. Many also insinuated that Edda's silhouette resembled Angelica rather than Rachele.

"Each legend, each lie, as incredible as it may be, always contains a part of truth," wrote Mussolini's son, Vittorio, in his book *Mussolini Intime*, in an attempt to clarify events once and for all. "It was suggested, for example, that Edda was the daughter of the Jewish Russian ... Angelica Balabanoff. It is true that Angelica Balabanoff and my father had known each other intimately.... Every evening, my father and the Russian Jew took the same way home on the way back from the newspaper and it often happened that they stopped for a few minutes together. It is then, without a doubt, that a legend was born according to which my sister was the daughter of Balabanoff."[29]

Whether an ironic twist of fate or a simple mistake, it turns out that the most widely circulated photo "of Angelica" that we see today is actually a photo of Rachele. It depicts a broadly smiling woman, wearing a fashionable cloche hat with a wide upturned brim and a pastel coat with a contrasting high fur collar, representing a fashionably dressed person that Angelica never was. Taken by socialite photographer Albert Harlingue during Rachele's time as the First Lady of Italy, copyright of the Roger Viollet photo agency, the photo is found on some of Angelica's recently reprinted memoirs and is widely used on the Internet in Wikipedia and other sources, making it difficult to understand who used the photo as Angelica's for the first time.

Unfortunately for the Russian revolutionary, the fall of Mussolini and her sudden fame failed to attract the much-needed attention to her book and a play she had written—*Traitor: Benito Mussolini and His Conquest of Power*—whose bilingual English-Italian edition came out in serial format over 10 issues in the summer of 1942. Angelica dreamt of making "the best publication about fascism," "read in the libraries and schools" and played in the theatres—her most favorite form of entertainment. But her play enjoyed only moderate success in Italy and none at all in the United States "except [among] some intellectuals I'm not particularly interested in," wrote Angelica.[30] Initial plans were to publish 10,000 copies. The printing of the play was swiftly reduced to 1,500.

As the war was over and the story of Mussolini slightly faded away, Angelica decided to go back to her "adoptive" country, where she had not been since 1914. Her anti-fascist lectures in the United States were no longer necessary, while her anti-communist work was of the utmost importance for Italy. The Red Army occupied part of Eastern Europe and Germany and was also stationed in Austria, and the danger of communism in Europe was more present than ever. The Italian Socialist Party split into those who supported Moscow and those who supported Washington, the latter headed by Giuseppe Saragat. This future president of Italy (1964–1971) was considered by Angelica to be the new coming politician and savior of postwar Italy. "Angelica's presence in Italy is necessary," he confirmed to Norman Thomas, looking for more support from the United States to fight the "commies."[31]

Angelica was ready to go. "I still feel very unsatisfied for not being able to work, to be of any use [in the U.S.]," she explained later her decision to leave the United States. "Here [in Italy] it is quite different.... This does not mean objectively that I am more useful but I can't say that I waste time."

Norman Thomas nominated her the "American Socialist Party Ambassador to Italian people." He created the Foundation of Angelica Balabanoff, based at 112 East 19th Street, Room 706, New York. The funds donated by Italian socialists were sufficient to pay for her trip to Rome

XXIV. The Foundation of Angelica Balabanoff

and make it possible for her to attend all indispensable events, meetings, and congresses throughout the country for a few years to come.

Instead of leaving happily for Italy, Angelica suddenly found herself under threat of deportation from the United States. During her 11-year stay in the country, she had had constant problems with her temporary visitor's visa as a war refugee. The visa was extended every year for the duration of the war, but once the war ended, deportation was immediate. But where? To Russia because she was Russian? Wasn't her life in danger there? To Austria, the country of which she was a citizen but which was partly occupied by the Russians? Would the Russians come for her now that there was no one else to protect her?

Her friends organized a support group. Representatives from the Civil Liberation Unit and the Common Council of American Unity started to write letters and memoranda to the House of Representatives and Department of Justice to establish an Act for the relief of Angelica. They looked for a congressman or a senator able to introduce a private bill "so that she may become an American citizen."

"Please do your best to introduce the bill, as the old lady is quite worried that she might be subject to deportation," requested Roger Baldwin's associates from the House of Representatives.[32]

Time passed, but "no one [...] introduced a bill for her."[33] After a year-long battle for her legal status, the National Refugee service had finally found a solution. They sent a letter to Ellis Island confirming that she was "Austrian and not an enemy alien." As such, Angelica received an extended return visa to the United States, "which implies the right to two extensions of six months each."[34]

Giorgio Giannelli, the only person alive today who knew Angelica well, maintained that Angelica did obtain an American passport. However, there are no official traces of her ever getting American citizenship or a passport.

Angelica was leaving America with a heavy heart: "I have found in America—where I expected to be and remain a 'stranger'—such friends, such comrades, such warm fraternal relationships," she confessed later to Ella Wolfe, "which gave me also the possibility to terminate my life as I began it—for and with the underprivileged."[35]

Legal procedures settled, in January 1947, Angelica boarded the S.S. *Vulcania* to go to Rome, leaving behind some of her books, a radio, a gramophone, and a bank account with a few hundred dollars.

"The first impressions of the boat were rather discouraging," she reported on the trip to her secretary Kate, writing on the *Vulcania* letterhead, "it was more like a hospital and I was afraid of the lack of cleanliness: during the war the soldiers used to be transported [in it].... On the other hand I was and am happy to travel like everybody else—'no classes, no distinction, no privileges....'"[36] At the age of 78, Angelica was ready to face the biggest danger of all—Communism, which was coming directly from her native land.

XXV

Under FBI Surveillance

Angelica left the United States for Italy. What else could happen to her in her life, apart from spending her remaining years reading books and making occasional speeches?

What happened was quite the opposite. Upon her arrival in Rome, the seemingly innocent and aged revolutionary created such an uproar among her Italian countrymen that she was immediately put under FBI surveillance. The "American Socialist Party Ambassador to Italy," as she was dubbed by Norman Thomas, went to her "adoptive" homeland with instructions from him to prevent an Italian Socialist party split into communists and socialists, wherein the communists might win the majority. Angelica arrived in the Eternal City just in time for a large socialist congress to which she was invited as a guest of honor and a survivor of Mussolini's regime; as such, she was invited to say a few words. Her openly anti-communist speech, when Russia had just won the war against fascism, sparked a mutiny. The FBI reported from Rome:

>> Department of State
>> Incoming Telegram
>> Plain

Control 3611
Rec'd January 13, 1947
8:45 p.m.
FROM / ROME via Army
TO : Secretary of State
NO : 97, January Twelfth
Reference my 66, January 12.

> Friday morning labor group and parliamentary group of Socialist Party submitted to Congress resolution support unity of the party.
>
> In the afternoon more speeches of foreign delegates were heard. The climax, however, came with the appearance on the rostrum of Angelica Balabanoff recently arrived from the U.S.A. She was greeted with great applause by the audience and with great affection.... She was obviously

touched by the overwhelming and dramatic reception given her by the Congress and spoke of her constant spiritual unity and sympathy with Italian socialism during her long exile. She then referred to the time when she had been forced to leave her own country because the "Russian Bolsheviks" had made it impossible to practice social democracy. The statement was interrupted with shouts of disagreement. To which she replied that for 45 years she had been speaking her own mind and that neither Fascists nor Communists had ever been able to shut her up.... She left the rostrum and the hall without applause and amidst the greatest conceivable confusion.
                        KEY
Note : Above message subject to correction.
EEC : PPM[1]

Angelica attracted the attention of the media, who knocked on her door to get more interviews, and she was recognized on the streets after her photos appeared in the press. Surprised by this turn of events as much as the FBI was, she reported to Kitty Crowe: "The first weeks [in Rome] I was frantically assailed by journalists, and you could see my picture everywhere. And why? Only because in a short speech I made, I said some true things, made statements which others do not choose—or do not dare to make...."[2]

This unfortunate fame was aggravated by Angelica's purported relations with Mussolini, which continued to raise many questions; besides, her slight American accent sounded annoying for someone who considered herself an Italian and wanted to take part in the politics of the country and added fuel to the fire of those against her. Though she did not realize it right away, her life was in imminent danger.

                          Telegram Sent
                          Department of State
     October 14, 1947
URGENT
AMEMBASSY
Rome
    Cortesi article in Oct 9 New York <u>Times</u> states that three Saragat's adherents were assaulted physically and one seriously injured in Rome yesterday by Communist gang. In your opinion, knowing the role played by Balabanoff and probably latent hostility of many years' standing against her for her anti–Communist speeches and actions, do you consider that her life may now be in danger?[3]

The reply about a week later only confirmed the seriousness of her situation.

XXV. Under FBI Surveillance

Department of State
Incoming Telegram
Rec'd October 20, 1947
1 09 p.m.
From: Rome
To: Secretary of State
No: 3300, October 18, Noon

Embassy believes Balabanoff may well be in danger at this time. Conclusion is not based on belief that Communist leadership would move against her, for to do so (*) her martyr. However, in spite of generally good discipline of the party there are irresponsible elements in it whose actions cannot be foretold as elections (EMBTEL 3242, October 15); unsettled conditions and heightened political feelings that may be anticipated during coming winter increase dangers from these elements.

NOTE: (*) Garbled portion; repetition on request[4]

The Department of State took action. The American Council in Rome provided her with an emergency exit visa and a boat ticket in case she chose to leave.

PRIORITY TRAVEL CERTIFICATE
American Council in Rome
Naples, Italy
Date: 27th October 1947.

Outside her home in the outskirts of Rome, 1961 (collection of Judy Kelly).

To : Angelica BALABANOFF

The Department of State at Washington had necessarily established a priority system for person[s] desiring to proceed to the United States on repatriation vessels provided by the department. Under that statement you are entitled to
Priority "F"
H.W. Carlson
American Consul[5]

But Angelica had no intention of using her ticket and escaping from Italy without a proper fight against the communists. The only thing that really interested her in this regard was having a permanent entry visa into the United States in case Russians invaded Italy or communists achieved their goals and wanted to imprison her for life. Norman Thomas and Roger Baldwin intervened on her behalf. After four years of administrative procedures, she received a confirmation from the Department of State that she would have an open-entry visa to the United States in case of imminent danger.

> August 23rd, 1951
> Miss Angelica Balabanoff
> Hotel Park Plaza
> 50–58 West Seventy-Seventh St.
> New York 24, New York
> Dear Comrade Balabanoff,
>   The Department of the State will look with sympathy upon your request for re-entry into the United States....
>   I informed them that you would most likely live out the remainder of your life in Italy, but that if there was[were] a war it would be imperative for you to be given a safe haven in the USA.
>   Fraternally yours,
>   Irving Salert[6]

Reassured that her visa to the United States had been maintained and that in case of Russian invasion she would be safely evacuated, Angelica continued her work in Europe. She knew that she lived "on borrowed time" and decided to make it as much quality time as possible, ready as ever to "swim against the stream."

XXVI

The Red Popessa

The two words that could describe Angelica and her weird and wonderful life better than others would be *the Red Popessa* (female Pope). They provide an exact definition of what she was all about: the enduring spiritual leader of the underprivileged.

Once settled in Rome, she maintained her regular lifestyle. The Red *Popessa* multiplied her traveling and speaking engagements. "I have spoken 22 times in 22 different locations," she wrote to Ella Wolfe, "leaving the hotel at 8.30 a.m. and returning at 12 p.m. "everywhere loudspeakers, windows open, most of the audience hidden, afraid of communist espionage...."[1]

Angelica would make her final speech two years before her death, asserting in a letter to one of her friends that "as far as I personally am concerned, I really should not complain nor do I so. At my very advanced age I have not yet had to say to myself or others 'when I was young' or 'if I were young'—as far as socialism is concerned and my reaction to the events, to the sufferings of mankind—injustice, slavery, demagogy—I am just as you have known me and before that."[2]

Quite astounding were Angelica's frequent changes of apartment in Rome. During her 20-year stay, she moved 13 times. From the picturesque and shadowy *via Aurora*, with the magnificent view of cypress trees and the Borghese gardens that swiftly inclined uphill, making one wonder how an elderly woman ever could have lived and walked there every day, she then moved to *via Azuni*, which might have reminded her of Moscow with high plane trees on every side of the road and with a room that had "more space" and where she could "keep her books," and then from that location to the touristic and scenic *via Margutta* near the Spanish steps where she had a "microscopic" room in a pretty, terra-cotta building covered with bindweeds, which was "not clean"; she had to "separate from her books" and in November "wear a coat inside the apartment."[3]

Equipped in winter with "warm underwear" and an "electric stove from friends," she started to work early in the morning "before the apartment was heated," often with a "hot water bottle on [her] knees," wishing that all "old and young" could be like her and considering herself a "spoilt" and "privileged" person.[4]

Despite the assurance of the perfect and happy life found in Angelica's letters, such frequent change of lodgings was rather surprising. It was as if she was afraid that someone would follow her. Her rooms were paid for by the Italian Socialist Party. She insisted that she did not want them to pay for her lodging while she was away on long trips. Or as possibly more than likely she was afraid of the Russians, thinking that they were after her?

For the first time in her life, Angelica had sufficient income to lead a

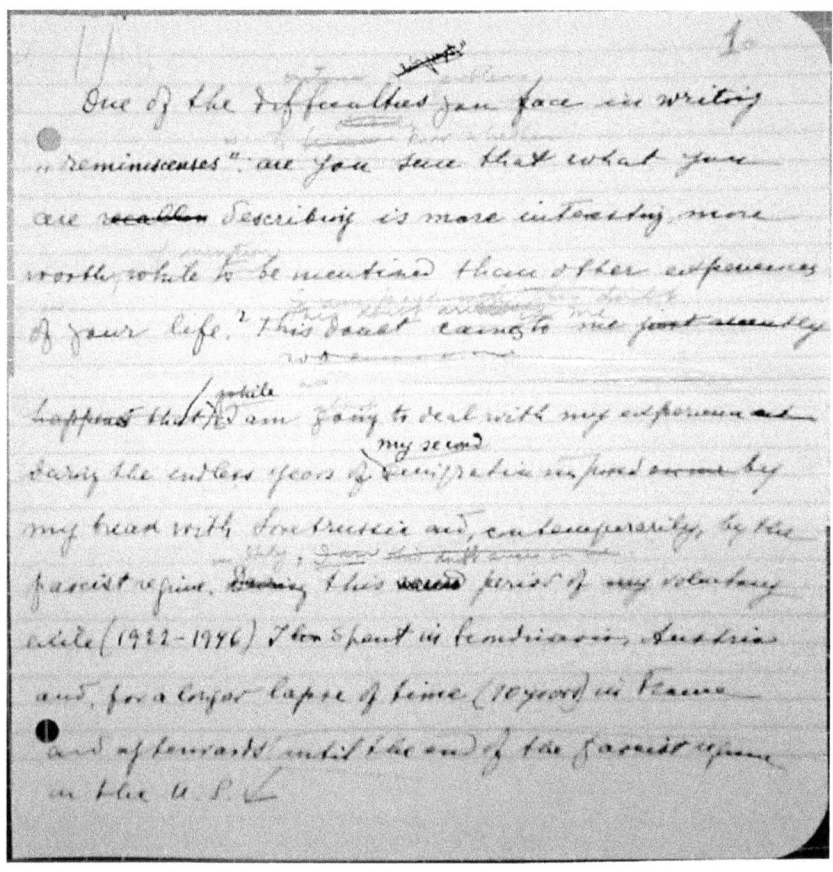

The first page of the memoirs written by Angelica, 1950s (IISH, author's photograph).

comfortable life. Not only was her room paid for, but Norman Thomas, who managed the Foundation of Angelica Balabanoff, sent her "every two months 200 D," about $2,000 today. She also received $50 monthly, about $500 today, as a lifetime pension from the Italian-American Fund for her anti-fascist propaganda campaign during World War II in the United States.[5]

But instead of spending this money on an apartment, vacations, or clothes, Angelica, of course, used it for the cause. She reported to Norman Thomas on her expenses: "In Italy," she wrote, "paying not only most of the fare of my very many lectures, but [I] also make some contributions to the needs of the party, of some comrade or needy person in general. Besides my lectures I wrote—and still am writing from here—articles for Italian socialists papers," which provided her with extra income.

More money arrived for Angelica in the form of donations and gifts from friends, associations, and various workers' foundations who loved her as a person and wanted to support her work. Roger Baldwin, the founder of the American Civil Liberties Union, remembered how during his stay in Rome he "helped her with a deposit of $500 from the DeSilver Fund," referring to a Foundation named after Albert DeSilver, one of the founding members of the ACLU, which supported Angelica, "only to find out that she was not as poor as I had gathered! She lived so frugally, she needed little, and evidently had saved the gifts her friends gave her."[6]

Besides being provided for financially, she received an incredible number of parcels with food and clothes from the United States and often did not have to buy much for herself.

> Junior Tins
> One carton as follows: Four cans each of
> Spinach
> Carrots
> Green Beans
> Mixed Vegetables
> Squash
> Sweet Potatoes
> Two cartons as follows: Six cans each of
> Peaches
> Applesauce
> Applesauce & Apricots
> Pears & Pineapple
> Pears
> Prunes
> Bananas with Pineapple
> Plums with Tapioca[7]

Such were the contents of the parcel Angelica received on a few occasions from her friend in New York, Frances Grant, a pioneer in U.S.-Latin American relations. The note for customs which accompanied the parcel explained: "The lady of the consignee in question lives in Rome. She is around eighty years of age and the reason she has to eat these baby foods in obvious. She can't chew.... Possibly could you have enough samples of the Junior tins to make three cases...."[8]

As usual, Angelica did not have any cooking facilities in her "new" and "comfortable" apartment. The parcel was "more than welcome," she reported to Frances. "Going to the market or purchasing in general," Angelica explained to her friend in a thank you letter, "is almost impossible to me.... Walking gets sometimes a little complicated.... Mostly there is an infinite number of cars and most of the motorists are incredibly undisciplined."[9]

Ella Wolfe sent so many gifts that Angelica begged her: "Do not use the care parcels [care packages], they contain many things which are abundant and most likely cheaper here. The contents of the parcels remain the same as during the war, e.g., sugar, soap, milk, lard—which one does not use anymore here, especially people like myself with no cooking facilities. I was really angry seeing how much you spent, the more as I know how much you work and how you use what you earn. Believe me my dear I don't need anything apart from your warm friendship."[10]

Angelica once confessed in a letter to Kitty Crowe that she wrote at some point during the summer of 1956 that she had received so much chocolate for Christmas and then again for

Posing for a photograph with the boys on one of the streets in Rome, 1953 (HIA/BWC, Box 2, Folder 61).

Easter that she still had some left, in spite of offering it regularly to friends and guests and consuming it herself.

One thing she never refused, however, were the items she had become most accustomed to in the United States and that were not yet available in postwar Italy: Lipton tea bags and paper towels, "since I am often travelling or stay out for an entire day."[11] Stationery also remained a much-appreciated gift: "the taste of the old friend who gave you that paper, or rather your taste for having such a friend..." marveled Angelica in her letter to Kitty upon receiving new writing paper from her.[12]

Provided for financially, professionally Angelica's life was far from being easy. Her relations with Russia were strained to the point that she had a recurrent fear of being kidnapped and sent back to the Soviet Union. After crossing her Russian "comrades" at the conferences a few times, she reported: "They say that I had to leave Russia because I betrayed them and because I was a spy, or they would say that I am not A.B. but another person paid to substitute for her or that the American government paid me 15,000 lira [about $100 today] a day and so on."[13]

Angelica next to Giuseppe Saragat, at the International Socialist Congress in Milan, translating his speech into different languages, including Japanese, October 1952 (collection of Giorgio Giannelli).

She understood only too well how lucky she had been to leave her country while Lenin was still alive. Summarizing her feelings in a letter to Ella Wolfe, she wrote:

> I was and I am privileged; I found what I was looking for: an approach to life and interpretation of events which fully satisfied me, and the possibility to live accordingly, not remaining a parasite as I was supposed to be, given the surroundings in which I was born, the rest came by itself...
>
> In comparison with such a life the rest has very little importance.... In my life I had two <u>very great</u> fortunes: I was able to leave the surroundings in which I was born, and have been still more fortunate having been able to leave Russia as soon as I felt and understood what was going on and maturing there, such good fortune!!![14]

Angelica, in the center, with Diva Benetti to her left and Maria Lombardo to her right, Milan, 1960s (collection of Marina Cattaneo).

Had she stayed there, her fate would have been doomed, along with that of the rest of her family—if not during the Stalin purges, then later during the massive killings of Jews in the Ukraine during World War II.

Angelica's political relations in Italy were more complicated than one might have hoped. She continued calling for a social revolution. But after the war, in the mind of the general public, revolution was associated with more bloodshed. No one heard or understood the "social" part of her call, and her speeches were not welcome. Her efforts to explain to workers that having "comfortable apartments and televisions" was a good achievement, but it was not the end of the fight, that there was a necessity for global changes in society that would prevent the abuse of human rights, and provide equality of wealth for all nations, were not understood.

"Life seems to want to prove to us," she wrote, "that as terrible as the past and present may seem—the future is still worse. To me all this is only another incentive to work, to encourage, to fight—as modest as the results may be."[15]

Angelica possibly foresaw a near future in which most of the wealth would belong to an even smaller group of people than during her time, making some nations much poorer than others, and in which socialism would need to be much more humanitarian. She realized that during her lifetime these changes would be impossible:

"No optimism, my dear friends, no illusions about what I may be able to achieve," explained Angelica to Ella, "only an almost selfish desire not to be a parasite."[16]

Misjudged, confronted by her past, she confessed to Ella in another letter that she regularly had "to defend [herself] against being considered or suspected of being a communist ... or to try to make believe that [she was] paid by America..." and was constantly reminded of her past with Mussolini.[17]

Not wanting to see her and her revolutionary speeches circulate, the Italian socialists even put her into a psychiatric clinic. "It was terrible," remembered Giorgio Giannelli, who found out about it and rushed to save his "surrogate mother." "I went to see her as soon as I heard about her ordeal. I was told that she was ill and put away. When I came to visit her it was a house for mad people. She was kept in a small room with bars on the windows." He told the authorities that he would write about it in the papers if they did not let her out. After nearly four months in the clinic, Angelica was liberated. She spent another two months in Giorgio's home to recover, and then she left. "Where did she go?" explained the journalist in one of his interviews, "she was like a nomad. She was always invited to big events, to give lectures in small towns. What did she do in my house? She spoke on the phone. People called her from everywhere. God knows in how many languages she talked."[18]

Nonetheless, Angelica was happy. She found her new ideal politician and man whom she could promote and support: Giuseppe Saragat. Let down by Lenin and Mussolini, she was sure that she had chosen a winner this time. Upon arrival in Rome from the United States, she became a member of the Socialist Party of Italian workers that Saragat had created. When Giuseppe Saragat was elected president of Italy in 1964, it was not least due to Angelica's incessant work.[19] She stood next to him on the podiums, barely coming to up to his shoulder, translating his speeches into foreign languages, to all nationalities present at the meetings, Japanese included.

Unwelcome in Italy, yet she was invited all over Europe to give speeches as a sort of icon of freedom fighters that could be moved around to support the cause. A close friend of Ben Gurion and Golda Meir, in 1961 she went to Israel. Possibly her first flight on a plane, the voyage was followed by a two-week stay in Tel-Aviv. She reported on her stay excitedly, emphasizing "not only attending many receptions organized by Ben Gurion … but … the visits and letters and … meetings with people who knew me in Europe or whose parents and relations were dead or had been assassinated were my parent's relations or others who had known my relations or had read my books.… I made most of my speeches in Yiddish!! I did not want to speak for the English- or Russian-speaking minority; not only did people understand me but the newspapers praised my Yiddish!!" continued Angelica, explaining to

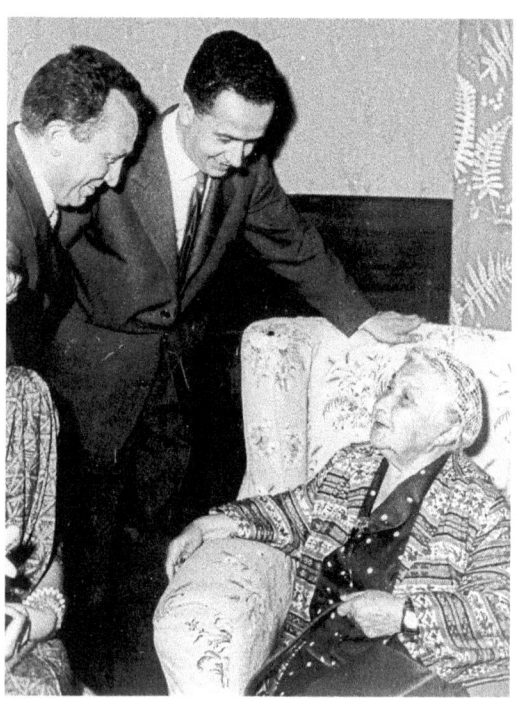

With Italian politicians Italo Viglianesi and Flavio Orlandi, 1960s (collection of Marina Cattaneo).

Ella that she had not spoken Yiddish "for [the] more than 60 years" since she had been "away from Russia...."[20]

Over the course of her life, Angelica had never received any awards. Considering that her work frequently had to be anonymous, she had never looked for any public recognition. But she received her accolades in so many other ways. Among her remaining correspondence is a letter from Giovanni Buitoni, the owner of the pasta business. In his letter dated 1959,

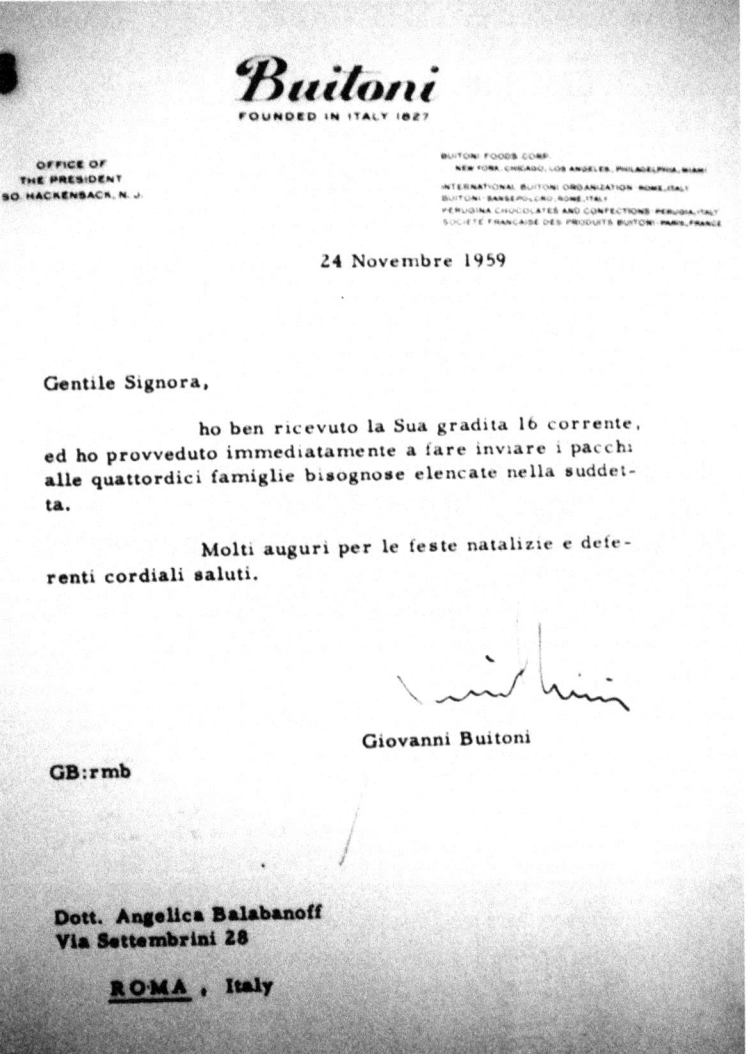

Giovanni Buitoni, letter to Angelica, 1959 (collection of Marina Cattaneo).

he confirmed to her that he had sent food parcels to 14 families in need, indicated on her list, and that he would continue to remain at her disposal.[21]

Gratitude for her lifelong deeds was best expressed by Norman Thomas, who wrote to Angelica: "It is the world which is a better place because you have been in it."[22]

One year before her death, having been suffering for some time from the "hardening of arteries," Angelica's health suddenly worsened and made her sometimes lapse "into a status of absence of mind and of blurred reasoning."[23] During the summer of 1964 she was taken to a nursing home near Rome. By coincidence it was a "commie" home with posters of known communists on the walls and staff singing *Bandiera Rossa* (Red Flag) in the evening. Rather curiously, the home was called *Rocca di Papa*, Rock of the Pope. "Situated at an altitude of 1200 feet," the air was much cooler there than in Rome, and hopes were high that she would at least partially recover.[24] But Angelica no longer realized what was going on around her and failed to recognize the posters of the known communists in her room, just happily nodding along to the rhymes of the communist songs.

The bill of $800 per month for her "living nurse medical assistance and so forth" was entirely paid by Giuseppe Saragat.[25] Upon leaving *Rocca di Papa*, she moved to her last residence, on 26 *Via Valchizone*, a home for socialist women, where she was taken care of by a few friends. "My wife," remembered Giorgio Giannelli, "helped her to take her shower. She was so small. It was like bathing a little pony."

Angelica would not be Angelica had she not been surrounded by mysteries until her last days.

"Before she died," recalled Marina Cattaneo, "she was calling her Mother. She was saying: '*Mamushka, Mamushka*,' we thought it meant 'Mama' in Ukrainian."[26]

So, not only did Angelica call out for Anna Hoffmann, after rebelling all her life against her mother's values and being cursed by her, but she called her in Russian, the language she had never used to address her mother. They used French as the language of communication in the family.

Angelica died on November 25 at 9:35 a.m. The funeral was attended by barely 200 people. Her coffin was carried from *via di Tritone* to the *Piazza del Popolo*, People's Square, passing by pretty Spanish Steps and the scenic and medieval *via del Babuino*. Notably absent was Giuseppe Saragat, who sent a telegram. *The New York Times* wrote an obituary of the one who "Attacked Lenin's Strategy," and "Turned Against Mussolini," "Found Mussolini; Turned on 'Isms' Later," said *The New York Herald Trib-*

Angelica's funeral, 1965. Ivan Matteo Lombardo is in the dark glasses (collection of Marina Cattaneo).

une. As with most foreigners and non-believers in Rome, she was buried in the Non-Catholic cemetery—a beautiful place with cypress trees, wildflowers, and three-colored cats. The cemetery boasts the tombs of the 19th-century English poets Shelley and Keats, as well as many known historical personalities who died in the Eternal City at a time when bodies were not transported back to their native land.

Angelica's possessions included 326 books, three mugs, a few articles of clothing, and two bank accounts, in Rome and New York. Her will stated "please burn all papers…" but most of her personal papers had either already been burnt by her, leaving many questions about her past unresolved, or given to The International Institute of Social History (IISH) in Amsterdam.[27]

To general astonishment, after her death, Giorgio Giannelli, the executor of her will, was contacted by the Council of the Austrian Embassy in Rome. Angelica was an Austrian citizen. She never obtained an Italian passport. Giorgio thought that this had been because she did not want the passport of the country that harbored a Pope; she also always maintained that she never wanted to ask anything from Saragat for herself.

Angelica's grave in Rome, at the Non-Catholic Cemetery (author's photograph).

The Austrian officials claimed their right to her inheritance. Her possessions being rather meager, the representatives took all the German books. The rest were donated to a library in Rome. The money from her account in Italy, 1,550,000 lira, was donated to the Humanitarian Institute in Milan to be used to establish a scholarship for gifted students. Her possessions in New York—a savings account with a few hundred dollars and some books—were handled by the executor of her will in the States, Norman Thomas. He gave the money for the cause of the underprivileged and books to a local library. All that is left of the eternal revolutionary today is a street and a music school named after her in Rome.

From a Letter of
Frances Grant to Angelica Balabanoff

"It must be a great source of real gratification to you to realize how much you have accomplished in your lifetime. I realize that, to a person like yourself whose objectives are so great, the accomplishment may seem comparatively little but that is only because you sights are set so high. We who see you and can appreciate your achievements, stand in constant admiration. For me, one of the most impressive things about you is the fact that you live your philosophy not merely articulate it."[28]

Afterword:
Ten Birth Dates

I would like to says a few words at the end about a laborious research I have been through to find Angelica's date of birth. Whether it was female coquetry, spy mania, or a craving for mystery, throughout her life she obstinately hid this date. She had used at least ten of them. Every time I came across a new document, I was sure to find a new date. They changed as often as she changed her country of residence. The dates varied from the 4th to the 26th, from May to August, and from 1869 to 1878. The revolutionary used every opportunity to modify it.

The cover page of Angelica's folder in the Swiss Federal Archives in Berne has two dates of birth—August 8, 1877, and May 4, 1875. One of her passports claimed her birth date as August 4, 1877; another stated July 14—obviously implying the day of surrender of the Bastille. When registering at the New University of Brussels, in the student registration form, she wrote a date that looked like it could have been April 26, 1897 or 1847. Later, when registering for the second year her of her studies, she neglected to put any date at all, while other students dutifully provided this information.

The French counter-espionage file started on Angelica in 1933 in Paris indicated May 4, 1875, as her date of birth in the Swiss file, probably relying on the information provided by the Swiss police. More dates appeared in her FBI file and in the obituaries, the "official" one considered that on her tombstone—August 4, 1877.

When questioned about her date of birth by the Swiss Federal agents, who realized that they had one date too many, she answered that she was "not sure herself about the exact date of birth."[1]

When I started this work in December of 2009, I was far from imagining that months would go by before I would be able to find the real date.

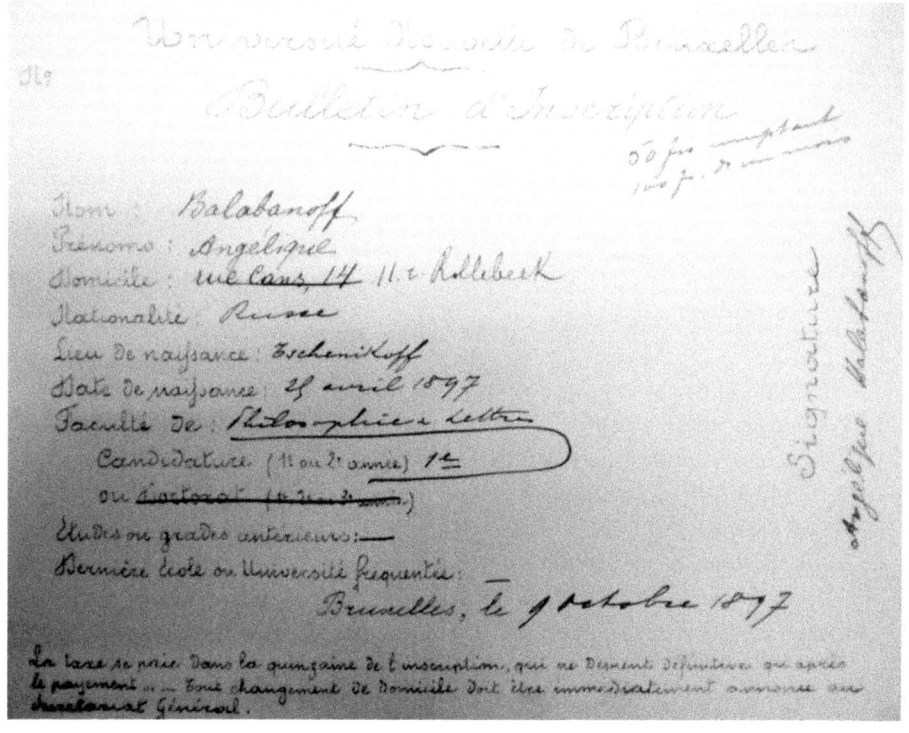

New University of Brussels, student registration form, October 1897. When registering, in the student registration form, Angelica wrote a date that looked like it could have been April 26, 1897, or 1847 (Archives, Bibliothèques et Patrimoine de l'ULB, Fonds de l'Université Nouvelle de Bruxelles [1849–1919], 01Z, author's photograph).

I was determined to find it. After all, why would a simple person need so many birth dates and what did she try to achieve by claiming to be younger than she really was?

Angelica maintained an extensive correspondence with numerous people, and I was hoping to find more information in one of her letters. Hundreds of letters addressed to her by her friends and colleagues exist and are mainly housed in the Institute of Social History in Amsterdam. At first it seemed impossible that none of them would have any mention of the real date. However, she had warned people on a number of occasions that she would destroy all documents that contained private information, her date of birth certainly included. She kept her word. After dedicating five days to reading through her letters in the archives in Amsterdam, I learnt a lot of interesting details about her life, but I came across no exact date of birth.

I hoped that Angelica's friends were more attentive to the possible historical importance of her correspondence. I was partly right. Even when she specifically asked them to "destroy it," they frequently turned her letters over to the archives in various universities in Europe and in the United States. I read through piles of pages written by Angelica in which she described her life, deeds, and emotions, but not her birth date. She appears to have never mentioned it to anyone.

My last hope was that as a known public figure, she must have celebrated her birthdays and received presents from friends and well-wishers from all over the world. To my surprise, Angelica celebrated her birthday publicly only once. It was on December 6, 1940, in New York, where she lived in exile during World War II. Her friends sponsored a dinner in the Hotel Diplomat to mark her 60th birthday and 40 years of working for the socialist cause. Both dates were symbolically rounded down.

In 1948, only eight years later, her friends decided to organize another public dinner to celebrate her 70th birthday and 50 years of working for the cause. This time, she refused any celebrations:

"One more banquet in a world in which hunger and want are rampant seemed singularly inappropriate at this time."[2] The dinner was cancelled, as was my opportunity to find out more about my heroine.

Angelica knew that she would not be able to avoid an obvious question: "When is your birthday?" For occasional celebrations she had invented herself a rule: "When people wanted to make me a surprise [*sic*] for my birthday, I asked them to make it in occasion of the Mayday."[3] Labor Day was the favorite holiday of the secretive revolutionary.

I was about to abandon my investigation when the tedious research finally yielded some results. Angelica's day and month of birth were mentioned in a letter, addressed to her by her niece Lida, a daughter of her elder brother Victor. The document is kept in the RGASPI (Russian State Archives of Social-Political History) in Moscow and miraculously survived being torn up and thrown away by its recipient. On May 8, (according to the Julian calendar) 1916, Lida sent birthday wishes to her aunt:

"I'm writing to you today because I, and all of us, think a lot about you and in our thoughts, we wish you all the best. I remember your birthday that we celebrated when we were together and would like to go back to this time.... I hope this letter will reach you and when you will be reading it, you will know that today we are with you in our thoughts, even though these greetings are belated."[4]

I thus had Angelica's date of birth—May 8. The year was more difficult to establish, but she made a few slips of the pen when writing to her friends. On January 15, 1959, she wrote to her American friend Kathleen Crowe: "I entered the ninth decade of life and do not feel tired or even old."[5] Therefore, all things considered, Angelica must have been born on May 8, 1869.

I tried to understand why she would have so many dates of birth. Such subterfuge did not match her image as an austere, unfashionable, and hard-line socialist. Part of the answer most certainly goes back to the time when she broke ties with her family and left Chernigov to live in Europe. How old was she at this moment—28, or around 19, as indicated her numerous passports? Surely, leaving at 19 sounded more unique and courageous, while being 28 made this act much less remarkable.

The question about her real age brought up another uncomfortable question for Angelica: that of a possible early marriage in the Ukraine, to her distant cousin and an ardent socialist, Mikhail Balabanoff, which I have already described in the chapter about her early years. Never in her life did Angelica refer to this marriage, making the whole issue questionable, though highly possible. Firstly, if she had left her native town at the age of 28, she was certain to have been married. The pressure of society for a woman to be married was too strong to resist, even for Angelica. Secondly, the marriage to a socialist cousin would explain Angelica's seniority in the Russian Communist Party, for which she had applied during the Russian Revolution in 1917. She was given 25-year seniority (!), dating her first work for the party to 1893, making her marriage to Mikhail Balabanoff and some early work for the socialist cause possible.

In the end, not only had my little investigation been successful, but I also found an explanation for the date of birth written on Angelica's tombstone in the Protestant cemetery in Rome. The date, August 4, 1877, was provided to the cemetery after her death by one of the executors of Angelica's will and her long-time friend, Ivan Matteo Lombardi. During my interview with his granddaughter, Marina Cattaneo, in Milan, she revealed to me: "A few days before her death Angelica asked my grandparents to declare this date as her official birth date."[6] Angelica simply chose the date that looked good to her. The Russian revolutionary had thus skillfully orchestrated all information related to this delicate matter from the beginning to the end.

Chapter Notes

Preface

1. Florence, R. *Marx's Daughters: Eleanor Marx, Rosa Luxemburg, Angelica Balabanoff.* New York: Dial Press, 1975.
Slaughter, J. "Humanism versus Feminism in the Socialist Movement: The Life of Angelica Balabanoff." *Social Science Journal* 14. Ed. Jane Slaughter and Robert Kern. Westport CT: Greenwood Press, 1981, pp. 179–194.
Mullaney, M. M. "The Female Revolutionary as Pariah." *Revolutionary Women: Gender and the Socialist Revolutionary Role.* New York: Praeger, 1983, pp. 149–189.
2. *Suisse-Russie. Contacts et ruptures.* Editions Paul Haupt Berne. Stuttgart: Vienne, 1956.

Introduction

1. AB. Letter to Ella Wolfe. October 2, 1961. HIA/BWC, Box 2, Folder 62.

Chapter I

1. "Chernigov." *Wikipedia.* July 12, 2011. http://ru.wikipedia.org/wiki/Chernigov.
2. *Ibid.*
3. Despite prominent origins of the Balabanoff family it is impossible to find Angelica's name in any of the parish birth registrars of Chernigov. Such documents are non-existent. Most of the churches and the parish documents had long since burnt, destroyed during the Russian Revolution in 1917 as unnecessary elements of the bourgeois and capitalist past. The constructions holding these documents being made out of wood, as most of the buildings in the region, had facilitated this destruction. For the entire town of Chernigov, there is only one parish birth registry that belonged to Voznesenskaya Church and there are no such records for the suburbs.
4. Balabanoff, A. Unexamined (circa 1920–1972). Saxe Commins Papers, Box 1, Folder 13. Manuscripts Division, Department of Rare Books and Special Collections, Princeton University Library, p. 3.
5. Balabanoff, A. *My Life as a Rebel.* Bloomington: Indiana University Press, 1973, pp. 5–6.
6. Saxe Commins Papers, pp. 7–8.
7. AB. Letter to Emma Goldman. July 7, 1925. IISH/EG.
8. Saxe Commins Papers, p. 3.
9. *Ibid.,* p. 10.
10. *Ibid.,* p 9.
11. *Ibid.,* p. 3.
12. Dickens, Ch. *David Copperfield.* London: Collins, 1968, p. 167.
13. Giorgio Giannelli. Personal Interview. December 27, 2011.

Chapter II

1. ISB—International Socialist Bureau, the permanent organization of the Second International, established in 1900. It was based in Brussels and met between congresses to manage and organize the work of the Second International and its subsequent congresses.
2. Balabanoff, A. *My Life as a Rebel,* p. 12.
3. AB. Letter to Ella Wolfe. September 2, 1956. HIA/BWC, Box 2, Folder 60.
4. *Ibid.,* p. 14.
5. *Ibid.,* p. 15.
6. AB. Letter to Célestin Demblon. January 16, 1878. Célestin Demblon Papers. Special Reserve Collection. Free University of Brussels, Brussels.
7. Demblon, C. *Les Wallonnes, Trois Miettes retrouvés.* Wallonie, Revue Mensuel, 2ème année 1887, des presses de H. Vaillant-

Carmanne, à Liége, p. 83. *op. cit.* (Tr. Maria Lafont: Let's Fly! oh! but faster, to the great ideal! Far from the churlish days, far from the past of the vassals, Madly! let's fly to the splendid future, Mystic, loving, garnet, orange, gay, lucid!).
   8. Balabanoff, A. *My Life as a Rebel*, p. 20.
   9. Balabanoff, CCXXXVIII, Minutes of the Exams, Faculty of Philosophy and Letters, Archives of the New University of Brussels, Free University of Brussels, Brussels.
   10. Lämmel, Roy. "Re: Request of Information on Angelica Balabanoff 1899." Message to the author. April 4, 2011. E-mail.
   11. Balabanoff, A. *My Life as a Rebel.* p. 21.
   12. The German Royal Family.

Chapter III

   1. Balabanoff, A. *My Life as a Rebel*, p. 22.
   2. Rosa Luxemburg. Letter to Clara Zetkin. June 4, 1907. Luxemburg, R. *Band 2 Gesammelte Briefe.* Berlin: Karl Dietz Verlag, 1993, pp. 294–295.
   3. AB. Letter to Célestin Demblon. January 16, 1878. Célestin Demblon Papers. Special Reserve Collection. Free University of Brussels.
   4. Balabanoff, A. *Impressions of Lenin.* Ann Arbor: University of Michigan Press, 1965, p. 6.
   5. The newspaper *Iskra* was published in Munich from 1900 to 1902, then moved to London in the spring of 1902. Its editorial board was spread around Europe but continued to have a significant Russian community.
   6. Kelly, Judy. "Re: Request of Information on Angelica Balabanoff." Message to the author. August 9, 2012. E-mail.
   7. Senn, A.E. *The Russian Revolution in Switzerland, 1914–1917.* Madison: University of Wisconsin Press, 1971, p. 122.
   8. Jean-Jacques Marie. Personal Interview. October 12, 2012.

Chapter IV

   1. Balabanoff, A. *My Life as a Rebel*, p. 27.
   2. AB. Letter to Kathleen Crowe. February 12, 1948. UT/KC.
   3. Saxe Commins Papers, p. 15.
   4. *Ibid.*, p. 17.
   5. CH-BAR#E21#1000/131, Nr. 7548, Elena Pensuti. N 11858. July 2, 1906. 1903–1906, SFA.
   6. AB. Newspaper interview. Undated. Folder 1, IISH/AB.
   7. *Suzanne Girault: A French Woman in the Russian Revolution.* Office of Radio and Television Broadcasts, France, Jean Balensi 1907–1967, Suzanne Girault Archives 1944–1968, 265J4. Dir. Georges Grauier. French Communist Party Archives. The Departmental Archives of Bobigny, Bobigny.
   8. CH-BAR#E21#1000/131, Nr. 5231, AB. June 30, 1906. 1904–1932, SFA.
   9. AB. Letter to Ella Wolfe. March 11, 1947. HIA/BWC, Box 2, Folder 60.
   10. *Op.cit.*, November 14, 1948. Box 2, Folder 60.
   11. *Op.cit.*, February 1, 1953. Box 2, Folder 60.
   12. AB. Letter to Kathleen Crowe. February 12, 1948. UT/KC.
   13. AB. Letter to Ella Wolfe. July 23, 1947. HIA/BWC, Box 2, Folder 61.
   14. AB. Letter to Ella Wolfe. December 30, (unclear) 1953. HIA/BWC, Box 2, Folder 61.
   15. Balabanoff, A. *My Life as Rebel*, p. 19.
   16. CH-BAR#E21#1000/131, Nr. 5231, AB. N 339. August 24, 1904. 1904–1932, SFA.

Chapter V

   1. Saxe Commins Papers, p. 23.
   2. Giorgio Giannelli. Personal Interview. December 27, 2011.
   3. Balabanoff, A. *My Life as a Rebel*, pp. 47–48.
   4. Olla, R. *Il Duce and His Women.* Richmond, UK: Alma Books, 2011, p. 67.
   5. Giorgio Giannelli. Personal Interview, *op. cit.*
   6. *Ibid.*, p 101.
   7. Saxe Commins Papers, pp. 20–21.
   8. CH-BAR#E21#1000/131, Nr. 8599, AB. N 5. February 13, 1904. 1903–1930, SFA.
   9. The Russian proverb "To firmly believe in something as if it was a stone wall," is an equivalent of the English saying "as if it was made of steel."

Chapter VI

   1. Pulina, Paolo. "Maria Giudice, una vita dedicata alle lottie sociali sindicali." *Il Lunedì.* November 17, 2003. http://www.cgil.pavia.it/centenario/maria_giudice.htm. 26 February 2012. tr. Federica Prina.
   2. Eschelman, N. G. "Forging a Socialist Women's Movement: Angelica Balabanoff in Switzerland." Ed. Caroli, B.B. *The Italian Immigrant Women in North America.* Toronto: The Multicultural History Society of Ontario, 1978, pp. 44–75, p. 55.
   3. Eschelman, N. G., p. 59.

4. Balabanoff, A. *La Chiesa al servizio del capitale, relazione di Angelica Balabanoff. I Preti e l'emigrazione*, relazione ... di Angelo Oliviero Olivetti. Lugano: Cooperativa tipografica sociale, 1904, p. 29.
5. Eschelman, N.G., p. 50.
6. CH-BAR#E21#1000/131, Nr. 8599, AB. August 6, 1904. 1903–1930, SFA.
7. Balabanoff, A. *La Chiesa al servizio del capitale, relazione di Angelica Balabanoff. I Preti e l'emigrazione*, relazione ... di Angelo Oliviero Olivetti. Lugano: Cooperativa tipografica sociale, 1904
8. Balabanoff, A. *My Life as a Rebel*, p. 35.
9. *Ibid.*, p. 37.
10. *Ibid.*
11. "Italian Unrest. Freethinkers and Strikers." *Nelson Evening Mail*. Issue 179, September 22, 1904: 3. National Library of New Zealand. http://www.paperspast.natlib.govt.nz/cgi
12. AB. Letter to Ella Wolfe. January 12, 1964. HIA/BWC, Box 2, Folder 62.
13. Saxe Commins Papers, pp. 19–20.

Chapter VII

1. CH-BAR#E21#1000/131, Nr. 5231, AB. *La Gazette de Lausanne*, N 19. January 23, 1906. 1904–1932, SFA.
2. Liffran, F. *Margherita Sarfatti: l'égérie du Duce*. Paris: Seuil, 2009, p. 146.
3. CH-BAR#E21#1000/131, Nr. 14194, *Nucleo-Socialista*, 1905–1907, SFA.
4. CH-BAR#E21#1000/131, Nr. 8599, AB. N 7/32. July 2, 1906. 1903–1930, SFA.
5. *Ibid.*
6. Balabanoff, A. *My Life as a Rebel*, pp. 77–78.
7. CH-BAR#E21 1000/131, Nr. 8599, AB. *Journal de Lausanne*. N 153. July 14, 1906. 1903–1930, SFA.
8. CH-BAR#E21 1000/131, Nr. 8599, AB. N 335, September 2, 1906. 1903–1930, SFA.
9. *Ibid.*, letter report addressed to the Prefect of the district of Neuchatel. October 27, 1906.

Chapter VIII

1. AB, file 19940508—art. 125, file 19940434—art. 39, n. 2941, The National Archives of France, Central Directorate of General Intelligence, Fontainebleau.
2. "La Camarade Angelica." *La Gazette de Lausanne*. November 7, 1918. Online archives, http://www.letempsarchives.ch/.

Chapter IX

1. Balabanoff, A. *Impressions of Lenin*, p. 7.
2. Balabanoff, A. *My Life as a Rebel*, pp. 54–55.
3. At the Second Congress of the Social Democratic Labour Party in London in 1903, there was a dispute between Vladimir Lenin and Julius Martov, two of SDLP's leaders. Lenin argued for a small party of professional revolutionaries with a large fringe of non-party sympathizers and supporters. Martov disagreed, believing it was better to have a large party of activists. Julius Martov based his ideas on the socialist parties that existed in other European countries, such as the British Labour Party. Lenin argued that the situation was different in Russia, as it was illegal to form socialist political parties under the Tsar's autocratic government. At the end of the debate Martov won the vote 28–23. Vladimir Lenin was unwilling to accept the results and formed a faction known as the Bolsheviks. Those who remained loyal to Martov became known as Mensheviks.
4. Rappaport, H. *Conspirator: Lenin in exile*. New York: Basic Books, c 2010.
5. Balabanoff, A. *Impressions of Lenin*, p. 17.
6. Rappaport, H., p. 167.
7. Balabanoff, A. *My Life as a Rebel*, pp. 74–75.
8. Balabanoff, A. *Impressions of Lenin*, p. 7.
9. *Ibid.*, p. 7.
10. *Ibid.*, p. 27.
11. Balabanoff, A. *My Life as a Rebel*, p. 93.
12. *Ibid.*, p. 94.

Chapter X

1. Rivera, D. *My Art Life – An Autobiography (with Gladys March)*, http://fr.scribd.com/doc/147888915/21613010-Diego-Rivera-My-Art-My-Life.
2. Milza, P. *Mussolini*. Paris: A. Fayard, 1999, p. 76.
3. Olla, R. *Il Duce and His Women*. Richmond: Alma Books, 2011, p. 116.
4. *Ibid.*, p. 5.
5. Balabanoff, A. *Traitor*. New York: G. Popolizio, 1942–1943, p. 61.
6. *Ibid.*, p. 82.
7. Sarfatti, M.G. *Mussolini l'homme et le chef*. Traduit de l'italien par Maria Croci et Eugène Marsan. Paris: A. Michel, 1927, p. 91.
8. Shepherd, N. A. *Price Below Rubies: Jewish Women as Rebels and Radicals*. London: Weidenfeld & Nicolson, 1993, p. 70.
9. *Ibid.*, p. 84.
10. La Vigne, C. *Anna Kuliscioff: From*

Russian Populism to Italian Socialism. New York: Garland, 1991, p. 219.
11. *Ibid.*, p. 217.
12. *Ibid.*, Anna Kuliscioff. Letter to Filippo Turati. November 28, 1912. From CTK EMS-T.
13. Saba, M. A. *Anna Kuliscioff: vita privata e passione politica.* Milan: A. Mondadori, 1993, p. 222.
14. Mullaney, M. M. "The Female Revolutionary as Pariah." *Revolutionary Women: Gender and the Socialist Revolutionary Role.* New York: Praeger, 1983, p. 179.
15. Liffran, F. *Margherita Sarfatti: l'égérie du Duce.* Paris: Seuil, 2009, p. 172.
16. *Ibid.*, p. 75.
17. Rivera, D. *My Art Life—An Autobiography (with Gladys March).*
18. Olla, R. *Il Duce and His Women*, pp. 125–126, from Leda Rafanelli, *Una Donna and Mussolini*, Milan: Rizzoli, 1946.

Chapter XI

1. Victor Balabanoff. Letter to AB. July 31, 1916. A.I. Balabanova, 286/51 RGASPI, Moscow.
2. Lida Balabanova. Letter to AB. July 31, 1916. A.I. Balabanova, *op. cit.*
3. AB. Letter to L.I. Balabanoff, 1903. A.I. Balabanova, *op. cit.*
4. *Ibid.*
5. Leonid Balabanoff. Letter to AB. January 3, 1915. Folder 172, IISH/AB.
6. CH-BAR#E21#1000/131, Nr. 8599, AB. *Journal de Jura*, N 42. N 324. February 20, 1914. 1903–1930. SFA.
7. *Journal du Jura* N 46, *op. cit.*
8. N 724, February 21, 1914, *op. cit.*
9. Lida Balabanova. Letter to AB. September 27/October 10, 1916. A.I. Balabanova. 286/51, RGASPI.
10. Balabanoff, A. *My Life as a Rebel*, p. 126.
11. Eschelman, N. G., pp. 47–48.

Chapter XII

1. Victor Balabanoff. Letter to AB. July 31, 1916. A.I. Balabanova, 286/51, RGASPI.
2. Lida Balabanova. Letter to AB. December 28, 1914. A.I. Balabanova, *op. cit.*
3. Rappaport, H., p. 272.
4. Farnsworth, B. *Alexandra Kollontai: Socialism, Feminism and Bolshevik Revolution.* Stanford: Stanford University Press, 1980, p. 57.
5. Balabanoff, A. *Impressions of Lenin*, p. 41.
6. Balabanoff, A. *My Life as a Rebel*, pp. 131–132.
7. *Ibid.*, p. 134
8. Clara Zetkin. Letter to AB. April 9, 1915. A.I. Balabanova. 286/51, RGASPI.
9. CH-Bar#21#1000/131, Nr. 8916, Robert Grimm. 1911–1934, SFA.
10. Balabanoff, A. *Impressions of Lenin*, p. 43.
11. Reminiscences, Unpublished. Miscellaneous material on different subjects written by AB destined for a publication of her memories, c. 1960, Folder 216, IISH/AB.
12. Balabanoff, A. *My Life as a Rebel*, p. 149.

Chapter XIII

1. By dating Angelica's work in the party back to 1893, the Bolsheviks had probably taken into account her marriage to Mikhail Balabanov, an active revolutionary, and some underground leftist work that she might have done during this time in Chernigov.
2. Balabanoff, A. *Impressions of Lenin*, p. 29.
3. Balabanoff, A. *My Life as a Rebel*, p. 175.
4. M. Litvinov. Letter to AB. Undated. A.I. Balabanova. 286/51, RGASPI.
5. Balabanoff, A. *My Life as a Rebel*, p. 173.
6. "L'agitatrice Balabanoff condamnée par les terroristes." *Le Matin.* 6 March 1918. On-line *Le Matin* Archives 1884–1944 http://gallica.bnf.fr/ark:/12148/cb328123058/date.
7. Service, R. *Lenin: A Biography.* Cambridge: Harvard University Press, 2010, p. 221.

Chapter XIV

1. AB. Letter to Ella Wolfe. December 6, 1959. HIA/BWC, Box 2, Folder 61.
2. "On Lenin." AB. Radio Interview. Radio Liberty, Munich, Germany, 1958. Columbia University, New York.
3. Balabanoff, A. *Impressions of Lenin*, p. 11.
4. Balabanoff, A. *My Life as a Rebel*, p. 192.
5. Raphael Abramovitch. Letter to AB. September 28, 1961. Folder 7, IISH/AB.
6. Boris Nikolaevsky. Letter to AB. July 4, 1959. Folder 98, *op. cit.*

Chapter XV

1. CH-BAR#E3120B#1997/17#4. L. Haas. Letter to Philippe Zutter. December 9, 1965. SFA.
2. Philippe Zutter. Letter to L. Haas. February 21, 1966, *op. cit.*

3. L. Haas. Letter to Philippe Zutter. February 28, 1966, op. cit.

Chapter XVI

1. *Suisse-Russie. Contacts et ruptures.* Editions Paul Haupt Berne. Stuttgart. Vienne. 1956.
2. CH-BAR#E21#1000/131, Nr. 8670, Rosa Bloch. February 18, 1921, 1919–1922, SFA.
3. "Undesired/Russia." *Gazette de Lausanne.* October 24, 1918. www.letempsarchives.ch/.
4. Balabanoff, A. *My Life as a Rebel,* p. 192.
5. CH-BAR#E21 1000/131, Nr. 8599, AB. N 99. October 26, 1918. 1903–1930, SFA.
6. CH-BAR#E21 1000/131, Nr. 8670, *op. cit.*
7. Balabanoff, A. *My Life as a Rebel,* p. 196.
8. "Fin de Greve à Berne." December 7, 1918. *La Gazette de Lausanne.* Online archives, www.letempsarchives.ch/.
9. Balabanoff, A. *My Life as a Rebel,* pp. 195–196.
10. *Ibid.*
11. Representative of Switzerland to Petrograd. Letter to the Federal Political Department. February 6, 1918. AF, E 2001 (B), 1/23, *Suisse—Russie. Contacts et ruptures, op. cit.*

Chapter XVII

1. Balabanoff, A. *My Life as a Rebel,* p. 201.
2. Mawdsley, E. *The Soviet elite from Lenin to Gorbachev: the Central Committee and its members, 1917–1991.* Oxford: Oxford University Press, 2000, p. 257.
3. AB. Letter to Emma Goldman. July 7, 1925. IISH/EG.
4. Margaret Grace Bondfield, Russian Diary, May 7–30, 1920, file 5 A2(1), Vassar College, CT.
5. Balabanoff, A. *Impressions of Lenin,* pp. 30–31.
6. Harrison, M. *Marooned in Moscow.* New York: Doran, 1921, p. 80.
7. Balabanoff, A. *Impressions of Lenin,* p. 45.
8. *Ibid.*
9. Harrison, M., p. 80.
10. AB. Interview. Radio Liberty, Munich, Germany, 1958, Columbia University, New York.
11. Balabanoff, A. *My Life as a Rebel,* p. 216.
12. Les Cahiers du CERMTRI, La Fondation de l'Internationale Communiste, Centre d'Etudes et de Recherches sur les Mouvements Trotskyste et Révolutionnaires Internationaux, N 133, May 2009, p. 65, Jules Humbert-Droz: L'Origine de l'Internationale Communiste.
13. AB. Radio Interview, *op.cit.*
14. Balabanoff, A. *My Life as a Rebel,* p. 220.
15. CH-BAR#E21#1000/131, Nr. 9691, Grigory Zinoviev. 1923, SFA.
16. Vaksberg, A. *Hotel Lux. Les parties frères au service de L'international communiste.* Paris: A. Fayard, 1993, pp. 16–18, tr. Maria Lafont.
17. Pierre Boichu. Personal Interview. September 10, 2012.

Chapter XVIII

1. Boichu, P. *Suzanne Girault Itineraire d'une Bolcheviuk française.* Mémoire de DEA d'Histoire. Diss. Jacques Girault. October 2000, p. 31.
2. Unpublished memoirs, Folder 216, IISH/AB.
3. AB. Letter to Boris Nikolaevsky. December 29, 1960. HIA/BWC, Box 2, Folder 58.
4. Boichu, P., pp. 33–34.
5. CH-BAR#E21#1000/131, Nr. 8599, AB. July 22, 1919. 1903–1930, SFA. Information concerning Angelica's nomination as the Governor of Odessa came from the reports in the SFA. I tried to reconfirm it with the State Archives of Odessa. Unfortunately, they did not have any information about Angelica in their files.
6. *Suzanne Girault: A French Woman in the Russian Revolution.* Office of Radio and Television Broadcasts, France, Jean Balensi 1907–1967, Suzanne Girault Archives 1944–1968, 265J4. Dir. by Georges Grauier. French Communist Party Archives. The Departmental Archives of Bobigny, Bobigny.
7. Balabanoff, A. *Impressions of Lenin,* p. 15.
8. *Ibid.,* p. 190.

Chapter XIX

1. Report 257 523. February 5, 1921. PP/AB.
2. CH-BAR#E21 1000/131, Nr. 8599, AB. N 100. January 28, 1920. 1903–1930, SFA.
3. Memo N 1224-SCR-2/11 of 15/2/21, PP/AB.
4. Report. Ministry of Internal Affairs. January 5, 1921. N 4750.U., *op. cit.*
5. Report. Police Division, Central Directorate of General Intelligence. N 768. February 5, 1921, *op. cit.*
6. Report. Ministry of Internal Affairs. September 27, 1921. N 3958.U., *op. cit.*

7. CH-BAR#E21#1000/131, Nr. 9063, Ivan Krasnopolsky. Minutes of the Hearing Process. November 26, 1923. 1923–1926, SFA.
8. CH-BAR#E21 1000/131, Nr. 8599, AB. January 15, 1920. 1903–1930, SFA.
9. The documents of the time refer to Turkestan, or the Turkestan Autonomous Soviet Socialist Republic of the Soviet Union created after the Revolution and which was eventually split into the Kazakh SSR (Kazakhstan), Kyrgyz SSR (Kyrgyzstan), Tajik SSR (Tajikistan), Turkmen SSR (Turkmenistan) and Uzbek SSR (Uzbekistan).
10. Balabanoff, A. *My Life as a Rebel*, pp. 238–239.
11. Gelb, B. *So Short a Time: A Biography of John Reed and Louise Bryant*. New York: W. W. Norton, 1973, p 268.
12. Balabanoff, A. *My Life as a Rebel*, pp. 244–245.
13. *Ibid.*, p. 252.
14. AB. Letter to Boris Nikolaevsky. January 25, 1954. HIA/BWC, Box 58, Folder 9.
15. Balabanoff, A. *My Life as a Rebel*, p. 245.
16. Goldman, E. *My Disillusionment in Russia*. London: Daniel, 1925, p. 26.
17. Goldman, E. *Living My Life*, Volume II. New York: Alfred A. Knopf, 1931, pp. 760–761.
18. Balabanoff, A. *My Life as a Rebel*, p. 249.
19. AB. Letter to Emma Goldman. June 23, 1933. IISH/EG.

Chapter XX

1. Cachin, M. *Carnets 1906–1947, Tome II, 1917–1920*, Editions établie et annotée par Gilles Canard, Brigitte Studer et Nicolas Werth. CNRS Editions, 1993, p. 452.
2. Gelb, B., p. 277.
3. Balabanoff, A. *Impressions of Lenin*, p. 114.
4. Goldman, E. *Living My Life*, p. 760.
5. Report N 13209/915/38. November 21, 1921, FO 371/6893. AB. The National Archives of the UK, London.
6. Balabanoff, A. *Impressions of Lenin*, p. 151.
7. Panné, JL. *Boris Souvarine, le premier désenchanté du communisme*. Robert Laffont, 1993, p. 99.
8. Balabanoff, A. *Impressions of Lenin*, p. 1.
9. *Ibid.*, pp. 151–152.
10. Report N 14042/915/38. December 19, 1921. AB. The National Archives of the UK, London.
11. Balabanoff, A. *Impressions of Lenin*, p. 152.

Chapter XXI

1. CH-BAR#E21 1000/131, Nr. 8599, AB. *Journal de Genève*. April 22, 1924. 1903–1930, SFA.
2. December 19, 1921, FO 371/6893, N 13209/915/38, AB. The National Archives of the UK, London.
3. Balabanoff, A. *My Life as a Rebel*, pp. 296–297.
4. *Ibid.*, p. 297.
5. Report of the Director of the General Service to the Police Commissioner. May 26, 1932. PP/AB.
6. Wolfe, B. D. "The Red Queen Victoria." *Strange Communists I Have Known*. New York: Stein & Day, 1965, p. 84.
7. FBI archives, Box 02, Rg No 65, Stack Area 230, Row 32, Compartment 42, Shelf 6, file 61, sub 4021, AB, Department of Justice, Washington, D.C..
8. AB. Letter to Ella Wolfe. October 2, 1961. HIA/BWC. Box 2, Folder 62.
9. AB. Letter to Emma Goldman. July 7, 1925. IISH/EG.
10. Emma Goldman. Letter to Fanny Barrett. April 16, 1936. Fannie Dorothy Garfinkle Barrett Papers, Reel 6, Arthur and Elizabeth Schlesinger Library on the History of Women in America, Radcliffe Institute, MA.
11. CH-BAR#E21 1000/131, Nr. 5231, AB. *Sentinelle*. N 7188. August 16, 1923. 1904–1932, SFA.
12. AB. Letter to Emma Goldman. July 7, 1925. IISH/EG.
13. Balabanoff, A. *Tears*. New York: E. Laub Publishing Co., 1943.There is no Sunshine, no Happiness at all in my Bereaved Soul, St. Tropez, 1928.
14. Unpublished Memoirs, Folder 216, IISH/AB.

Chapter XXII

1. Reminiscences. Folder 216–220, IISH/AB.
2. Ministry of Internal Affairs. July 13, 1926, N 6303 and October 23, 1926, N 267 523, PP/AB.
3. AB. Letter to Emma Goldman. December 1925, IISH/EG.
4. CH-BAR#E21#1000/131, Nr. 5231, AB. September 11, 1925. 1904–1932, SFA.
5. Report. July 25, 1931. SAR/AB.
6. Report. February 15, 1934, AB, *op. cit.*
7. AB. Letter to Emma Goldman. June 14, 1934. IISH/EG.
8. Report. April 11, 1931. SAR/AB.
9. *Op. cit.*, March 15, 1929.

10. Albert Tosoni-Pittoni. Personal Interview. July 20, 2012.
11. *Women in World History: A Biographical Encyclopedia.* Ed. Commire, A. Detroit: Yorkin Publications, Sarfatti, Margherita, p. 803.
12. Sarfatti, M. *Mussolini: L'Homme et le Chef,* p. 98.
13. "L'Ere Nouvelle." February 18, 1927. 267.523. PP/AB.
14. AB. Letter to Emma Goldman. July 7, 1932. IISH/EG.
15. Marina Cattaneo. Personal Interview. February 14, 2011.

Chapter XXIII

1. Report. March 7, 1934, SAR/AB.
2. *Op.cit.,* April 25, 1934.
3. *Op.cit.,* June 8, 1934.
4. AB. Letter to Emma Goldman. August 26, 1934. IISH/EG.
5. Report. June 27, 1934. SAR/AB.
6. *Ibid.*
7. AB. Letter to Emma Goldman. August 26, 1934. IISH/EG.
8. Balabanoff, A. *Tears.* New York: E. Laub Publishing Co., 1943. Paris, 1933. (And I would like when the time comes For me to trespass to the other side I remain quiet and calm And shall not cry, And those who will see me die Will keep from my death only one memory: MY SMILE ... tr. Maria Lafont.)
9. CH-BAR#E21#1000/131, Nr. 5231, AB. September 1934. 1904–1932, SFA
10. Poem *Mothers,* Golf Juan, 1927. Collection of Marina Cattaneo.
11. AB. Letter to Emma Goldman. August 26, 1934. IISH/EG.
12. Anonymous letter. Undated. N 267.523. 1929. PP/AB.
13. Alexander Berkman. Letter to AB. March 17, 1930. Alexander Berkman Papers, IISH.
14. Report. July 25, 1931, SAR/AB.
15. AB. Letter to Emma Goldman. October 9, 1931. IISH/EG.
16. *Op.cit.,* October 5, 1931.
17. *Op.cit.,* October 1, 1935.
18. *Op.cit.,* September 7, 1935.
19. *Op.cit.,* November 29, 1929.
20. Chamber of Commerce and Industry of Marseille Provence: CCIMP, http://www.ssmaritime.com/Excalibur.htm, June 13, 2013.

Chapter XXIV

1. AB File, Sidney Hook Collection, HIA.
2. Brochure describing the Park Plaza, circa 1939, New York Historical Society.
3. Fooltner, H. *New York, City of Cities.* Philadelphia: J.B. Lippincott, 1937, p. 269.
4. Alma Lutz, Guide to AB papers, 1941–1947, Folder 8, Balabanoff 1.8, Archives and Special Collections, Vassar College, CT.
5. *Ibid.*
6. *Ibid.*
7. AB. Letter to Lola Maverick Lloyd. April 3, 1936. NYPL/LML.
8. Norman Thomas. Letter to AB. June 25, 1936. NYPL/NT.
9. Fooltner, H., p. 298, *op. cit.*
10. AB. Letter to Emma Goldman. March 16, 1936. IISH/EG.
11. *Ibid.*
12. Bank Savings Account Book, Folder 2, IISH/AB.
13. AB. Letter to Emma Goldman. February 8, 1939. IISH/EG.
14. AB. Letter to Lola Maverick Lloyd. January 19, 1937. NYPL/LML.
15. Leon Trotsky. Letter to AB. February 3, 1937. N 7314, Trotsky Collection, HIA.
16. AB. Interview. Radio Liberty, Munich, Germany, 1958, Columbia University, New York.
17. The New York Times. August 3, 1938.
18. The New York Herald Tribune. August 7, 1938, p. 5.
19. AB. Letter to Charles Zimmerman. October 3, 1938. 5780:014, Box 3, 86, Charles Zimmerman papers, Kheel center, Cornell University, Ithaca.
20. Schlisinger Library, The Mendelsohn Papers, Reel 6, Correspondence, from Emma Goldman to Bill and Lillian Mendelsohn, July 26, 1939.
21. AB. Letter to Lola Maverick Lloyd. 26 June 1937. NYPL/LML.
22. New York Post, July 26, 1943. The Herald Tribune, July 27, 1943.
23. Saxe Commins Papers, p. 24.
24. New York Post, July 27, 1943.
25. Saxe Commins Papers, p. 20.
26. Balabanoff A. *Tears.* New York: E. Laub Publishing Co., 1943.
27. Mussolini, R. *La Mia Vita con Benito,* p. 31.
28. Ciano, E. *Témoignage pour un homme.* Propos recueillis et traduits de l'italien par Albert Zarca. Paris: Stock, 1975, p. 35.
29. Mussolini, V. *Mussolini Intime,* pp. 105–107.
30. AB. Letter to Nelson, ILGWU, L158, 51801054 Box 1, 811, April 1943, Charles Zimmerman Papers, Kheel center, Cornell University.
31. AB. Letter to Norman Thomas. January 1946. NYPL/NT.
32. Clifford Forster. Letter to Irene Silvey. September 24, 1937. Roger N. Baldwin Pa-

pers. Box 3, Folder 11, Public Policy Papers, Department of Rare Books and Special Collections, Princeton University Library.
33. Cecilia Razovsky Davidson. Letter to Roger Nash Baldwin. September 12, 1944. *Op. cit.*
34. AB. Letter to Norman Thomas. October 19, 1949. NYPL/NT.
35. AB. Letter to Roger Nash Baldwin. January 31, 1953. Roger Nash Baldwin Papers, *op. cit.*
36. AB. Letter to Kathleen Crowe. January 3, 1947. UT/KC.

Chapter XXV

1. Report to the Secretary of State. January 13, 1947. Reg No 59, Stack Area 250, Row 36, Compartment 28, shelf 7, AB, Department of State, Washington, D.C.
2. AB. Letter to Kathleen Crowe. January 20, 1947. UT/KC.
3. Department of State to the U.S. Embassy in Rome. October 14, 1947. Telegram. Reg No 59, Stack Area 250, Row 38, Compartment 17, shelf 2, AB, Department of State, Washington, D.C.
4. Telegram to the Secretary of State. October 20, 1947. Reg No 59, Stack Area 250, Row 38, Compartment 17, shelf 2, AB, *op. cit.*
5. H.W. Carlson. Letter to AB. October 27, 1947. Collection of Giorgio Giannelli.
6. AB, Box 103, File 18, Guide to Jewish Labor committee records, Part II, Holocaust, ERA Files, WAG025.2, Tamiment Library, New York.

Chapter XXVI

1. AB. Letter to Ella Wolfe. Undated. HIA/BWC, Box 2, Folder 62.
2. AB. Letter to Shmarya Kleinman. June 28, 1960. Shmarya Kleinman Collection, Walter P. Reuther Library Detroit, MI.
3. AB. Letter to Ella Wolfe. September 2, 1956. HIA/BWC, Box 2, Folder 60.
4. AB. Letter to Ella Wolfe. March 11, 1956 (?).HIA/BWC, Box 2, Folder 60.
5. Luigi Antonioni. Letter to AB. April 27, 1954. Collection of Marina Cattaneo.
6. Roger Baldwin personal note preceding AB papers in his collection, Roger N. Baldwin Papers, Box 3, Folder 11. Public Policy Papers, Department of Rare Books and Special Collections, Princeton University Library.
7. Frances Grant. Letter to Frederick Gonzalez. October 22, 1958. Frances Grant personal papers, Special Collections and University Archives, Rutgers University Libraries, NJ.
8. *Ibid.*
9. AB. Letter to Frances Grant. September 23, 1958. Frances Grant personal papers, *op. cit.*
10. AB. Letter to Ella Wolfe. Between January and August 1958. HIA/BWC, Box 2, Folder 62.
11. AB. Letter to Ella Wolfe. December 6, 1954, *op. cit.*
12. AB. Letter to Kathleen Crowe. Undated. UT/KC.
13. AB. Letter to Norman Thomas. April 1953. NYPL/NT.
14. AB. Letter to Ella Wolfe. December 12, 1962. HIA/BWC, Box 2, Folder 62.
15. AB. Letter to Frances Grant. January 15, 1953. Frances Grant personal papers, *op. cit.*
16. AB to Ella Wolfe. December 4, 1954. HIA/BWC, Box 2, Folder 60.
17. AB. Letter to Ella Wolfe. February 23, 1954, *op. cit.*
18. Giorgio Giannelli. Personal Interview. December 28, 2011.
19. *Ibid.*
20. AB. Letter to Ella Wolfe. Undated. HIA/BWC, Box 2, Folder 60.
21. Giovanni Buitoni. Letter to AB. November 24, 1959. Collection of Marina Cattaneo.
22. Norman Thomas. Letter to AB. December 19, 1961. NYPL/NT.
23. Ivan Matteo Lombardo. Letter to Harry Goldberg. July 15, 1964. HIA/ BWC, Box 2, Folder 9.
24. *Ibid.*
25. *Ibid.*
26. Marina Cattaneo. Personal Interview. February 14, 2011.
27. From the will of AB. Collection of Marina Cattaneo.
28. Francis Grant. Letter to AB. April 2, 1953. Frances Grant personal papers, *op. cit.*

Afterword

1. CH-BAR#E4320B#1975/40#188, AB. Report. City Police of Zurich. May 20, 1949. SFA.
2. Margaret DeSilver. Letter to Georgia Llyod. April 8, 1948. Georgia Lloyd papers. Manuscripts and Archives Division. The New York Public Library. Astor, Lenox, and Tilden Foundations.
3. AB. Letter to Ella Wolfe. April 16, 1957. HIA/BWC, Box 2, Folder 61.
4. Lida Balabanova. Letter to AB. May 8, 1916. A.I. Balabanova, 286/51. RGASPI.
5. AB. Letter to Kathleen Crowe. January 15, 1959. UT/KC.
6. Marina Cattaneo. Personal Interview. February 14, 2010.

Bibliography

Archives

Belgium
GOB—Grand Lodge of Belgium, Brussels
ULB—*Université Libre de Bruxelles* (Free University of Brussels)
  • New University of Brussels Archives
  • Special Reserve Collection/Célestin Demblon Papers

Canada
Thomas Fisher Rare Book library, University of Toronto, Toronto
  • Ms. Claude Stewart Collection of Kathleen Crowe/Angelica Balabanoff papers

France
CCIMP—Chamber of Commerce and Industry of Marseille Provence, Marseille
  • Information on S.S. Exeter
CERMTRI—Centre d'Etudes et de Recherches sur les Mouvements Trotskyste et Révolutionnaires Internationaux (Centre for Study and Research on the International Trotskyist and Revolutionary Movements), Paris
  • Microfilms of *Nashe Slovo* (Our Word), 1914–1916
Préfecture de Police, Remembrance and Cultural Affairs Division, Paris
  • Angelica Balabanoff file
The Departmental Archives of Bobigny, Bobigny
  • Suzanne Girault papers
The National Archives of France, Fontainebleau
  • Central Directorate of General Intelligence/Angelica Balabanoff file

Germany
Humbert University
University of Leipzig

Great Britain
The National Archives of the UK, London

Italy
Foundation of Anna Kuliscioff, Milan
State Central Archives, Rome
  • Angelica Balabanoff file
University of Sapienza, Rome

Netherlands
IISH—International Institute of Social History, Amsterdam
  • Anželika Balabanova papers
  • Lidia Dan papers
  • Emma Goldman papers
  • Alexander Berkman papers

Russia
RGASPI—Russian State Archive of Social and Political History, Moscow
  • Angelica Balabanoff Personal letters
GARF—State Archive of the Russian Federation, Moscow
  • Angelica Balabanoff file

Switzerland
SFA—The Swiss Federal Archives, Berne
Files of:
  • Angelica Balabanoff
  • Rosa Bloch
  • Maria Giudice
  • Robert Grimm
  • Alexander Krasnopolsky
  • Elena Pensuti
  • Benito Mussolini
  • Alfredo Talamini
  • Grigory Zinoviev
  • Nucleo-Socialista
Swiss Railways SBB/CFF Heritage Foundation, Berne
  • Swiss Railways Archives

Ukraine

State Archives of Chernihiv Oblast, Chernigov

State Archives of Odessa Region, Odessa

United States

Arthur and Elizabeth Schlesinger Library on the History of Women in America, Radcliffe Institute, Cambridge, MA
- Lillian and William Mendelsohn papers
- Fannie Dorothy Garfinkle Barrett papers
- Leon Malmed and Emma Goldman papers
- Frank Adelaide Schulkind papers/Angelica Balabanoff letters

Beinecke Rare Book & Manuscript Library, Yale University, New Haven, CT
- Serge Victor papers

FBI, Washington, D.C.
- Angelica Balabanoff file

HIA—Hoover Institution Archive, Stanford University, Stanford, CA
- Herman Axelbank Motion Picture Film Collection
- Bertram David Wolfe Collection
- Sidney Hook Collection
- Trotsky Collection

Kheel Center, Cornell University, University, Ithaca, NY
- Charles Zimmerman papers
- Fannia Cohn papers

Mudd Manuscript Library, Princeton, NJ
- Roger Nash Baldwin papers
- American Civil Liberties Union Records, The Roger Baldwin Years

New York Historical Society, New York, NY

NYPL—New York Public Library, New York, NY
- Manuscripts and Archives Division. Astor, Lenox, and Tilden Foundations
  ◊ Georgia Lloyd papers
  ◊ Lola Maverick Lloyd papers
  ◊ Norman Thomas papers
  ◊ Erich Fromm papers

Princeton University Library, Manuscripts Division, Department of Rare Books and Special Collections Princeton, NJ
- Saxe Commins papers

Rutgers University Libraries, Special Collections and University Archives, Newark, NJ
- Frances Grant's personal papers

Tamiment Library, New York, NY
- Holocaust, ERA Files

Vassar College, Archives and Special Collections, Poughkeepsie, CT

- Margaret Grace Bondfield papers
- Alma Lutz papers

Walter P. Reuther Library, Detroit, MI
- Shmarya Kleinman Collection

Interviews

France

Pierre Boichu, Paris
Jean-Jacques Marie, Paris
Albert Tosoni-Pittoni, Paris

Italy

Marina Cattaneo, Milan
Giorgio Giannelli, Rome
Roberto Olla, Rome

United States

Judy Kelly, VT, by e-mail

Newspapers

Gazette de Lausanne. On-line archives, www.letempsarchives.ch/.

il Lunedì. On-line archives, http://www.cgil.pavia.it/centenario/maria_giudice.htm.

Le Matin. On-line archives 1884–1944, http://gallica.bnf.fr/ark:/12148/cb328123058/date.

Nelson Evening Mail. National Library of New Zealand. On-line archives, http://www.paperspast.natlib.govt.nz/cgi.

Radio Program

Angelica Balabanoff. Radio Interviews. Radio Liberty, Munich, Germany, 1958. Columbia University, New York, NY.

Suzanne Girault: A French Woman in the Russian Revolution. Office of Radio and Television Broadcasts, France, Jean Balensi 1907–1967, Suzanne Girault Archives 1944–1968, 265J4. Dir. by Georges Grauier. French Communist Party Archives. The Departmental Archives of Bobigny, Bobigny.

Books

Balabanoff, A. *Impressions of Lenin*. Ann Arbor: University of Michigan Press, 1965.

_____. *La Chiesa al servizio del capitale*, relazione di Angelica Balabanoff. I Preti e l'emigrazione, relazione ... di Angelo Oliviero Olivetti. Lugano: Cooperativa tipografica sociale, 1904.

_____. *My Life as a Rebel*. Bloomington: Indiana University Press, 1973.
_____. *Tears*. New York: E. Laub Publishing Co., 1943.
_____. *Traitor: Benito Mussolini and His "Conquest of power."* New York: G. Popolizio, 1942–1943.
Boichu, P. *Suzanne Girault Itineraire d'une Bolchevik française*. Mémoire de DEA d'Histoire. Diss. Jacques Girault. October 2000.
Cachin, M. *Carnets 1906–1947, Tome II, 1917–1920*. Editions établie et annotée par Gilles Canard, Brigitte Studer et Nicolas Werth, CNRS Editions, 1993.
Ciano, E. *Témoignage pour un homme. Propos recueillis et traduits de l'italien par Albert Zarca*. Paris: Stock, 1975.
Clements, B.E. *Bolshevik Women*. Cambridge: Cambridge University Press, 1997.
_____ *Bolshevik Feminist. The Life of Aleksandra Kollontai*. Bloomington: Indiana University Press, c1979.
Dickens, Ch. *David Copperfield*. London: Collins, 1968.
Eschelman, N. G. "Forging a Socialist Women's Movement: Angelica Balabanoff in Switzerland." In *The Italian Immigrant Women in North America*. Ed. Caroli, B.B. Toronto: The Multicultural History Society of Ontario, 1978, pp. 44–75.
Farnsworth, B. *Alexandra Kollontai: Socialism, Feminism and Bolshevik Revolution*. Stanford: Stanford University Press, 1980.
Florence, R. *Marx's Daughters: Eleanor Marx, Rosa Luxemburg, Angelica Balabanoff*. New York: Dial Press, 1975.
Fooltner, H. *New York, City of Cities*. Philadelphia: J.B. Lippincott, 1937.
Goldman, E. *My Disillusionment in Russia*. London: Daniel, 1925.
Goldman, E. *Living My Life*. Volume II. New York: Alfred A. Knopf, 1931.
Gelb, B. *So Short a Time: A Biography of John Reed and Louise Bryant*. New York: W. W. Norton, 1973.
Harrison, M. *Marooned in Moscow*. New York: Doran, 1921.
LaVigna, C. *Anna Kuliscioff: From Russian Populism to Italian Socialism*. New York: Garland, 1991.
Les Cahiers du CERMTRI *La Fondation de l'Internationale Communiste*, Centre d'Etudes et de Recherches sur les Mouvements Trotskyste et Révolutionnaires Internationaux, N 133, May 2009.
Liffran, F. *Margherita Sarfatti: l'égérie du Duce*. Paris: Seuil, 2009.
Luxemburg, R. *Band 2 Gesammelte Briefe*. Berlin: Karl Dietz Verlag, 1993.
Mawdsley, E. *The Soviet elite from Lenin to Gorbachev: the Central Committee and its members, 1917–1991*. Oxford: Oxford University Press, 2000.
McNeal, R. *Bride of the Revolution*. Ann Arbor: University of Michigan Press, 1972.
Milza, P. *Mussolini*. Paris: A. Fayard, 1999.
Mussolini, R. *La mia vita con Benito*—1st ed. Milano: Mondadori, 1948.
Mussolini, V. *Mussolini intime*. Adaptation de Jean-Paul Sautet. Paris: Éditions France-Empire, 1973.
Mullaney, M. M. "The Female Revolutionary as Pariah." In *Revolutionary Women: Gender and the Socialist Revolutionary Role*. New York: Praeger, 1983, pp. 149–189.
Panné, JL. *Boris Souvarine, le premier désenchanté du communism*. Robert Laffont, 1993.
Rappaport, H. *Conspirator: Lenin in exile*. New York: Basic Books, 2010.
Rivera, D. *My Art Life—An Autobiography (with Gladys March)*, http://fr.scribd.com/doc/147888915/21613010-Diego-Rivera-My-Art-My-Life.
Saba, M. A. *Anna Kuliscioff: vita privata e passione politica*. Milano: A. Mondadori, 1993.
Sarfatti, M.G. *Mussolini l'homme et le chef....* Traduit de l'italien par Maria Croci et Eugène Marsan. Paris: A. Michel, 1927.
Service, R. *Lenin: A Biography*. Cambridge: Harvard University Press, 2010.
Senn, A.E. *The Russian Revolution in Switzerland, 1914–1917*. Madison: University of Wisconsin Press, 1971.
Shepherd, N. *A Price Below Rubies: Jewish Women as Rebels and Radicals*. London: Weidenfeld & Nicolson, 1993.
Slaughter J. "Humanism versus Feminism in the Socialist Movement: The Life of Angelica Balabanoff." In *Social science Journal 14*. Ed. by Jane Slaughter and Robert Kern. Westport, CT: Greenwood Press, 1981, pp. 179–194.
Stites, R. *The Women's Liberation Movement in Russia. Feminism, Nihilism and Bolshevism 1860–1930*. Princeton: Princeton University Press.
Suisse-Russie. Contacts et ruptures. Editions Paul Haupt. Stuttgart: Vienne, 1956.
Vaksberg, A. *Hotel Lux. Les parties frères au service de L'international communiste*. Paris: A. Fayard, 1993.
Wolfe, B. D. *Strange Communists I have known*. New York: Stein & Day, 1965.

Wolikow, S. *L'Internationale Communiste (1919–1943): Le Komintern Ou le Rêve Déchu du Parti Mondial de la Révolution.* Paris: Les Éditions de l'Atelier/Éditions Ouvrières, 2010.

Women in World History: A Biographical Encyclopedia. Ed. Commire, A. Detroit: Yorkin Publications, 1999.

Index

Abramovitch, Raphael 117, 220
Adler, Friedrich 166, 169, 170
Alexander III 23
Amsterdam 2, 15, 140, 150, 211, 214, 225
Andreeva, Maria 75
Anselme, Jacques Bernard d' 141
Arbeiderbladet 169, 182
Armand, Inessa 36, 100, 112, 131
Avanti! 5, 12, 82–84, 86, 87, 90, 94, 95, 97, 101, 109, 159, 175; in Paris 174, 190; in Vienna 170, 173

Balabanoff, Isaac (father) 17–19, 21, 39, 91
Balabanoff, Leon (brother) 18, 92, 93
Balabanoff, Leonid (nephew) 93, 188, 220
Balabanoff, Samuil (brother) 18, 92, 93
Balabanoff, Sergei (brother) 18, 92, 104, 105, 107
Balabanoff, Victor (brother) 18, 92, 97, 215, 220
Balabanov, Mikhail (husband) 24, 216, 220
Balabanova, Anna (sister) 18, 22, 34, 91, 104, 105, 144–146, 167, 168, 181
Balabanova, Lida (niece) 92–94, 98, 215, 220, 224
Balabanova-Hoffmann, Anna (mother) 18–25, 91, 93, 158, 210
Baldwin, Roger Nash 185, 195, 200, 203, 223, 224, 226
Barcelona 179, 180
Basel 40
Bebel, August 76
Bergnac, Yvonne de 82
Berkman, Alexander 11, 12, 182, 223, 225
Berlin 12, 31–36, 38, 76, 79, 132, 140, 149, 150, 164, 167, 175, 184, 218
Bernardy, Amy 58
Berne 2, 15, 31, 44, 48, 54, 59, 67–69, 95, 97, 98, 100, 101, 106, 118, 119, 124, 125, 127, 128, 213, 221, 225, 227
The Berne International Women's Conference 98, 100, 101
Berzin, Yan 124–127
Bissolati, Leonida 82

Bloch, Rosa 122–123, 126, 221, 225
Bloody Sunday 75
BOI 9, 71
Bolsheviks 16, 77, 78, 79, 100, 103–105, 108, 111, 114, 117, 124, 131, 132, 141, 142, 144, 151, 168, 198, 219, 220
Bondfield, Margaret Grace 131, 221, 226
Bonomi, Ivano 82
Bosporus 167
Branting, Hjalmar 160, 161, 165
Brissago 181, 183
Brooklyn 191
Bruno, Giordano 4, 63, 157
Brussels 2, 6, 11, 15, 23, 24, 26–32, 35, 38, 150, 157, 183, 213, 214, 217, 218, 225
Bryant, Louise 11, 13, 158, 182, 222
Buitoni, Giovanni 209, 224
Byron, George Gordon 179

Cabrini, Angelo 82
Cagnoni, Egisto 67
California 191
Cattaneo, Marina 5, 33, 206, 208–211, 216, 223, 224, 226
Central Asia 151–153
Chaplin, Charlie 152
Cheka 16, 132, 138, 144, 147
Chekhov, Anton 110, 137
Chernigov 1, 2, 6, 9, 17–20, 22–26, 28, 37, 42, 48, 70, 91–93, 111, 131, 137, 140, 144, 158, 186, 190, 216, 217, 220
Chicago 37
Chicherin, Georgy 135
Cold War 36
Cologne 150
Comintern 14, 16, 137–141, 144, 147, 149, 150, 153, 155, 170; *see also* Third International
Commins, Saxe 6, 217–219, 223, 226
Connecticut 191
Constantinople 140, 146, 150, 166–168, 181
Cossy, Robert 65, 68
Crowe, Kathleen (Kitty) 4, 11, 15, 45, 187, 198, 204, 216, 218, 224, 225

229

230 Index

Dalser, Ida 89
De Felice, Renzo 84
Demblon, Célestin 11, 28–30, 64, 157, 217, 218, 225
Dickens, Charles 21, 217
Drapeau Rouge 142
Il Duce 9, 50, 51, 53, 79, 83, 87, 89, 174, 175, 178–180, 218–220
Duma 75, 102
Dzerzhinsky, Felix 16, 147, 149

Eberlin, Hugo 136
Eisenstein, Sergei 142
S.S. *Exeter* "Four Aces" 183, 184, 225

FBI 7, 9, 71, 154, 166–168, 185, 197, 198, 213, 222, 226
Fels, Joseph 77, 78
Forli 80–82, 87, 88
Foundation of Angelica Balabanoff 13, 185, 194, 203
Foundation of Anna Kuliscioff 5, 225
Free University of Brussels 6, 15, 217, 218, 225
freemasons 28, 156, 161
The Freethinkers Congress of Rome 62, 63, 219
Fromm, Erich 7, 185, 226
FSB 3, 4
Funi, Achille 88

Gailland, Ugo 67
Geneva 23, 45, 52–54, 67, 75, 79, 123, 124, 151
Giannelli, Giorgio 4, 27, 51, 56, 65, 72, 119, 137, 142, 190, 195, 205, 207, 210, 211, 217, 218, 224, 226
Girault, Suzanne 42, 143–146, 155, 218, 221, 225, 226
Giudice, Maria 11, 55, 67, 218, 225, 226
Gola, Emilio 88
Goldman, Emma 4, 11, 15, 154, 155, 159, 169, 170, 173, 174, 179, 182, 187, 188, 190, 217, 221–223, 225
Gorki 114–116
Gorky, Maxim 12, 75–77, 79, 171
Grant, Frances 204, 212, 224, 226
Grimm, Robert 12, 99, 101, 102, 105, 121, 123, 126, 173, 181, 220, 225
Gulag 188
Gurion, Ben 33, 208

Harlingue, Albert 194
Highgate Cemetery 30
Hitler, Adolf 177
Hohenzollern family 32
Hook, Sidney 185, 223, 226
Hoover, Edgar 154
Hotel National 127–129, 138, 147, 149, 153, 154, 158, 161
Humboldt University 31

Hyde Park's Speaker's Corner 30
Hyndman, Henry 30

Illinois 191
IISH 2, 15, 187, 189, 202, 211, 225
"Impressions of Lenin" 35, 100, 218–222
Iskra 36, 218

Jaroslavsky, Emelian 164, 165
Jonas, Emil 37
Jonas, Renee 37

Kaplan, Fanny (Dora) 110, 112, 113, 115–117
Kautsky, Karl 51
Keats, John 8, 211
KGB 3, 9, 71
Kharkov 22, 91, 92, 144, 145
Kiev 2, 135, 136, 140, 141, 146, 149
Kilbom, Karl 161, 163
Kochubeevna, Motrya 25, 158
Kokoschka, Oscar 88
Kollontai, Alexandra 12, 97, 106, 159, 189, 220
Konstanz 126, 127
Kremlin 111–114, 117, 127, 129, 130–132, 135, 138, 139, 147, 151–154, 156, 158, 161, 183
Krestinsky, Nikolay 151, 152
Kreuzlingen 126
Krupskaya, Nadezhda 12, 34, 36, 37, 98, 100, 114–117, 131, 153
Kuliscioff, Anna 5, 12, 14, 83, 85, 86–88, 90, 159, 171, 219, 220, 225

Labriola, Antonio 12, 38, 39, 63, 64
Landolt Café 75, 151
Lausanne 43–45, 50–52, 65, 66–69, 71, 94, 123, 125, 219, 221, 226
Leipzig 31, 225
Lenin, Vladimir 1–3, 9–13, 16, 23, 32–38, 52, 70, 73–76, 78, 79, 81, 83, 89, 98, 100–120, 124, 130–138, 140, 143–154, 158–161, 163, 164, 166, 167, 176–177, 186, 188, 189, 206, 208, 210
Litvinov, Maxim 109, 220
Lloyd, Lola Maverick 15, 186, 188, 224, 226
Lombardo, Ivan Mattheo 33, 211, 224
Lombardo, Maria 33, 206
London 2, 16, 30, 76, 77–79, 151, 162, 218, 219, 225
Lotta di Casse 79
Lugano 44, 45, 57–60, 64, 70, 72, 76
Lunacharsky, Anatoli 103
Lutz, Alma 185, 186, 223, 226
Luxemburg, Rosa 13, 34, 35, 38, 100, 218
Lyle, Lane 185

Majorca 179, 180
Manhattan 191
Mann, Tom 30
Martov, Julius 13, 16, 76, 78, 97, 219

Index

Marx, Karl 16, 30, 31, 82, 161
Meir, Golda 33, 208
Mensheviks 13, 16, 77, 78, 219
Milan 5, 33, 79, 80, 81, 84, 85, 87–89, 93, 155, 159, 171, 173, 176, 205, 206, 212, 216, 225, 226
Minneapolis 191
Misiano, Francesco 33
Montreux 18, 23, 144
Morgari, Oddino 102
Moscow 2–4, 11, 15, 16, 18, 35, 42, 52, 78, 92, 105, 111–116, 127–140, 144, 146, 149, 152–155, 158, 159, 161, 163, 165, 166, 171, 182, 194, 201, 215, 225
Munich 36, 189, 218
Mussolini, Benito 1, 5, 7, 9, 10, 12, 13, 33, 46, 49, 50–54, 66, 73, 74, 79–90, 94–96, 116, 139, 156, 165, 168–171, 173–181, 183, 188, 189, 191–194, 197, 198, 207, 208, 210, 225
Mussolini, Edda 9, 13, 87, 193
Mussolini, Rachele 13, 87, 175, 176, 193, 194
Mussolini, Vittorio 193
"My Life as a Rebel" 1, 4, 38, 51, 172, 190

Naine, Charles 102
Narodnaya Volya 22
Nervi 70–72
New Hampshire 191
New University of Brussels 6, 11, 23, 26, 28, 30, 32, 213, 214, 225
New York 2, 4, 10, 11, 15, 17, 166, 167, 182, 183–186, 189–191, 194, 198, 200, 204, 210–212, 215, 226
Nicolas II 66, 102
Nikolaevsky, Boris 117, 220, 221, 222
NKVD 9, 71
Non-Catholic Cemetery 7, 8, 211, 212, 216

October Revolution 1, 12, 35, 78, 91, 107
Odessa 2, 140–146, 150, 168, 221, 226
Olla, Roberto 53, 226
Oss, Fernanda 89
Oulianov, Alexander 23
Oulianov, Anna 34, 35

Paradiso 57
Paris 2–4, 6, 7, 11, 15, 17, 38, 50, 52, 79, 88, 89, 97, 146, 150, 157, 171–175, 177, 179–181, 183, 184, 188, 213, 225, 226
Paris Commune 50, 52, 157
Pensuti, Elena 38, 41, 218, 225
Petrograd 97, 104–106, 108, 110, 139, 140, 155, 176, 221; *see also* St. Petersburg
Pirro, Count 146, 147, 149
Pittoni, Valentino 65, 166
Pivert, Marceau 37
Plekhanov, Georgy 77, 78
Poland 126, 127

Polotti, Giulio 5
Popote 175, 184
Pravda 164, 174
Princeton University Library 6
PSI 14, 15, 33, 39, 40, 41, 48, 54, 67, 83–88, 90, 95, 102, 136, 153, 156, 171, 175, 184

Radek, Karl 107, 134
Rakovsky, Christian 13, 134, 135, 137, 140, 188
Random House 6
Réclus, Elie 27
Réclus, Elisée 27, 30
Red Orient Mission 151
Red Terror 2, 35, 111, 116, 131, 147, 149
Reed, John Silas 11, 13, 33, 152, 153, 158
Reggio Emilia 82
Remembrance and Cultural Affairs Section of the *Préfecture de Police* 7, 15, 172, 225
RGASPI 4, 15, 92, 215, 225
Riazanov, David 161, 163, 188
Rimbaud, Arthur 179
Rivera, Diego 82, 88, 89
Robermont Cemetery 29
Roger Viollet Agency 194
Romani, Romolo 88
The Romanov family 102, 110
Rome 2, 4, 5, 7, 10, 14, 15, 17, 38, 41, 42, 45, 63, 64, 66, 74, 78, 118–120, 194, 195, 197–199, 201, 203, 204, 208, 210–212, 216, 225
RSDLP 16, 76, 77

Sadoul, Jacques 136, 141–143, 146
St. Gall 40–42, 45, 48, 51, 55, 58, 59, 124
St. Petersburg 2, 18, 70, 75, 92–94, 139, 143; *see also* Petrograd
Sapienza University 38, 39, 63, 64, 225
Saragat, Guiseppe 2, 10, 194, 198, 205, 208, 210, 211
Sarfatti, Margherita 13, 46, 66, 84, 87, 175, 191
sealed trains 103
Second International 16, 156, 158, 217
SFA 15, 43, 47, 48, 99, 122, 225
Shelley, Percy Bysshe 8, 211
Socialdemokraten 169, 182
Stabio 60, 61
Stalin, Joseph 1, 9, 10, 33, 38, 79, 130, 133, 138, 161, 164, 165, 168–170, 181, 185, 188, 189, 191, 207
State Archives of Chernihiv Oblast 6, 91, 226
Stockholm 11, 104–110, 111–115, 140, 150, 152, 161, 163, 165, 171
Ström, Frederik 161, 163
Su, Compagne! 55–59, 63, 67, 70
Switzerland, strike 6, 115, 118, 119, 121, 123–126

Tagore, Rabindranath 33, 157
Talamini, Alfredo 38, 41, 225
Tel-Aviv 208
Terni 71, 72
Ter-Petrosian 79
Terracini, Vittorio 177–180
Third International 16, 106, 135, 136, 138, 156; *see also* Comintern
Thomas, Norman 7, 13, 15, 119, 185, 187, 194, 197, 200, 203, 210, 212, 223, 224, 226
Tiflis 78
Tosoni-Pittoni, Albert 83, 84, 173, 174, 226
"The Traitor: Benito Mussolini and His Conquest of Power" 83, 194
Treves, Claudio 85, 86
Trotsky, Leon 1, 4, 7, 9, 10, 13, 33, 38, 76, 78, 104, 108, 136, 138, 152, 155, 163, 165, 169, 170, 185, 189, 190, 223, 226
Trotsky, Olga 69
Turati, Filippo 14, 84–86, 90, 159, 171
Turgenev, Ivan 110
Turkestan Republic 151–154, 222
Twain, Mark 75

Ufa 34
United Kingdom 71, 100, 109, 161, 162, 165, 182, 222, 225
United States 2, 7, 10, 11, 14, 31, 75, 79, 109, 133, 141, 146, 152, 154, 156, 166, 167, 168, 172, 181–188, 191, 194, 195, 197, 199, 200, 203, 205, 208, 215
University of Berne 31
University of Leipzig 31, 225

Valldemossa 180
Vandervelde, Emile 27
Vatican 63
Victor, Serge 166, 226
Vienna 157, 164, 166–170, 172, 173, 175, 184
Vinogradov, Vladimir 133
Vittorio Emmanuel II 82, 85
Vorovsky, Vatslav 14, 108–110, 137, 170

Wagner, Adolph 31–33
Wolfe, Bertram 4, 10, 14, 15, 112, 191, 226
Wolfe, Ella 10, 14, 44, 45, 64, 113, 195, 201, 204, 206, 207, 209

Zaira 176
Zetkin, Clara 14, 34, 35, 98, 100
Zimmerwald Conference 12, 101, 105–107, 119, 136
Zinoviev, Grigory 14, 69, 76, 137, 139, 140, 149, 150, 153, 155–157, 165, 188, 225
Zurich 40, 45, 52, 54, 85, 102, 121, 123, 149, 173

www.ingramcontent.com/pod-product-compliance
Ingram Content Group UK Ltd.
Pitfield, Milton Keynes, MK11 3LW, UK
UKHW041943140426
5217IPUK00014B/633